SEVENTY-EIGHT DEGREES OF WISDOM

An in-depth analysis of the Tarot, examining all aspects of the cards – their origins, symbolism, psychological resonances and historical, mythological and esoteric background, including instructions on how to give readings.

BY THE SAME AUTHOR:

Alqua Dreams
Godmother Night
Golden Vanity
Tarot Tales
Temporary Agency
Unquenchable Fire

The Body of the Goddess
The Dali Tarot
Fabrications
The Haindl Tarot
Le Jeu Divinatoire
The New Tarot
Shining Woman Tarot
Tarot Readings and Meditations
Teach Yourself Fortune Telling
The Vertigo Tarot

SEVENTY-EIGHT DEGREES OF WISDOM

A BOOK OF TAROT

RACHEL POLLACK

WEISERBOOKS
San Francisco, CA / Newburyport, MA

This edition first published in 2007 by
Red Wheel/Weiser, LLC
With offices at:
500 Third Street, Suite 230
San Francisco, CA 94107
www.redwheelweiser.com

Copyright © Rachel Pollack 1980, 1983, 1997
Original Dutch edition of *Seventy-eight Degrees of Wisdom: Part I, The Major Arcana*
published by Uitgeverij W. N. Schors – Amsterdam, 1980
Published by the Aquarian Press as
Seventy-eight Degrees of Wisdom: Part I, the Major Arcana and
Part II, the Minor Arcana and Readings, 1980 (1995) and 1983
All rights reserved. No part of this publication may be
reproduced or transmitted in any form or by any means,
electronic or mechanical, including photocopying,
recording or by any information storage and retrieval system,
without permission in writing from Red Wheel/Weiser, LLC.
Reviewers may quite brief passages.
Published in 1997 by Thorsons,
an imprint of HarperCollins*Publishers*, ISBN: 0-7225-3572-4

ISBN-10: 1-57863-408-3
ISBN-13: 978-1-57863-408-8

**Printed in Great Britain by
Clays Ltd, St Ives plc**

To Marilyn, who taught me so much by becoming my student; to Edie, the best reader I know; and for Joan Goldstein, who knows that the best cards are the ones that tell the truth.

CONTENTS

PART THREE READINGS

PREFACE TO THE 1997 EDITION

In the winter of 1969–70 I was teaching English at the State University of New York in the town of Plattsburgh, near the Canadian border. Plattsburgh in winter becomes horrifically cold, often -30°C (-22°F). Linda, one of my fellow teachers, did not drive, and even though she lived only a ten-minute walk from campus, would sometimes wait an hour or two for someone to drive her home. One day in early 1970 Linda offered to do a Tarot reading for me if I gave her a lift. I had never seen Tarot cards. I knew of them only from T. S. Eliot's poem *The Wasteland*, with its 'Madame Sosotris … the wisest woman in Europe/With a wicked pack of cards.'

I remember nothing of that first reading other than the impact the cards had on me. I knew of nothing like them – their bright colours, their vivid yet mysterious scenes, their strange figures with exotic names: the Magician, the High Priestess, the Hanged Man … Linda was not an experienced reader. For many of the cards she consulted a book. Rather than lessen the allure, this only heightened it, for the cards and the text seemed a kind of art form all its own.

Tarot books were simple in those days. Commonly they would describe the card, oddly repeating what you could see with your own eyes, though with subtle points that seemed to open the way to a greater story. 'In a state of dejection, a woman and child are ferried across the water to a calm shore' (*A Complete Guide to the Tarot*, Eden Gray). But who are these people? Why are they dejected? What waits for them on that 'calm shore'? Following these descriptions, the books would give formulas for fortune-telling, phrases such as 'Journey to a new home' (Gray). The possibility of discovering secrets and predicting the future attracted me, but the cards themselves, and the words that went with them, told me that I must find a set for myself.

It was not easy to find Tarot cards. Only a couple of years later they would begin appearing everywhere, but at that time it took several weeks of searching before I could locate a deck in an odd little shop in Montréal, a place even colder that Plattsburgh. Along with the cards I bought Eden Gray's book, whose work gives simple formulas yet also openings to the Tarot's deeper levels (for the card described above she characteristically adds, 'Also a journey in consciousness'). Gray's descriptions captured the special wonder of Pamela Smith's Rider edition drawings, with their delicate cartoon-like images concealing a vast system of symbolism and philosophy. Some time later I found a copy of A. E. Waite's own book on the cards, *The Pictorial Key to the Tarot*, which contained allusive and complex statements on the trumps, but also pages with the individual pictures and, under them, the same kind of descriptions as given by Eden Gray.

Like Linda, I began reading with the cards in one hand and the book in the other. Some of those early 'readings' still astound me when I think of them. In particular, I seemed to uncover my friends' extra-marital affairs.

At the end of the year, Linda asked me for a reading. She was taking a leave of absence to teach for a year in Copenhagen and wondered what the cards predicted for her. I told her she would marry a Danish man and not return. She laughed, having resigned herself to the life of a spinster. The following Spring the school received her resignation. Due to her impending marriage to a Danish teacher, she would be staying in Copenhagen.

If the readings intrigued me, something else excited me more. One afternoon another teacher came by, and we went through the cards one by one, ignoring the book now and just playing with the pictures. Russ was a poet and I wrote fiction. Ignoring the conceptual structures as well as the predictive formulas, we just looked for stories, working from the pictures but also Gray's and Waite's descriptions. I remember the moment when I realized that the

Tarot opened to worlds beyond their surface scenes and 'official' symbolism. We were looking at the ten of Pentacles, and especially the white-haired man in his coat of many colours. He looks like a beggar, I thought, but clearly he is much more. And no one see him, only the dogs. Odyssesus! I thought. The old man is Odysseus, returned to his home after 20 years and disguised as a beggar, to be recognized only by his ancient dog. When I looked at Waite's description I discovered themes similar to those in the *Odysssey*, in particular the need for security versus the desire for adventure and risk.

I did not think that Smith and Waite and deliberately coded Odysseus into the ten of Pentacles. That would have been far less interesting than the other possibility, that we could discover figures from mythology and literature in these pictures, these openings to different worlds.

So began my study of the cards, not from texts or symbolism or diagrams, but from the pictures themselves. To a great extent, the material in this book does not derive from teachers on Tarot (I never studied with anyone or took any classes) but just from working with the cards: looking at them, thinking about what is going on, considering the number and the imagery, comparing the cards to characters and stories in myth and popular culture – and doing readings.

In those days a long-time split still existed in the Tarot world. On one side stood the grand tradition of the occultists, from Antoine Court de Gébelin down through the Hermetic Order of the Golden Dawn and its descendants. On the other we found the tradition of readings, almost despised by the occultists. To some extent, this reflected a gender split as well. The great esoteric writers were almost all men (Dion Fortune being the most famous exception). Tarot readers were mostly women. It is not an accident that when most people visualize a Tarot reader, they see a woman in a headscarf.

In the 1980s a group of writers, primarily women, began to take Tarot in a new direction. Such people as Mary Greer, Angeles Arrien, James Wanless and Gail Fairfield began with a knowledge of the occult tradition (and also the ideas and techniques of psychology and counselling) but focused their work on the undeveloped potential of readings to illuminate human experience. *Seventy-eight Degrees of Wisdom*, originally published in two parts in 1980 and 1983, was one of the first books in this movement. Following the traditional method of card-by-card explanations rather than the emphasis on techniques in such books as Mary Greer's *Tarot for Yourself* or Gail Fairfield's *Choice-centred Tarot*, *Seventy-eight Degrees of Wisdom* nevertheless attempted to give people a tool to understand and ultimately transform their lives.

The book and its ideas evolved over time. A year after my friend Linda moved to Denmark, my partner Edith and I also moved to Europe, expecting to stay a year or two. I returned to the United States 19 years later. (Edith remained in Europe, where she teaches Tarot and reads professionally. She is, and has always been, as the Dedication to this book says, the best reader I know.) We took our cards with us, laying them out on tent floors by candlelight, carrying them in our backpacks through rainstorms and snow until they took on the look of a deck handed down through generations.

In France we met a group of artists renovating a medieval chateau. They looked with astonishment at our Rider pack, just as we were amazed to discover the *game* of Tarot that they played with a set of cards showing elaborate courtly figures but little symbolism.

Every year, when we visited our friends and family back in New York, we brought our cards with us. In the Summer of 1975 Edith and I spent several days at a beach house with her cousin and a few friends. The first evening, Marilyn, a therapist, asked me if I would teach her about the cards. Over the next few days we spent hours on the beach, going over the symbolism and philosophy, examining the structure, comparing the messages in the cards to ideas in psychology. At the end of that time we each had learned something. Marilyn felt comfortable enough with the cards to begin using them for her clients, and I discovered that I had something to teach.

A year and a half later, I needed a job. I had been working part-time while continuing to write, but the work I was doing had ended, and after considering teaching English at a Berlitz school I decided to do something more radical. I went to the Kosmos Meditation Center and asked to teach a class on Tarot.

The programme committee listed to my ideas, and then asked if I would do a sample reading. Usually I hate doing public readings, especially as a challenge, but there was obviously no choice. The only woman on the committee volunteered. When we laid out the cards I saw such heartbreak that I knew the only thing I could do was read the cards as if no one else existed in that room but her and me. 'Have you suffered a great deal of pain over a relationship?' I asked her, and she began to cry. The reading described the situation in depth, including ways for her to go on with her life. When we finished there was silence for a moment, than the head of the committee asked me 'When would you like to begin your class?' Only months later did I learn of the complex relationship between him and the woman who had offered herself for the reading.

The class ran for two years. Out of it came a small but dedicated community of Tarotists, several of whom moved deeply into studies of Kabbalah. To organize the class I needed to develop and codify my understanding of the cards. Along the way I decided to transform my class notes into a book. When I had enough material to show a publisher, I went to speak to Warren, an American who was managing Amsterdam's finest esoteric bookstore. I asked him if he could suggest a likely publisher. 'Well,' he said, 'we might be interested.' The store's owner, Nick Schors, primarily a dealer in rare books, had decided to branch out into original works.

Thus, *Seventy-eight Degrees of Wisdom* began as a discussion on a beach in New York and came to life first in a Dutch translation. I am indebted always to Nick for taking a chance on an unknown writer, and for the various international editions he and his son David have arranged for this book – including the English edition by the Aquarian Press.

For various reasons, earlier editions of this work were published in two volumes. Part II, The Minor Arcana, opened up the study of the cards even more than Part I (on the Major Arcana), for at that time (and even today) very few Tarot books gave serious attention to the suit cards. And yet, I had thought for a long time that a single volume would be a good idea. For one thing it would make the book easier to use, for people who found two volumes awkward to consult. This new edition has also given me the chance to make some changes. In the 18 years since Part I was published, I have continued to work with Tarot and to learn its history. While the book remains substantially the same – I would not radically alter something so many people have found helpful – I have gone through both parts carefully, revising whatever stood out in the light of new knowledge.

One thing I might have done differently if I were writing the book now: in Part I, I used the idea of ancient European initiations based around the story of the Holy Grail and its attendant objects. I am less convinced now that such secret groups actually existed. The Grail may have been a wholly literary invention (though based on earlier Celtic mythology). Nevertheless I have let these passages stand, for the idea of Grail Mysteries and initiations forms a valuable Tarot myth.

At the time I first wrote *Seventy-eight Degrees* virtually no Tarot books compared different decks. While I focused on the Rider pack, I tried to use other cards for contrast and to illuminate symbols. Since writing the book I have created my own deck, *Shining Woman Tarot*. I decided not to bring it in here (or any other decks created since 1980) so that the book would retain its original character.

In the years since *Seventy-eight Degrees of Wisdom* I have written ten further books on Tarot. But this book will always remain special, not just because it was my first non–fiction book (my first novel came out the same year), but also because of the many people who have told me how much the book has meant to them, how it has helped them use the cards to change their lives. I remember one woman in particular, Aster (a name that means Star). Aster had suffered neurological damage in an airplane so that reading often produced intense headaches. Refusing to give up her plans she had enrolled in medical school, persuading the school to allow her to take all her exams orally, and persuading her friends to take turns reading her her study material so she could memorize it. But Aster only spent half the year in school. The rest of the time she lived on the Greek island of Mykonos, where she supported herself reading Tarot cards – on the beach. Shortly after I met Aster, I went to a party at her apartment. Her shelves held very few books, for after all she could hardly read. But among the few books, two volumes stood out by their tattered look, worn from constant use. They were, of course, her copies of *Seventy-eight Degrees of Wisdom*.

In honour of their different ways of showing faith in this Book of Tarot, I dedicate this new comprehensive edition to Nick Schors and Aster Schelp.

PART ONE

THE MAJOR ARCANA

INTRODUCTION

ORIGINS OF THE TAROT

Around the middle of the fifteenth century, not so long after the first written references in Europe to cards of any kind, an artist named Bonifacio Bembo painted a set of unnamed and unnumbered cards for the Visconti family of Milan. These pictures comprise the classic deck for an Italian game called 'Tarocchi': four suits of fourteen cards each, plus twenty-two cards showing different scenes and later called 'trionfi' – in English, 'triumphs', or 'trumps'.

Now, of these twenty-two images many can be interpreted as simply a catalogue of medieval social types, such as (to give them their later names) 'the Pope' or 'the Emperor', or else common medieval moral homilies, such as 'the Wheel of Fortune'. Some represent virtues, like 'Temperance' or 'Fortitude'. Others show religious-mythological scenes, such as the dead rising from the grave at the trumpet call for 'the Last Judgement'. There is even a card depicting a popular heresy, the image of a female pope, which we can describe as a joke on the Church with rather deeper significance than most ecclesiastical humour. Still, we can view this heretical picture as deeply rooted in popular culture, and therefore obvious to someone representing medieval 'types'.

One figure, however, stands out as rather strange. It shows a young man hanging upside down by his left leg from a simple wooden frame. His hands are held casually behind his back to form a triangle with his head at the bottom, his right leg is bent behind his knee to produce the figure of a cross, or else the numeral four. The face appears relaxed, even perhaps entranced. Where did Bembo derive this image? It certainly does not represent a criminal hanged at the gallows, as some later artists have assumed. In Italy traitors were sometimes hanged upside down, and in fact many modern Italian decks call this card *L'Apezzo*, the Traitor. But there is no evil implicit in Bembo's figure. The young man appears beautiful, and at peace.

Christian tradition describes St Peter as being crucified upside down, ostensibly so he could not be said to be copying his Lord. The Elder Edda describes the god Odin hanging from the World Tree for nine days and nights, not as a punishment, but in order to receive enlightenment, the gift of prophecy. But this mythological scene itself derives from the actual practice of shamans, medicine men and women, in such places as Siberia and North America. In the initiation and training the candidates for shamanism are sometimes told to hang upside down. Apparently the reversal of the body produces some sort of psychological benefit, in the way that starvation and extreme cold will induce radiant visions. The alchemists – who, with the witches, were possibly the survivors of the shamanist tradition in Europe – also hung themselves upside down, believing that elements in the sperm vital to immortality would thus flow down to the psychic centres at the top of the head. And even before the West began to take Yoga seriously everyone knew the image of the yogi standing on his head.

Did Bembo simply wish to represent an alchemist? Then why not use the more common image, that of a bearded man stirring a cauldron or mixing chemicals? The picture, titled 'the Hanged Man' in subsequent decks and later made famous by T.S. Eliot in *The Wasteland*, appears not so much as an alchemist as a young initiate in some secret tradition. Was Bembo himself an initiate? The special crossing of the legs would suggest so. And if he included one reference to esoteric practices, might not other images, superficially a social commentary, in reality represent an entire body of occult knowledge? Why, for instance, did the original deck contain twenty-two cards, not say, twenty or twenty-one or twenty-five, all of which are more commonly given significance in Western culture? Was it chance, or did Bembo (or perhaps others whom Bembo simply copied) wish to slyly represent the esoteric meanings connected to the twenty-two letters of the Hebrew alphabet? And yet, if any evidence exists anywhere connecting Bembo or the Visconti family to any occult group no one has produced it for public scrutiny.

A brief look at the stunning correspondences between the Tarot and the body of Jewish mysticism and occult knowledge, called collectively the Kabbalah, will demonstrate the way in which Bembo's cards seem almost to demand an esoteric interpretation, despite the lack of hard evidence. The Kabbalah dwells very deeply on the symbolism of the Hebrew alphabet. The letters are connected to the paths of the Tree of Life and they are each given their own symbolic meanings. Now, the Hebrew alphabet contains, as noted, twenty-two letters, the same number as the trumps of Tarocchi. The Kabbalah also goes deeply into the four letters of God's unpronounceable name, YHVH. They represent the four worlds of creation, the four basic elements of medieval science, four stages of existence, four methods of interpreting the Bible, and so on. There are four court cards in each of Bembo's four suits.

Finally, the Kabbalah works with the number ten – the Ten Commandments and ten Sephiroth (stages of emanation) on each of the four Trees of Life. And the four suits contain cards numbered from one to ten. Do we wonder then that Tarot commentators have claimed that the deck originated as a pictorial version of the Kabbalah, meaningless to the masses, but highly potent to the few? And yet, in all the thousands of pages of Kabbalistic literature, not one word appears about the Tarot.

Occultists have claimed secret sources for the cards, such as a grand conference of Kabbalists and other Masters in Morocco in 1300, but no one has ever produced any historical evidence for such claims. Even more damning, Tarot commentators themselves do not mention the Kabbalah until the nineteenth century. And of course, the names and numbers sequence, so vital to their interpretations, came after the original images.

If we accept Carl Jung's idea of basic spiritual archetypes structured into the human mind we can perhaps say that Bembo unconsciously tapped hidden springs of knowledge, allowing later imaginations to make the conscious connections. And yet, such exact and complete correspondences as the twenty-two trumps, the four court cards and ten pip cards in the four suits, or the position and ecstatic face of the Hanged Man, would seem to strain even such a potent force as the Collective Unconscious.

For years Tarrochi was seen primarily as a game for gambling, and to a much lesser extent as a device for fortune-telling. Then, in the eighteenth century, an occultist named Antoine Court de Gébelin declared the Tarot (as the French called the game) to be the remnant of the Book of Thoth, created by the Egyptian god of magic to convey all knowledge to his disciples. Court de Gébelin's idea appears far more fanciful than factual, but in the nineteenth century another Frenchman, Alphonse Louis Constant, known as Eliphas Lévi, linked the cards to the Kabbalah, and since then people have looked deeper and deeper into the Tarot, finding more and more meanings, wisdom, and even, through meditation and deep study, enlightenment.

Today, we see the Tarot as a kind of path, a way to personal growth through understanding of ourselves and life. To some the Tarot's origin remains a vital question; for others it only matters that meanings have accrued to the cards over the years.

For Bembo (and whoever his predecessors might have been) did create an archetype, whether consciously or from deep instinct. Beyond any system or detailed explanations, the images themselves, changed and elaborated over the years by different artists, fascinate and entrance us. In this way they draw us into their mysterious world which ultimately can never be explained, but only experienced.

DIFFERENT VERSIONS OF THE TAROT

Most modern Tarots differ very little from those fifteenth-century sets of cards. They still contain seventy-eight cards divided into the four suits, Wands, Cups, Swords, and Coins or Pentacles, called collectively the 'Minor Arcana', and the twenty-two trumps, known as the 'Major Arcana' (the word 'arcanum' means 'secret knowledge'). True, some of the pictures have changed considerably, but each version usually keeps the same basic concept. For example, there are several widely varying versions of the Emperor, but they all represent some idea of an Emperor. In general, the changes have tended towards the more symbolic and the more mystical.

This book uses as its primary source the Tarot of Arthur Edward Waite, whose very popular Rider pack (named after its British publisher) appeared in 1910. Waite was criticized for changing some of the trump cards from their accepted version. For instance, the common picture of the Sun shows two children holding hands in a garden. Waite changed it to one child on a horse riding *out* of a garden. The critics claimed Waite was altering the card's meaning to his personal vision. This was probably the case, since Waite believed more strongly in his own ideas than those of anyone else. But few people stopped to consider that the earliest version of the Sun, that of Bembo, in no way resembles the supposed 'traditional' version. Indeed, it seems closer to Waite's; the picture shows a single miraculous child flying through the air, holding up a human head radiating light.

The most striking change Waite and his artist, Pamela Colman Smith, made was to include a scene on all the cards, including the numbered cards of the Minor Arcana. Virtually all previous decks, as well as many later ones, have simple geometric patterns for the 'pip' cards. For example, the ten of Swords will show ten swords arranged in a pattern, much like its descendant, the ten of spades. The Rider pack is different. Pamela Smith's ten of Swords shows a man lying under a black cloud with ten swords stuck in his back and legs.

We do not really know who actually designed these cards. Did Waite himself conceive them (as he undoubtedly did the Major Arcana), or did he simply tell Smith the qualities and ideas he wanted and allow her to invent the scenes? Waite's own book on the Tarot, *The Pictorial Key to the Tarot*, makes little real use of the pictures. In some cases, such as the six of Swords, the picture suggests far more than Waite's stated meaning, while in others, particularly the two of Swords, the picture almost contradicts the meaning.

Whether it was Waite or Smith who designed the pictures, they had a powerful effect on later Tarot designers. Almost all decks with scenes on every card rely very heavily on the pictures in the Rider pack.

Waite called his deck the 'rectified Tarot'. He insisted that his pictures 'restored' the true meanings of the cards, and throughout his book he scorns the versions of his predecessors. Now, by 'rectified' many people will think Waite's membership in secret societies gave him access to the 'original' secret Tarot. More likely, he simply meant that his pictures gave the cards their deepest meanings. When he so drastically altered the card of the Lovers, for instance, he did so because he thought the old picture insignificant and his new one symbolic of a deep truth.

I do not mean to suggest that Waite's cards are simply an intellectual construction, like a scholar rearranging some speech of Hamlet's in a way which makes more sense to him. Waite was a mystic, an occultist, and a student of magic and esoteric practices. He based his Tarot on deep personal experience of enlightenment. He believed his Tarot to be right and the others wrong because it represented that experience.

I have chosen the Rider pack as my source for two reasons. First, I find many of its innovations extremely valuable. The Waite-Smith version of the Fool strikes me as more meaningful than any of the earlier ones. Secondly, the revolutionary change in the Minor Arcana seems to me to free us from the formulas that dominated the suit cards for so long. Previously, once you read and memorized the given meanings of a Minor card you could not really add to it; the picture suggested very little. In the Rider pack we can allow the picture to work on the subconscious; we can also apply our own experience to it. In short, Pamela Smith has given us something to interpret.

Above I wrote that I chose the Rider pack as my 'primary' source. Most books on the Tarot use one deck alone for illustrations. This self-limitation perhaps stems from a desire to represent the 'true' Tarot. By choosing one deck and not another we are really declaring that one is correct and the other is false. Such a declaration matters most to those writers, like Aleister Crowley or Paul Foster Case, who consider the Tarot a symbolic system of objective knowledge. This book, however, looks upon the cards more as an archetype of experience. Seen that way no deck is right or wrong, but is simply a furthering of the archetype. The Tarot is both the total of all the different versions over the years, and an entity apart from any of them. In the cases where a version other than Waite's will deepen the meaning of a specific card we will look at both images. In some cases, Judgement for instance, or the Moon, the differences are subtle; in others, the Lovers, or the Fool, the difference is drastic. By looking at several versions of the same experience we heighten our awareness of that experience.

DIVINATION

Today, most people see the Tarot as a means of fortune-telling, or 'divination'. Strangely, we know less historically about this aspect of the cards than any other. Judging by the comparatively few historical references to divination as opposed to gambling, the practice did not become common until some time after the introduction of the cards themselves. Possibly the Romany, or 'gypsies', came across the game of Tarocchi on their travels in Europe and decided to use the cards for fortune-telling. Or individuals developed the concept (the earliest written references are individual interpretations, though they might have derived from some earlier system, not written down but in general use) and the Romany took it from them. People used to believe that the Romany themselves brought the cards from Egypt. The fact is, the Romany probably came from India, and they arrived in Spain a good hundred years after Tarot cards were introduced in Italy and France.

In the section on readings we will consider just what divination does, and how such an outrageous practice could possibly work. Here we can simply observe that people can and have told fortunes with anything – the smoky innards of slaughtered beasts, bird patterns across the sky, coloured stones, tossed coins, anything. The practice stems from the simple desire to know, in advance, what is going to happen, and more subtly, from the inner conviction that everything is connected, everything has meaning and that nothing occurs at random.

The very idea of randomness is really very modern. It developed out of the dogma that cause and effect is the only valid connection between two events. Events without this logical joining are random, that is, meaningless. Previously, however, people thought in terms of 'correspondences'. Events or patterns in one area of existence corresponded to patterns in other areas. The pattern of the zodiac corresponds to the pattern of a person's life. The pattern of tea leaves in the bottom of a cup corresponds to the outcome of a battle. Everything is connected. The idea has always claimed its adherents, and recently even some scientists, impressed by the way events will occur in series (like a 'run of bad luck'), have begun to look seriously at it.

If we can use anything for fortune-telling why use the Tarot? The answer is that any system will tell us *something*; the value of that something depends on the inherent wisdom of the system. Because the Tarot pictures carry deep significance all by themselves, the patterns they form in readings can teach us a great deal about ourselves, and life in general. Unfortunately, most diviners over the years have ignored these deeper meanings, preferring simple formulas ('a dark man, one disposed to help the querent'), easily interpreted and quickly digested by the client.

The formula meanings are often contradictory as well as blunt, with no indications of how to choose between them. This situation holds true especially for the Minor Arcana which is the bulk of the deck. Almost no works on the Tarot have treated this subject fully. Most serious studies, those which deal with the deep meanings of the Major Arcana, either do not mention the Minor cards at all, or simply throw in another set of formulas at the back, as a grudging addition for those readers who will insist on using the deck for fortune-telling. Even Waite, as mentioned, simply gives his own formulas to the remarkable pictures drawn by Pamela Smith.

While this book will deal extensively with the concepts embodied in the cards and their symbolism it will also look carefully at the application of these concepts to Tarot readings. Many writers, notably Waite, have denigrated divination as a degenerate use of the cards. But the proper use of readings can greatly increase our awareness of the cards' meanings. It is one thing to study the symbolism of a particular card, it is something else to see that card in combination with others. Many times I have seen specific readings open up important meanings that would not have emerged in any other way.

Readings teach us a general lesson as well, and a very important one. In a manner no explanation can possibly equal, they demonstrate that no card, no approach to life, is good or bad except in the context of the moment.

Finally, giving readings gives each person a chance to renew his or her instinctive feeling for the pictures themselves. All the symbolism, all the archetypes, all the explanations given in this book or any other can only prepare you to look at the pictures and say, 'This card tells me …'

CHAPTER ONE

THE FOUR CARD PATTERN

UNITY AND DUALITY

Through its long history the Major Arcana has attracted a great many interpretations. Today, we tend to look upon the trumps as a psychological process, one that shows us passing through different stages of existence to reach a state of full development; we can describe this state, for the moment, as unity with the world around us, or perhaps liberation from weakness, confusion, and fear. The full Arcana describes this process in detail, but to get an understanding of it as a whole we need look at only four cards; four basic archetypes arranged in a graphic pattern of evolution and spiritual awareness.

If you have your own deck of Rider Pack Tarot cards* remove the Fool, the Magician, the High Priestess, and the World, and place them in the diamond pattern shown overleaf. Look at them for a while. Notice that while both the Fool and the World show dancing, joyful figures, the Magician and the High Priestess are stationary and unmoving in their positions. If you glance through the rest of the Major Arcana you will notice that all the trumps but 0 and 21 are drawn as if staged for a still photograph,

---

* In other decks, particularly those older than Waite's, the Fool appears very different from the one shown here. The chapter on the symbolism of the Fool (page 24) will deal with this alternative tradition.

THE FOOL.

THE MAGICIAN.

THE HIGH PRIESTESS

THE WORLD.

rather than say, a motion picture. They present themselves as fixed states of existence.

But there is a difference between the two dancers. The Fool rushes forward richly clothed; the figure in the World is naked. The Fool looks about to leap into the lower world from some high distant country; the World paradoxically appears outside the material universe, the Dancer suspended in a magical wreath of victory.

Note also the numbers of the four cards. 0 is not strictly a number at all, rather it represents the absence of any specific number, and therefore we can say that it contains all numbers within itself. It symbolizes infinite potentiality. All things remain possible because no definite form has been taken. 1 and 2 are the first genuine numbers, the first reality; again, a fixed state. They form the archetypes 'odd' and 'even', and therefore represent all opposites, male and female, light and dark, passive and active, etc. But 21 combines these two numbers in one figure.

Look at their postures. The Magician raises a magic wand to heaven. Besides the ideas of spirit and unity, the phallic wand symbolizes maleness. The High Priestess sits between two pillars, a vaginal symbol as well as a symbol of duality. These two pillars appear again and again in the Major Arcana, in such obvious places as the temple in the Hierophant, and in more subtle ways, like the two lovers on card 6, or the two sphinxes harnessed to the Chariot. But now look at the World. The dancer, a female figure (though some decks represent her as a hermaphrodite) carries two magic wands, one in each hand. The male and female are unified, and more, their separate qualities are subordinated to the higher freedom and joy shone in the light way the dancer holds these powerful symbols.

Clearly, then, while the horizontal line, the Magician and the High Priestess, shows a duality of opposites, the vertical line, 0 and 21, shows a unity, the Fool being some sort of perfect state before duality, and the World giving us a glimpse of the exhilarating sense of freedom possible if only we can reconcile the opposites buried in our psyches.

The Tarot, like many systems of thought, indeed like many mythologies, symbolizes duality as the separation of male and female. The Kabbalists believed that Adam was originally hermaphroditic, and that Eve only became separate from him so that they might regard each other as independent beings. In most cultures, to a greater or lesser degree, men and women see each other as very distinct, almost separate societies. Today, many people think of each person as having both masculine and feminine qualities, but previously such an idea was found only in esoteric doctrines of unification.

If we picture duality dramatically as male and female, or black and white, we also experience more subtle splits in our ordinary lives, especially between our hopes, what we imagine as possible, and the reality of what we achieve. Very often the actions we take turn out not to fulfil our hopes for them. The marriage gives less than the total happiness expected, the job or career brings more frustration than fulfilment. Many artists have said that the paintings on the canvases are never the paintings they envisioned; they never can express what they really wanted to say. Somehow the reality of life is always less than the potential. Acutely aware of this, many people agonize over every decision, no matter how small or great, because they cannot accept that once they take an action in one direction they have lost the chance to go in all the other directions previously open to them. They cannot accept the limitations of acting in the real world.

The split between potentiality and reality is sometimes seen as the separation between mind and body. We sense that our thoughts and emotions are something distinct from our physical presence in the world. The mind is unlimited, able to go anywhere in the universe, backwards or forwards in time. The body is weak, subject to hunger, tiredness, sickness. Attempting to resolve this separation people have gone to philosophical extremes. Behaviourists have claimed that 'mind' does not exist; only the body and the habits it develops are real. At the other end, many mystics have experienced the body as an illusion created by our limited understanding. Christian tradition defines the 'soul' as the immortal 'true' self, existing before and after the body that contains it. And many religions and sects, such as the Gnostics and some Kabbalists, have considered the body a prison, created by the sins or mistakes of our fallen ancestors.

At the source of all these dualities we feel we do not know ourselves. We sense that deep down our true nature is something stronger, freer, with great wisdom and power; or else a thing of violent passions and furious animal desire. Either way, we *know* that this true self hides, or perhaps lies buried deep inside our normal, socially restricted personalities. But how do we reach it? Assuming the essential self to be a thing of beauty and power, how do we liberate it?

The disciplines we call the 'occult sciences' begin with a strong awareness of all these splits and limitations. They then go on, however, to another idea, that there exists a key, or a plan, to bring everything together, to unify our lives with our hopes as we release our latent strength and wisdom. People often confuse the purposes of spiritual disciplines. Many think the Tarot is for fortune-telling, that alchemists want to become rich by changing lead to gold, that Kabbalists work spells by saying secret words, and so on. In reality, these disciplines aim at a psychological unification. The 'base metal' that the alchemist wishes to change to gold is himself. Accepting the doctrine that we have fallen from a perfect state to a limited one the occultist does not believe we must simply wait passively for some future redemption by an outside agent. On the contrary, he or she believes it our responsibility to bring about that redemption by finding the key to unity.

The Tarot depicts a version of that 'key'. It is not *the* key, just as it is not really a secret doctrine. It represents a process, and one of the things it teaches us is that we make a mistake when we assume that unification comes through any simple key or formula. Rather, it comes through growth and increased awareness as we travel step by step through the twenty-one stages of the Major Arcana.

The Fool represents true innocence, a kind of perfect state of joy and freedom, a feeling of being one with the spirit of life at all times; in other words, the 'immortal' self we feel became entrapped in the confusions and compromises of the ordinary world. Perhaps such a radiant self never really existed. Somehow we experience our intuition of it as something lost. Virtually every culture has developed a myth of a Fall from a primeval paradise.

'Innocence' is a word often misunderstood. It does not mean 'without guilt' but rather a freedom and a total openness to life, a complete lack of fear that comes through a total faith in living and in your own instinctive self. Innocence does not mean 'asexual' as some people think. It is sexuality expressed without fear, without guilt, without connivance and dishonesty. It is sexuality expressed spontaneously and freely, as the expression of love and the ecstasy of life.

The Fool bears the number 0 because all things are possible to the person who is always ready to go in any direction. He does not belong in any specific place; he is not fixed like the other cards. His innocence makes him a person with no past, and therefore an infinite future. Every moment is a new starting point. In Arabic numerals the number 0 bears the shape of an egg, to indicate that all things emerge from it. Originally the zero was written as a dot; in Hermetic and Kabbalistic tradition the universe emerged from a single point of light. And God in the Kabbalah is often described as 'nothingness' because to describe God as any *thing* would be to limit Him to some finite fixed state. Those Tarot commentators who argue whether the Fool belongs before, after, or somewhere between the other cards seem to be missing the point. The Fool is movement, change, the constant leap through life.

For the Fool no difference exists between possibility and reality. 0 means a total emptiness of hopes and fears, and the Fool expects nothing, plans nothing. He responds instantly to the immediate situation.

Other people will receive his complete spontaneity. Nothing calculated, nothing held back. He does not do this deliberately, like someone consciously deciding to be wholly honest with a friend or a lover. The Fool gives his honesty and love naturally, to everyone, without ever thinking about it.

We speak of the Fool as 'he' and the World Dancer as 'she' because of their appearance in the pictures, but both can be a woman or a man with really no change. Just as the Fool does not experience a separateness from the physical world so he or she does not experience any isolation from the 'opposite sex'. The Fool and the Dancer are psychic hermaphrodites, expressing their complete humanity at all times, by their very natures.

Now look again at the four card pattern. See how the Fool splits into the Magician and the High Priestess, who must be brought back together again to form the World. The two cards represent the splitting up of the Fool's innocence into the illusion of opposites. The World shows us a restored unity, but a higher and deeper unity achieved through the growth outlined in the other eighteen cards. The fool is innocence, but the World is wisdom.

INNOCENCE AND FREEDOM

The Fool teaches us that life is simply a continuous dance of experience. But most of us cannot maintain even brief moments of such spontaneity and freedom. Due to fears, conditioning, and simply the very real problems of daily life, we necessarily allow our egos to isolate us from experience. Yet within us we can sense, dimly, the possibility of freedom, and therefore we call this vague feeling of a loss, a 'fall' from innocence. Once we lose that innocence, however, we cannot simply climb back to the level of the Fool. Instead, we must struggle and learn, through maturity, self-discovery, and spiritual awareness, until we reach the greater freedom of the World.

The Magician represents action, the High Priestess passivity, the Magician maleness, the High Priestess femaleness, the Magician consciousness, the High Priestess unconsciousness.

By 'consciousness' we do not mean the high awareness of the World, but rather the powerful yet limited consciousness of ego as it creates an outer universe of boundaries and forms. This description does not mean to denigrate or belittle the Magician's creative force. What greater creativity is there than giving shape to the chaos of experience? It is the Magician who gives life its meaning and purpose. Healers, artists, and occultists have all focused on the Magician as their patron card. Nevertheless, his power represents an isolation from the freedom of the Fool or the understanding of the World.

In the same way, the High Priestess indicates, in her unconsciousness, a very deep state of intuitive awareness. And yet, her inner knowledge does not belong to that radiant centre of nothingness that enables the Fool to act so freely.

The High Priestess represents the archetype of inner truth, but because this truth is unconscious, inexpressible, she can maintain it only through total passivity. This situation shows itself in life in numerous ways. We all carry within us a dim sense of who we are, of a genuine self never seen by other people and impossible to explain. But the women and men who throw themselves into competition, careers, responsibilities, without working at the same time to increase self-knowledge, often discover at some point that they have lost the sense of who they are, and what they once wanted in life. Now, directly opposite to these people, the Buddhist monk or nun withdraws from the world because the slightest involvement will distract them from the centre of their meditations.

Both the Magician and the High Priestess bear an archetypal purity. In a way, they have not lost the Fool's radiance, they have simply split it up into light and darkness. In the traditional split of Western and Eastern religion the Magician represents the West, with its emphasis on action and historical salvation, the High Priestess the East, the way of separation from the world and time. Yet those who have gone deepest in both traditions will combine these elements.

The High Priestess sits between the pillars of light and dark. Though she herself symbolizes the dark passive side, her intuition can find a balance between the two. This is less paradoxical than it sounds. If we sense our lives as filled with opposites which we cannot resolve, we can react in either of two ways. We can rush back and forth, going from one extreme to the other, or we can do absolutely nothing. Sit in the middle, not seduced in either direction, but passive, allowing the opposites to go on around you. Except, of course, that this too is a choice, and eventually we lose that balance and that inner knowledge simply because life continues on around us.

In Kabbalist imagery the High Priestess represents the Pillar of Harmony, a force which reconciles the opposing Pillars of Mercy and Judgement. Therefore she sits between the two pillars of the temple. But without the ability to blend in the active force of the Magician, the High Priestess's sense of harmony becomes swept away.

As archetypes, the Magician and the High Priestess cannot exist in our lives any more than the Fool can. Inevitably, we mix up these elements (rather than blend them) and thereby experience their lesser forms, as confused action, or else insecure and guilt ridden passivity. In other words, the purity of the two poles becomes lost because life muddles them together.

The purpose of the Major Arcana is twofold. First of all, by isolating the elements of our lives into archetypes it enables us to see them in their pure forms, as aspects of psychological truth. Secondly, it helps us to truly resolve these different elements, to take us step by step through the different stages of life until it brings us to unity. In reality, perhaps the innocence symbolized by the Fool never existed. Somehow we experience as something lost. The Major Arcana tells us how to get it back.

CHAPTER TWO

THE OVERVIEW

THE CARDS AS A SEQUENCE

Most interpreters of the Major Arcana take one of two approaches: either they consider the cards as separate entities or they look at them as a sequence. The first approach looks at each card as representing different qualities or situations of importance to a person's spiritual development. The Empress represents the soul glorified in nature, the Emperor mastery of self, etc. This system considers the numbers on the cards as part of their symbolic language. The number 1 belongs to the Magician not because he comes first but because that number signifies ideas – unity, will power – appropriate to the concept of the Magician.

The second approach looks upon the trumps as a progression. The Magician is 1 because his qualities form the starting point of the growth pattern figured in the other cards. Card number 13, say, belongs at just that point, between the Hanged Man and Temperance, and no other. Each new trump builds upon the previous one and leads the way to the next.

In general, I have followed the second method. While the number symbolism should not be neglected it is equally important to see where each card fits in the overall pattern. Comparisons with other numbers can also help us to see the limitations as well as the virtues of each card. For instance, number 7, the Chariot, is often spoken of as 'victory'. But what kind of victory? Is it the total liberation of the World, or something narrower, but still of great value? Looking at the card's position can answer these questions.

The interpreters who have taken this approach have usually looked for some place to divide the trumps for easier comprehension. The most common choice is the Wheel of Fortune. As the number ten, it symbolizes a completion of one cycle and a beginning of another. Also, if you place the Fool at the beginning this divides the cards neatly into two groups of eleven. Most important, the idea of a turning wheel symbolizes a change of outlook, from a concern with external things, such as success and romance, to the more inward approach depicted in such cards as Death and the Star.

Despite the value of seeing the Major Arcana as two halves, I have found that the trumps divide even more organically into three parts. Setting the Fool apart as really a separate category all by itself (and setting it apart allows us to see that it belongs everywhere and anywhere) gives us twenty-one cards – three groups of seven.

The number seven has a long history in symbolism: the seven planets of classical astrology, seven as a combination of three and four, themselves archetypal numbers, seven pillars of wisdom, the seven lower stations of the Tree of Life, seven openings in the human head, seven chakras, and of course, seven days in the week. Most of the meanings of seven derive from the fact that before the telescope people could see seven 'planets' in the sky, that is, seven moving objects: the Sun, the Moon, Mercury, Venus, Mars, Jupiter and Saturn. Though the idea of the seven-day week comes from ancient Israel, which may have got it from Babylon, the European names for the days come from the planets as personified in the Roman and Norse gods.

One particular aspect of seven relates it directly to the Tarot. The Greek letter *pi* stands for a ratio that exists in all circles between the circumference and the diameter. No matter how large or small the circle, the two will always work out to the same fraction, 22/7. And the Major Arcana with the Fool comes to twenty-two, just as without the Fool it reduces to seven. Also, twenty-two times seven equals one hundred and fifty-four (154 adds up to ten, linking it to the Wheel), and one hundred and fifty-four divided by two, for the two Arcana, comes to seventy-seven, the entire Tarot with the Fool again set aside.

Like the Kabbalistic conception of God the point is nothing, yet the entire circle radiates from it. And the Fool's number, 0, has been represented as a point as well as a circle.

The best reasons for the division into three groups lie within the Major Arcana itself. First, consider the picture symbolism. Look at the first card in each line. The Magician and Strength are both obviously cards of power, but so is the Devil. The Magician and Strength are linked by the infinity sign above their heads, while the Devil bears a reversed pentacle. If you look at the Devil's posture, one arm up, one arm down, you will see the picture is in some ways a parody of the Magician, with the torch pointing down instead of the wand pointing up. In some decks card 15 carries the title of 'Black Magician'. (In many decks Justice, not Strength is number 8. If you look at the posture of the figure in Justice you will see an even closer resemblance to the Magician and the Devil.) The same kind of vertical correspondences apply all the way through the three lines.

THE THREE AREAS OF EXPERIENCE

The division into three allows us to see the Major Arcana as dealing with three distinct areas of experience. Briefly, we can call these: consciousness, the outer concerns of life in society; subconscious, or the search inward to find out who we really are; and superconscious, the development of a spiritual awareness and a release of archetypal energy. The three levels are not forced categories. They derive from the cards themselves.

The first line, with its concentration on such matters as love, social authority, and education, describes the main concerns of society. In many ways the world we see mirrored in our novels, films, and schools is summed up by the first seven cards of the Major Arcana. A person can live and die and be judged a success by everyone around him or her without ever going beyond the level of the Chariot. Many people, in fact, do not reach that level at all.

Modern depth psychology concerns itself with the second line of trumps, with their symbols of a hermit-like withdrawal into self-awareness followed by a symbolic Death and rebirth. The angel of

Temperance at the end represents that part of ourselves which we discover to be essentially real after the illusions of ego, defensiveness, and rigid habits of the past are allowed to die away.

Finally, what of the last line? What can go beyond finding our true selves ? To put it simply, these seven cards depict a confrontation and finally a unity with the great forces of life itself. The other cards, formerly seen as so important, become merely the preparation for the great descent into darkness, the liberation of light, and the return of that light to the sunlit world of consciousness.

To most readers the last line will seem too vague and fanciful. We can call this subject matter 'religious' or 'mythical' but these words too remain hard to grasp.

The vagueness in our minds perhaps speaks more about ourselves and our time than about the subject. Any society automatically teaches its people, just by the language it uses, to make certain assumptions about the world. Examples in our culture would include the value and uniqueness of individuals, the reality and overwhelming importance of love, the necessity of freedom and social justice, and, more complex, but just as strong, the basic separateness of each person. 'We are born alone and we die alone.' Our society, built upon the materialist eighteenth and nineteenth centuries, does not merely reject the notion of 'superconsciousness' or 'universal forces', we do not really know what they mean.

When we deal with the last line of the Major Arcana, then, we deal with an area uncomfortable to many of us. It will make the task of understanding these cards harder – and perhaps more rewarding. Working with these ancient pictures can bring us knowledge neglected in our education.

CHAPTER THREE

THE OPENING TRUMPS: SYMBOLS AND ARCHETYPES

(a)   (b)

Figure 1

THE FOOL

We have already looked at the Fool in one aspect, the image of a spirit totally free. But we can look at the Fool from another side – the leap into the archetypal world of the trumps.

Imagine yourself entering a strange landscape. A world of magicians, of people hanging upside down, and of dancers in the bright air. You can enter through a leap from a height, through a dark cave, a labyrinth, or even by climbing down a rabbit hole chasing a Victorian rabbit with a pocket watch. Whichever way you choose, you are a fool to do it. Why look into the deep world of the mind when you can stay safely in the ordinary landscape of job, home and family? Herman Melville, in *Moby Dick,* warned his readers not to take even a step outside the ordinary path laid out for you by society. You might not get back again.

And yet, for those willing to take the chance, the leap can bring joy, adventure, and finally, for those with the courage to keep going when the wonderland becomes more fearsome than joyous, the leap can bring knowledge, peace, and liberation. Interestingly, the Fool archetype appears more in mythology than in structured religion. An institutionalized Church can hardly urge people beyond the limits of institutions. Instead, the churches offer us a safe haven from the fears of life. Mythology leads directly into the heart of those fears, and in every culture the mythological landscape contains the image of the Trickster – pushing, goading, jabbing the kings and heroes whenever they turn away from the inner world of truth.

In the King Arthur legends Merlin appears not only as a sorcerer and wise man but as a trickster. Constantly he appears before Arthur in disguise, as a child, a beggar, an old peasant. The young king, already seduced into pompousness by his high social position, never recognizes Merlin until his companions point out that he has been tricked again. More important than laws or military strategy is the ability to see through illusions. The Taoist masters were famous for playing tricks on their disciples.

The Fool archetype has even found social expression, as the real court jester. We all know the image from *King Lear* of 'the fool', permitted to tell the king truths no one else would dare to express. Today, our comedians and satirists enjoy something of the same privilege.

In many countries a yearly carnival releases all the wildness repressed through the rest of the year. Sex is freer, various laws are suspended, people go in disguises and the King of Fools is chosen to preside over the festival. Today, in Europe and North America, April the first remains 'April Fool's Day', a time for tricks and practical jokes.

The picture beside that of the Rider pack shows the Fool as conceived by Oswald Wirth. An older tradition than that of Waite, it pictures the archetype as a grotesque wanderer. This image has been interpreted variously as the soul before enlightenment, a newborn child entering the world of experience and the principle of anarchy. Elizabeth Haich has provided an interesting interpretation of Wirth's grotesque image of the Fool. Placing him between Judgement and the World, she describes the Fool as what the outside world sees when it looks upon someone who is truly enlightened. Because the Fool does not follow their rules or share their weaknesses, he appears to them in this ugly distorted way. Haich describes the Fool's face as a mask, put there not by himself but by the outside world. The last card, the World, presents the same enlightened person, but viewed from inside, that is, by himself.

In some early Tarot decks the Fool appeared as a giant court jester, towering over the people around him. His title was 'the Fool of God'. The term has also been used for idiots, harmless madmen, and severe epileptics, all of whom were thought to be in touch with a greater wisdorn precisely because they were out of touch with the rest of us.

The archetype persists in modern popular mythology as well. By their fantastic primitive nature comic books often reflect mythological themes better than novels. In *Batman* the hero's strongest enemy is called the Joker, a figure who has no past and is never seen without the wild make-up of a joker in a deck of cards. The joker is not descended from the Fool as I, and other Tarotists, have assumed. It was invented by a New York poker club as a 'wild card' to make the game more interesting. It does, however, call forth the same archetype as the Fool, being based on the court jester. The rivalry of Batman and the Joker sends a clear message to their readers: do not rebel against social values. Support law and order. In recent years the magazine has described the Joker as insane rather than criminal. To society the way of the Fool, instinct rather than rules, is a dangerous insanity.

So far we have looked at the Fool as the 'other', prodding us from complacency with his jokes and disguises. As the 'self' he represents that long tradition of the foolish brother or sister, despised by the older brothers and sisters, yet finally able to win the princess or the prince through instinctive wit and kindness.

Curiously the image of the Fool as self occurs more in fairy tales than myths. We look at myths as representing forces larger than ourselves; the simpler fairy tale allows us to express our own foolishness.

Like 'Boots' or 'Gluck' in the fairy tale, always accompanied by various animal helpers, the Fool in almost every deck walks with a companion. In Waite the figure is a leaping dog, in others a cat or even a crocodile. The animal symbolizes the forces of nature and the animal self of man, all in harmony with the spirit who acts from instinct. Mythological dogs are often terrifying, for example, the Hound of Hell chasing lost souls. But it is really the same beast; only our attitude changes. Deny your inner self and it becomes ferocious. Obey it and it becomes benign.

Waite's Fool holds a white rose. Roses symbolize passion, while white, the traditional colour of purity, together with the delicate way the flower is held, indicate the passions raised to a higher level. The Greeks saw Eros, the god of love, as a trickster, making the most proper people act ridiculous. But those who already express their folly will not be thrown by love. The Greeks also spoke of Eros, in other forms, as the animating force of the universe.

The bag behind him carries his experiences. He does not abandon them, he is not mindless, they simply do not control him in the way that our memories and traumas so often control our lives. The bag bears the head of an eagle, symbol of the soaring spirit. His high instinct fills and transforms all experience. The eagle is also the symbol of Scorpio raised to a higher level, that is, sexuality raised to spirit. This idea of the connection between sex and spirit will come up again with the card of the Devil.

Over his shoulder the Fool carries a stick, like a tramp. But this stick is actually a wand, symbol of power. The Magician and the Chariot driver also carry wands, but self-consciously, with a powerful grip. The Fool and the World Dancer hold their wands so casually we hardly notice them. What could be more foolish than to take a magic wand and use it to carry your bags? We can imagine a fairy tale in which the foolish younger brother finds a stick by the side of the road and carries it, not recognizing it as the lost wand of a wizard, and therefore not being destroyed like his two older brothers who tried to wield it for their own profit.

The Fool's wand is black; the others are white. For the unconscious Fool the spirit force remains always in potential, always ready, because he is not consciously directing it. We tend to misunderstand the colour black, seeing it as evil, or negation of life. Rather, black means all things being possible, infinite energy of life before consciousness has constructed any boundaries. When we fear blackness or darkness we fear the deep unconscious source of life itself.

Like the joker, the Fool really belongs anywhere in the deck, in combination with and between any of the other cards. He is the animating force giving life to the static images. In the Major Arcana he belongs wherever there is a difficult transition. Hence his position at the beginning, where there is the transition from the everyday world of the Minor Arcana to the world of archetypes. The Fool also helps us jump the gap from one line to the next, that is, from the Chariot to Strength, from Temperance to the Devil. To reach the Chariot or Temperance requires great effort and courage, and without the Fool's readiness to leap into new territory we would likely stop with what we have already achieved.

The Fool belongs as well with those cards of difficult passage, such as the Moon and Death (observe the winding road on each of these two), where he urges us on despite our fears.

In the Minor Arcana the Fool relates first of all to Wands – action, eagerness, movement without thought. But it connects as well to Cups, with their emphasis on imagination and instinct. The Fool, in fact, combines these two suits. Later we will see that this combination, fire and water, represents the way of transformation.

Finally the question arises of the Fool's place in divinatory readings. I have already mentioned the importance of readings for a fuller understanding of the cards. Even more, they help us apply the wisdom of the cards to our daily lives. In readings the Fool speaks to us of courage and optimism, urging faith in ourselves and in life. At difficult times, when we come under pressure from people around us to be practical, the Fool reminds us that our own inner selves can best tell us what to do.

The Fool can often symbolize beginnings, courageously leaping off into some new phase of life, particularly when that leap is taken from some deep feeling rather than careful planning.

These belong to the Fool in its normal position. We must also consider the 'reversed' meanings, that is, when the way we have mixed the cards makes the Fool come out with the feet on the top. Reversed meanings are controversial among Tarot commentators. Those who give formulas as meanings usually just turn the formula around, a simplistic method which has led several interpreters to abandon the whole idea of reversed meanings. But we can also look at reversals as deepening the meaning of the card as a whole. In general, a reversed card indicates that the qualities of that card have become blocked, distorted or channelled in another direction.

For the Fool a reversal means first of all a failure to follow your instincts. It can mean not taking a chance at some crucial time, because of fear or depending too much on plans and the practical advice of others.

Another reversed meaning of the Fool will appear at first to contradict the one just given. Recklessness, wildness, crazy schemes all seem the opposite of over-caution. And yet, they originate from the same weakness, a failure to act from inside. The reckless person superimposes a conscious or artificial foolishness on his life both because he does not trust the unconscious to act as a guide and because is also afraid of doing nothing.

This second reversed meaning suggests another dimension to the Fool – the awareness that great chances must be taken only at the proper time. There are, after all, many times when caution is needed, and times when it is better to do nothing at all. The basic thing any oracle teaches us is that no action or attitude is right or wrong, except in its proper context.

As we go further into the Tarot we will see that this concept of the proper time permeates the cards and is, in fact, the true key to their correct use. The card in the Rider pack that falls exactly in the middle of the three lines, that is, Justice, means a proper response.

Figure 2

THE MAGICIAN

The Magician emerges very directly from the Fool in the image of the trickster-wizard. As mentioned above, Merlin fulfils both these roles (as well as that of teacher and wise man), and many other myths make the same connection. Earlier Tarot decks pictured trump number one as a conjurer rather than a magus, or even a juggler tossing coloured balls in the air. Charles Williams described him as a juggler tossing the stars and planets.

Most modern images of the trump follow Waite's wizard, raising a magic wand to bring into reality the spirit force – the energy of life in its most creative form. He holds the wand carefully, aware of that psychic power the Fool carried so lightly on his shoulder. Thus, the Magician, as the beginning of the Major Arcana proper, represents consciousness, action and creation. He symbolizes the idea of manifestation, that is, making something real out of the possibilities in life. Therefore, we see the four emblems of the Minor Arcana – lying on a table in front of him. He not only uses the physical world for his magical operations (the four emblems are all objects used by wizards in their rituals), but he also creates the world, in the sense of giving life a meaning and direction.

The Magician stands surrounded by flowers to remind us that

the emotional and creative power we feel in our lives needs to be grounded in physical reality for us to get any value from it. Unless we make something of our potentials they do not really exist.

'In the beginning, God created the heaven and the earth.' The Bible begins at the moment the spirit descends into physical reality. For us, in the physical world, we can talk of nothing before this moment. In the linking of the Tarot with the Hebrew alphabet the Fool often receives the first letter *Aleph. (Aleph* bears no sound; it is a silent carrier of vowels, and therefore symbolizes nothingness. It is the first letter of the Ten Commandments.) This would assign the second Hebrew letter, *Beth,* the first letter with an actual sound, to the Magician. *Beth is* the first letter of Genesis.

Look at Waite's picture of the Magician. He is not casting spells, or conjuring up demons. He simply stands with one hand raised to heaven and the other pointed to the green earth. He is a lightning rod. By opening himself up to the spirit he draws it down into himself, and then that downward hand, like a lightning rod buried in the ground, runs the energy into the earth. Into reality.

We see many accounts of the 'descent of the spirit' in the Bible, in other religious texts and in contemporary religious experience. People 'speak in tongues' in Pentecostal churches, they scream and shout and roll on the floor at Gospel meetings. The priest giving communion sees himself as a 'vessel' or channel for the Holy Ghost. But we can see this experience in much simpler, non-religious, terms as well. People tremble with excitement at sporting events. 'I'm so excited I could burst!' In a new love affair or at the start of a new career, we feel a power filling us. You can sometimes see people at the opening of some important phase of their lives, tapping their legs up and down, half bouncing in their seats, filled with some energy they cannot seem to discharge. And writers and artists, when their work is going well, will experience themselves as almost passive channels for a spirit-like force. The word 'inspiration' originally meant 'filled with a holy breath', and derives from the same root as 'spirit'.

Notice that of all these examples all but the priest and the artist are seized with a frenzy. The possessed church-goer and the teen-ager about to burst at a football game share the feeling that their bodies are overwhelmed by a power too great for it. Far from being gentle the surge of energy can be almost painful. The person in religious fervour shouts and leaps about in order to release an unbearable energy.

The life force that fills the universe is not gentle or benign. It must be discharged, grounded in something real, because our bodies, our selves, are not meant to contain it, but only pass it on. Thus, the artist does not join in the physical frenzy because she or he is discharging that power into the painting. Similarly the priest passes the power into the bread and wine.

We function best as a channel for energy. Unless we follow the path of the High Priestess in withdrawing from the world, we live our lives most fully when we create or are active. 'Create' does not mean simply art, but any activity that produces something real and valuable outside of ourselves.

Many people experience feelings of being powerful so infrequently they try to hold on to them. By doing nothing they hope to preserve their magic moments. But we can really hold on to power in our lives only by constantly discharging it. By releasing creative power we open ourselves up to receive a further flow. However, by trying to hold on to it, we block the channels and the sense of power, which is really life itself, withers within us. The spectator at the football game, even the possessed church-goer, will find their excitement gone after the event that triggered it has ended. But the craftsman or scientist or teacher – or, for that matter, the Tarot reader – will find the power increase over the years the more they discharge it into physical reality.

When we look at the Magician those of us who feel a lack or a flatness in our lives will be drawn to the wand raised towards heaven. But the real magic rests in that finger pointing to the earth. That ability to create gives him his title. His image stems not only from the trickster-conjurer, but also from the archetypal hero. In our culture this would be Prometheus, who brought the heavenly fire down to weak and cold humanity.

In the West we tend to see wizards as manipulators. They learn secret techniques or make deals with Satan in order to gain personal power. This somewhat decadent image comes partly from the magicians themselves, since they make charms to find buried treasure, but also from the Church, which sees magicians, who deal directly with the spirit instead of going through the official priest-hood, as competitors. The Tarot and all occult sciences are in a sense revolutionary, because they teach direct salvation, in this life, through your own efforts.

We can get a different concept of the Magician through the image of the shaman, or medicine man. Because no hierarchical Church has arisen to banish the shamans they have not become isolated from the community. They serve as healers, teachers, and directors of the soul after death. Like the wizards, the shamans study and learn complicated techniques. Their magical vocabulary is often much larger than the everyday vocabulary of the people around them. None of this training, however, is used to manipulate the spirit or for personal gain. Rather, the shaman only seeks to become a proper channel, both for himself so he will not be over-whelmed, and for the community so he can serve them better. He knows the great power that will enter him at moments of ecstasy and he wants to make sure it does not destroy him and make him of no use to the people around him.

Like the wizard the shaman has developed his will to the point where he can direct the fire that fills him. At the same time he remains open, allowing his ego to dissolve under the direct onslaught of the spirit. It says something about our culture that our wizards stand inside magic circles to make sure the demons cannot touch them.

We can apply the shaman attitude to our use of the whole Tarot deck. We study the cards, learn the symbolic language, even spec-ific formulas, in order to give a direction to the feelings they arouse in us. But we must not forget that the true magic lies in the images themselves and not the explanations.

The divinatory meanings of the Magician derive from both hands, the one which receives the power and the one which directs. The card means first of all an awareness of power in your life, of spirit or simple excitement possessing you. It can also mean, depending on its position and your reaction to it, someone else's power affecting you. Like the Fool, the card refers to beginnings, but here the first actual steps. It can mean both the inspiration to begin some new project or phase of life, and the excitement that sustains you through the hard work to reach your goal. For many people the Magician can become a strong personal symbol for the creative force throughout their lives.

Secondly, the Magician means will-power; the will unified and directed towards goals. It means having great strength because all your energy is channelled in a specific direction. People who seem always to get what they want in life are often people who simply know what they want and can direct their energy. The Magician teaches us that both will-power and success derive from being conscious of the power available to everyone. Most people rarely act; instead they react, being knocked from one experience to the next. To act is to direct your strength, through the will, to the places where you want it to go.

The Magician reversed signifies that in some way the proper flow of energy has become disrupted or blocked. It can mean a weakness, a lack of will or a confusion of purpose that leads to doing nothing. The power is there, but we cannot touch it. The card reversed can mean the lethargic apathy that characterizes depression.

The reversed trump can also mean power abused, a person who uses his or her very strong character to exert a destructive influence on others. The most direct example of this would of course be the psychic aggression of 'black magic'.

Finally, the Magician reversed indicates mental disquiet, hallucinations, fear and particularly fear of madness. This problem arises when the energy or spirit fire enters a person who does not know how to direct it into an outer reality. If we do not ground the lightning it can become trapped in the body and force itself on our awareness as anxiety or hallucinations. Anyone who has ever gone through a moment of total panic will know that acute mental anxiety is a very physical experience, a feeling of the body running wild, like a fire out of control. The word 'panic' means 'possessed by the god Pan', himself a symbol of magical forces.

Think again of the lightning rod. It not only attracts the bolt but runs it into the dirt. Without that connection to the earth the lightning would burn down the house.

Several writers have commented on the relationship between shamanism and what the West calls 'schizophrenia'. Shamans are often not so much chosen as found. If, in our culture, a young person experiences visions, fearful hallucinations, we do not know what to do with such experiences other than to try and stop them, by drugs and self-control. But in other cultures, such people receive training. This is not to say that madness does not exist or is not recognized in archaic cultures. Rather, the training is meant to prevent madness by channelling the experiences into a productive direction.

The initiates learn, through study with an established shaman, and through physical techniques such as fasting, how to understand, structure and finally direct these visionary experiences towards the service of the community. The Magician reversed should not be banished or confined; instead, we must find the way to turn it right side up.

Figure 3

THE HIGH PRIESTESS

Bill Butler, in *The Definitive Tarot* has commented on the historical-legendary sources for this female archetype. Throughout the Middle Ages the story persisted that a woman was once elected Pope. Disguised for years as a man, this supposed 'Pope Joan' made her way through the Church hierarchy to the top position, only to die in childbirth during an Easter celebration.

Pope Joan was most likely a legend; the Visconti Papess was real. In the late thirteenth century an Italian group called the Guglielmites believed that their founder, Guglielma of Bohemia, who died in 1281, would rise again in 1300 and begin a new age in which women would be popes. Jumping ahead they elected a woman named Manfreda Visconti as the first papess. The Church graphically ended this heresy by burning Sister Manfreda in 1300, the year of the expected new age. Some one hundred and fifty years later the same Visconti family commissioned the first set of Tarot cards as we know them. Among these unnumbered and unnamed trumps appeared a picture of a woman later decks titled 'The Papess'.

The name persisted until the eighteenth century when Court de Gebelin, believing the Tarot to originate in the Isis religion of ancient Egypt, changed the name to the High Priestess. Today both names exist (as well as 'Veiled Isis'), and the Waite image of the card derives directly from the Isis priestess's symbolic clothing, particularly the crown representing the three phases of the moon.

The Pope Joan legend and Manfreda Visconti are not simply historical curiosities. They illustrate a major social development in the Middle Ages, the reintroduction of the female and feminine principles into religion and cosmology. The images and the concepts associated with the masculine role had dominated both the Church and Jewish religion for centuries. As a result ordinary people experienced the religions of the priests and rabbis as remote, harsh, and unapproachable, with their emphasis on sin, judgement, and punishment. They wanted qualities of mercy and love. And they identified these with women. Like a mother shelters her child from the somewhat distant strictness of the father, a female diety supposedly would intrude for the pathetic sinners against the unremitting judgement of the Father.

It is interesting to realize that in many ways the Church saw Christ, as the Son, in exactly that role of introducing love and compassion. Yet, the people demanded a female. Even the idea of the Church as 'Mother Church' did not go far enough. Finally, the Church capitulated by raising the Virgin Mary almost to the level of Christ himself.

Many writers and scholars believe that the elevation of Mary – as well as the priests' costume of long skirts – originated in the

Church's desire to assimilate a persistent goddess religion from the days before Christianity. If this is true it would indicate not so much a cultural conservatism as the power of the female archetype to maintain a hold and partially triumph against suppression.

In Judaism the official religion of the rabbis managed to resist any insurgent feminism. The people's need, however, took hold in another area: the long tradition of the Kabbalah. The Kabbalists took a term from the Talmud, 'Shekinah', which meant God's glory manifest in the physical world, and revised it to make it God's anima, or female side. The Kabbalists also revised the idea of Adam, making him originally hermaphroditic. The separation of Eve from Adam, even the separation of the Shekinah from God, became images of isolation and exile, sometimes connected to Adam and the sin of disobedience.

So far we have looked at the benign motherly qualities of female mythological figures. Historically, however, female deities have always shown a dark, hidden side as well. To introduce the female at all is to introduce the whole archetype. The Tarot splits up the feminine archetype into two trumps and actually assigns the benign qualities to the second one (trump 3), the Empress. The High Priestess herself represents a deeper, more subtle aspect of the female; that of the dark, the mysterious and the hidden. As such, she connects to the virgin side of the Virgin Mary, the pure daughter side of the Shekinah (who was pictured simultaneously as mother, wife, and daughter).

We should realize that this assigning of qualities to women comes mostly from men and male ideas. The Kabbalists, the occultists, and the Tarot designers, all deplored the separation of men and women into categories and taught unification as a final goal. This is shown by the World dancer of the Tarot. They were ahead of the established religion which even debated whether women had souls at all. Nevertheless, men still made the categories. To men, women have always appeared mysterious, strange, and, when safely in their mother role, loving and merciful. Women seem alien to men, more subtle in their thinking and non-rational. In our time, constant novels and films have pictured simple men manipulated by cunning women.

The fact that the menstrual cycle lasts about as long as the lunar cycle links women to that remote silvery body. Menstruation itself, a copious bleeding from the genitals, with no loss of life, has simply terrified men through the centuries. Even today superstitious Jews believe that one drop of menstrual blood will kill a plant. The fearful mystery of birth further connected women to the idea of darkness. The foetus grows and the soul enters it in the warm moist darkness of the womb. Motherhood linked women to the earth, and there too darkness dominates. Seeds lie in the ground through the dark dead winter, to emerge as food under the warm reassuring rays of the sun which, in many cultures, is considered as male.

Just as the sun's rays penetrate the earth so the male organ penetrates the female to leave a seed in her mysterious womb. We can easily see how men came to view themselves as active and women as both passive and mysterious. People often link passive with 'negative' or that is, inferior and weak. But passivity contains its own power. It gives the mind a chance to work. People who only know action never get a chance to reflect on what that action has taught them. In a deeper sense, passivity allows the unconscious to emerge. Only through withdrawal from outer involvement can we allow the inner voice of vision and psychic forces to speak to us. It is precisely to avoid this inner voice that many people never rest from action and movement. Our society, based completely on outer achievement, fosters a terror of the unconscious, yet without its wisdom we can never fully know ourselves or the world.

The High Priestess represents all these qualities: darkness, mystery, psychic forces, the power of the moon to stir the unconscious, passivity, and the wisdom gained from it. This wisdom cannot be expressed in rational terms; to try to do so would be to immediately limit, narrow, and falsify it. Most people at some time have felt they understood something in such a deep way that they could never manage to explain it. Myths serve as metaphors for deep psychic feelings; yet the myths themselves, like the explanations given by theologians and anthropologists, are only symbols. The High Priestess signifies inner wisdom at its deepest level.

She sits before two pillars, representing both the temple of Isis and the ancient Hebrew temple in Jerusalem, the dwelling place of God on earth, in other words, the home of the Shekinah. A veil hangs between the two pillars, indicating that we are barred from entering the place of wisdom. The image of the veiled temple or sanctuary appears in many religions. The Shekinah was indeed said to dwell within the veiled ark of the temple.

Now, most people assume we are somehow forbidden to pass the pillars of the High Priestess. In reality, we simply do not know how to. To enter behind the veil would be to know consciously the irrational wisdom of the unconscious. That is the goal of the entire Major Arcana. Look carefully at Smith's picture. You can see what lies behind the veil by looking between the veil and the pillars. And what lies behind is water. No great temple or complex symbols, simply a pool of water, a line of hills, and the sky. The pool signifies the unconscious and the truth hidden there. The water is motionless, the secrets in its darkest depths, hidden under a smooth surface. For most of us, at most times, the turbulent unconscious remains hidden under a placid layer of consciousness. We cannot enter the temple because we do not know how to go into ourselves; therefore we must travel through the trumps until we reach the Star and the Moon, where we can finally stir up the waters and return with the wisdom to the conscious light of the Sun.

The temple introduces the image of the two pillars, and the theme of duality and opposites. The image occurs again and again through the trumps, in such obvious places as the Hierophant's church pillars or the two towers of the Moon (the pillars of the High Priestess seen from the other side), but also in more subtle ways, such as the two sphinxes of the Chariot, or the man and woman of the Lovers. Finally, Judgement, with the child rising between a man and a woman, and the World, holding two wands, resolves the duality by uniting the inner mysteries with the outer awareness.

The letters 'B' and 'J' stand for Boaz and Jakin, the names given to the two main pillars of the temple in Jerusalem. Obviously, the dark Boaz stands for passivity and mystery while Jakin symbolizes action and consciousness. Notice, though, that the letters carry the reverse indications, a white B and a black J. Like the dots in the Tao symbol the letters signify that duality is an illusion, and each extreme carries the other imbedded inside it.

In her lap she holds a scroll marked 'Tora'. This name refers to the Jewish law, the Five Books of Moses which is usually spelled

'Torah' in English. This particular spelling allows the word to serve as an anagram for 'Taro'. As the ultimate subject of all Kabbalistic meditations (like Christ's crucifixion for Christian mystics) the Torah carries a great deal of esoteric significance. The Kabbalists believed that the Torah read on Saturday mornings in the synagogues was only a representation, a kind of shadow of the true Torah, the living word of God that existed before the universe and contains within it all true existence. The Tora held by the High Priestess, rolled up and partly concealed in her cloak, therefore signifies a higher knowledge closed to us with our lower understanding. We can describe it also as the psychic truths available to us only in the distorted form of myths and dreams.

Earlier we spoke of the Fool coming in at crucial moments of change to push us along. The gap between the High Priestess and the Empress is one such moment. We can too easily be seduced by the dark coolness of the second trump, even if we never really penetrate its secrets. The person beginning in spiritual discipline often prefers to stay at the visionary level rather than go through the slow hard work needed to advance. Many people in more ordinary situations will find life too overwhelming, too vast and demanding, for them to take part. We can best use the High Priestess's passivity as a balance to the outward-looking attitude of the Magician, but many people find the passive side extremely attractive. It represents an answer to struggle, a quiet retreat instead of the harsh glare of self-exposure when we involve ourselves openly with other people.

But the human mind does not work like that. It requires passion and it needs to connect itself to the world. If we cannot penetrate the veil the temple remains for us an empty place, devoid of meaning. The person who tries to live a completely passive life becomes depressed, more and more trapped in a cycle of apathy and fear.

Virtually all moon goddess religions feature myths of the goddess's ferocious side. Ovid tells the story of Actaeon, a hunter, and therefore a figure who properly belonged to the world of action. He happened one day to see a stream and decided to follow it to its source (again, water as a symbol of the unconscious). Thus he became separated from his dogs and the other hunters, and when he had reached the source, away from the active world, he saw a group of maidens. Among them, naked, stood the virgin goddess,

Diana. Now, if Actaeon had returned immediately to the outer world he would have found his life enriched. Instead, he allowed Diana's beauty to fascinate him; he stayed too long, and the goddess, discovering that a man had seen her nakedness (compare the High Priestess's layers of clothing with the Star maiden's nudity) turned Actaeon into a stag. When he ran away, terrified, his own dogs tore him to pieces.

Here the Fool comes in (and remember the Fool's dog, leaping at his side), reminding us to dance lightly away from both these visions, the Magician as well as the High Priestess, until we are truly ready to assimilate them.

The divinatory meanings of the High Priestess deal first with a sense of mystery in life, both things we do not know, and things we cannot know. It indicates a sense of darkness, sometimes as an area of fear in our lives, but also one of beauty. A period of passive withdrawal can enrich our lives by allowing things inside to awaken.

As an emblem of secret knowledge the trump indicates that feeling of intuitively understanding the answer to some great problem, if only we could express that answer consciously. More specifically, the card can refer to visions and to occult and psychic powers, such as clairvoyance.

In its most positive aspect the High Priestess signifies the potential in our lives – very strong possibilities we have not realized, though we can sense them as possible. Action must follow or the potential will never be realized.

Despite its deep wisdom the card can sometimes carry a negative meaning. Like most of the trumps, the High Priestess's value depends on the context of the other cards. Negatively the trump indicates passiveness at the wrong time or for too long, leading to weakness, fear of life and other people. It shows a person with strong intuition who cannot translate feelings into action, or a person afraid to open up to other people. Whether the good or bad aspect of the card comes up in a particular reading depends on the surrounding cards and of course the reader's intuition (we partake of the High Priestess every time we read the cards). Very often both meanings will apply. Human beings have more than one side.

The High Priestess is an archetype, a single-minded picture of one aspect of existence. When we reverse it we bring in the missing qualities. The card reversed signifies a turn towards passion, towards a deep involvement with life and other people, in all ways, emotionally, sexually and competitively. However, the pendulum can swing too far, and then the card reversed can symbolize a loss of that most precious knowledge: the sense of our inner selves.

THE WORLDLY SEQUENCE

THE MAJOR ARCANA AND PERSONAL GROWTH

The first line of the Major Arcana takes us through the process of maturity. It shows the stages of a person's growth from a child, to whom mother is all loving and father all powerful, through education, to the point where the child becomes an independent personality. At the same time these cards deal with a much wider development, of which the individual development is a microcosm. They depict the creation of human society, out of both the archetypes of existence and the chaotic energy of nature.

While they set the principles for the whole deck, the Magician and the High Priestess apply very specifically to the first line. The movement between opposites is the basic rhythm of the material world. Nothing exists absolutely in nature. In the words of Ursula Le Guin, 'Light is the left hand of darkness and darkness the right hand of light.' When we move from the two principles to the Empress we are seeing the opposites mingle together in nature to produce the reality of the physical universe.

The middle three cards of the line are a set. They show us a triad of nature, society, and.the Church. They also signify mother, father, and education. In ancient Egypt the godhead was often viewed as a trinity. The persons changed from place to place and through the years, but they were usually a female and two males, with the female viewed as supreme. In the Tarot, nature, symbolized by the

Empress, is the underlying reality, while her consorts, symbolized by the Emperor and the Hierophant, are human constructs.

The last two cards of the line represent the problems of the individual, love and sorrow, surrender and will. At some point each one of us must learn to distinguish ourselves from the outer world. Before this time personality remains a vague and formless creation of parents and society. Those who never make the break become cut off from a full life. For most people the medium by which they break from their parents is the emergence (Freudians and perhaps occultists would say 're-emergence') of the sexual drive at puberty. It is no accident that children rebel from their parents in ideas, habits, and dress at the same time that their bodies grow towards maturity.

The development of individuality is only a part of growth. Each person must find his or her personal goals and achievements. At the same time he or she will sooner or later face sorrow, sickness, and the general weakness of a life governed by old age and death. Only when we reach a full understanding of the outer life of humanity can we hope to reach inwards for a deeper reality.

Figure 4

THE EMPRESS

As stated in the previous chapter the Empress represents the more accessible, more benign aspects of the female archetype. She is motherhood, love, gentleness. At the same time she signifies sexuality, emotion and the female as mistress. Both motherhood and sex derive from feelings that are non-intellectual and basic to life. Passions rather than ideas. The High Priestess represented the mental side of the female archetype; her deep intuitive understanding. The Empress is pure emotion.

Like the Cunning Woman, we see her reflected in our movies and novels as the exasperating female, who both frustrates and delights, because her thought processes follow no rational development. Many women find this image insulting, partly because it represents values and approaches judged as negative by our patriarchal society, and partly because people make the error of assuming that women and men should personally express these archetypal ideas. But the social images are crippling in another way as well. They are trivial. The Empress, along with such mythological counterparts as Aphrodite or Ishtar or Erzulie, represent something very grand. They signify the passionate approach to life. They give and take experience with uncontrolled feeling.

Until we learn to experience the outer world completely we cannot hope to transcend it. Therefore the first step to enlightenment is sensuality. Only through passion, can we sense, from deep inside rather than through intellectual argument, the spirit that fills all existence.

Many people see religion as an alternative to the natural world, which they view as somehow impure or dirty. Though our cultural tradition fosters this duality it is really an illusion, and the person who approaches spirituality with this motivation to escape will likely never achieve a very developed understanding. The body, and the natural world, are realities that must be integrated rather than denied.

In the mythology of Buddhism we find that the gods manipulated Prince Siddhartha's father into providing his son, Gautama, with every sensual satisfaction. The father believed that pleasure would prevent his son from renouncing the world and becoming a

Buddha. The scheme backfired, because only after he had completely experienced sensuality could the prince leave it behind. After renouncing the world Gautama joined the ascetics, the other pole. But he reached enlightenment only when he had rejected both extremes for the Middle Way. Thus, we can see the Buddha in the World dancer who holds both the Magician and the High Priestess lightly in her hands.

As a combination of 1 and 2 the number 3 signifies synthesis and harmony. The natural world combines the Magician and the High Priestess in an indivisible unity of life and death, darkness and light. The idea of emotion also brings together the Magician archetype of activeness with the High Priestess archetype of instinct.

Consider as well the process of creation. The Magician symbolizes the energy of life, the High Priestess the possibilities of future development. The reality of the Empress results from their combination. Recently Carl Sagan demonstrated that life on earth might have begun when a lightning bolt struck the primordial sea. Thus again, from the lightning of the Magician striking the waters of the High Priestess, comes the natural world.

The symbolism of the Waite-Smith Empress reflects the idea of nature, with all its force and glory. The Empress herself, voluptuous and sensual, suggests passion. Her shield is a heart with the sign of Venus, the Roman version of the Great Goddess. Throughout the ancient world the goddess ruled, as Demeter, Astarte, Nut, until the patriarchal invaders demoted her to wife (and finally banished her altogether with an all-male godhead). At the Empress's feet grows a field of grain; the goddess ruled agriculture, and in North-Western Europe was called the 'Corn Goddess'. She wears a necklace of nine pearls, for the nine planets, while her crown contains twelve stars for the signs of the zodiac. In short, she wears the universe as her jewellery. The Great Mother is not the forms of nature, but the underlying principle of life. The stars are six-pointed, a symbol much older than its current use as a social emblem for Judaism. The six-pointed star combines two triangles; the upwards one symbolizes fire, the downwards one water. Again, the Empress combines trumps 1 and 2 in a new reality.

A river flows from the trees behind her to disappear beneath her seat. This river is the force of life, running like a great current beneath all the separate forms of reality, and experienced most fully when we give ourselves to unrestrained passion. Deep in our selves we can sense the rhythm of a river, carrying us forward through experience until, with death, our individual lives return to the sea of existence.

The river symbolizes also the unity of change and stability. The water in it is never the same, yet it always remains a particular river, with its own special qualities. Human beings change from day to day, the cells of our bodies die and new ones take their place, yet we always remain ourselves.

The number 3 produced by the combination of 1 and 2 brings out yet another idea. Just as the numbers 1 and 2 stood specifically for male and female, so the number 3 signifies the child produced by their joining together. The child is born as a creature of nature, unburdened with ego and personality, experiencing the universe directly, without controls or labels. It is only as we grow older that we learn to put barriers between ourselves and life. It is one of the goals of the Tarot to return us to that natural state of directly experiencing the world around us.

But if the Empress signifies the child she also stands for the mother. Motherhood is the basic means by which life continues throughout nature. And because the physical bond of the mother and child is so direct, mother love, in its strongest form, is pure feeling, given without intellectual or moral considerations. (This is, of course, an ideal, and in reality such love may come more from the male parent than the female, or sadly, not at all.) Throughout history people have identified motherhood with nature, so that the term 'Great Mother' for the earth itself appears all over the world, and even today we speak vaguely of Mother Nature.

In readings the Empress represents a time of passion, a period when we approach life through feelings and pleasure rather than thought. The passion is sexual or motherly; either way it is deeply experienced, and in the right context can give great satisfaction. In the wrong context, when analysis is needed, the Empress can mean a stubborn emotional approach, a refusal to consider the facts. She can indicate another problem as well: self-indulgent pleasure when restraint is needed. Usually, however, she indicates satisfaction and even understanding gained through the emotions. The reversed meanings of the cards also have their positive and negative contexts. On the one hand it can signify a retreat from feeling, either rejecting your emotions or attempting to suppress your desires, particularly sexual. However, just as the High Priestess, upside down, added the missing element of involvement, so the Empress reversed can mean a new intellectual awareness, especially the solving of some complicated emotional problem by calmly thinking it through.

In their right side up and reversed meanings trumps 2 and 3 are mirrors of each other. It sometimes happens that in a reading both will appear, upside down. This means that the person expresses both emotional and intuitive mental aspects, but in a negative way. Rationality comes as a reaction to excessive emotional involvement, while a feeling of isolation or coldness leads to passion. If the two aspects of the goddess can be experienced right side up the person will achieve a more stable and rewarding balance.

(a)

(b)

Figure 5

THE EMPEROR

For each child its parents are archetypes. Not just mother and father, but Mother and Father. Because our mothers give us life and feed us and shelter us we tend to see them as figures of love and mercy (and get very upset when they act harshly or coldly). But the Father, especially in traditional times when the sex roles were stricter, remained more remote, and therefore a figure of severity. It was the father who bore the authority and thus became the judge, the father who punished (and the mother who intervened) and the father who taught us the rules of society and then demanded obedience. To the child the father is in many ways indistinguishable from society as a whole, just as the mother is nature itself. One of the painful moments of maturity for many people comes when they discover the limited humanity of their parents.

In Freud's scheme of mental development the father and the rules of society become directly linked. The infant psyche demands constant satisfaction, particularly in its desires for food and physical pleasure from the mother. (Freudians may claim the child desires actual intercourse with its mother, but the situation holds even if the child seeks only the pleasure of being held against the mother's body.) By interfering in the child's relationship to its mother the father arouses the child's hostility, and for the still unrepressed infant, this means a desire to do away with the interference altogether. The urge to destroy the father, however, cannot be consummated or even recognized, and so the psyche, to relieve the terrible dilemma, identifies itself with the Father image, creating a 'super-ego' as a new guide for the self (replacing the 'id' – the urges and desires which led to such a crisis). But what form does this super-ego take? Precisely that of the rules of society, traditionally learned under the father's guidance.

Trumps 3 and 4 of the Tarot represent the parents in their archetypal roles. But just as the Empress signified the natural world, so the Emperor carries the wider significance of the social world 'married' to nature. He symbolizes the laws of society, both good and bad, and the power that enforces them.

In ancient times, where the Goddess reigned, the king performed a special function. New life can only come from death;

therefore, each winter, the Goddess's representatives sacrificed the old king, very often dismembering him and planting the pieces in the ground, thereby mystically fertilizing the earth. Later, when the male dominated religions took over, the king came to symbolize the rule of law which had clamped a lid of repression on what seemed to the patriarchs as the monstrous and chaotic darkness of the old order. We see this drama (much like Freud's substitution of super-ego for id) in many myths; such as Marduk, national hero of Babylon, killing Tiamat, the original mother of creation, because she is giving birth to monsters. Whether or not we see the old ways as monstrous or the new as civilized, the Emperor symbolizes the abstraction of society replacing the direct experience of nature.

In Rome, the concept of law versus chaos was carried to the point where stability, or 'law and order' to use the modern term, became virtues in themselves, apart from the inherent morality of those laws. No progress can be made in conditions of anarchy (runs the argument); bad laws need to be changed, but first the law must be obeyed at all costs. Any other approach can only destroy society. Today, we see this viewpoint embodied in an abstraction we call the 'system'. The Romans saw it more concretely in the personal figure of the Emperor, whom they described as the father of all his people.

In the Emperor's best aspect he indicates the stability of a just society that allows its members to pursue their personal needs and development. The natural world is chaotic; without some kind of social structure we could each spend all our lives fighting to survive. Society allows us both to work together and to benefit from the experience of those who !ived before us.

Stability allows spiritual development as well. In many countries society supports the churches (though whether this arrangement furthers spirituality is arguable); in some Eastern countries monks are free to pursue their studies because laymen fill their beggar bowls. Without this social custom they would have to spend their time working to get bread.

In its more negative aspects the Emperor represents the power of unjust laws in a society where stability takes precedence over morality. Once we establish law and order as supreme then a corrupt ruler becomes a disaster. But if the entire system is corrupt, producing only bad rulers, then stability becomes the enemy of morality. The value of the symbol of the Emperor depends a very great deal on time and place. In an unjust society the Emperor's power hinders, rather than helps, personal development. A great many people have gone to gaol for attacking unjust laws.

Even at its best, however, the Emperor remains limited. Over the spontaneity of the Empress he has laid a network of repression. If we lose touch with our passions then life becomes cold and barren. The Rider pack Emperor (see Fig. 5a) is drawn as old and stiff, dressed in iron, representing the sterility of a life rigidly governed by rules. The river which flowed so powerfully through the Empress's garden has here become a thin stream, barely able to penetrate a lifeless desert.

The card's other symbolism reflects its dual aspects. He holds an *ankh*, Egyptian symbol of life, to indicate that under the law he bears the power of life and death, and will hopefully use it well. Four rams, symbols of Aries, adorn his throne while at the crown's peak he bears the sign of Aries (unfortunately resembling a propellor). Now, Aries symbolizes force, aggression and war, but as the first sign of the zodiac it also signifies the new life of spring, which can emerge from the stability of a just society.

As the middle card of the first line of the Major Arcana the Emperor represents a crucial test. In the process of growing up it is indeed the rules of society that many people find most difficult to surmount. We must absorb these rules, as well as our society's traditions and beliefs, then go beyond them to find a personal code of conduct. This does not mean the attitude 'rules are made to be broken'. People who feel compelled to flaunt all laws remain as bound to those laws as the person who follows them blindly.

Because of the father's role in teaching us acceptably social behaviour, people who are trapped at the level of the Emperor are often people who have never really accepted the ordinary humanity of their father. They may recognize it rationally but it disturbs and haunts them. Similar problems plague those people for whom the Empress remains their mother's, rather than their own, passions and sensuality.

The idea of the Emperor as that of the limited values of social structure arises mainly from Waite and his followers. The picture on the right at the start of this section, from Paul Foster Case's Builders of the Adytum (BOTA) deck drawn by Jessie Burns Parke, illustrates another tradition. Here the Emperor symbolizes the sum total of spiritual knowledge. He is drawn in profile (this is much more common than the Rider pack full-face image), linking him to the Kabbalist image for God as the 'Ancient of Days', a seated king in profile. (The Ancient's face was never visible, only his crown with a radiance beneath.)

The Emperor's arms and legs form an equilateral triangle over a cross, the alchemical sign for fire. This figure is later reversed (in Waite as well as Case) in the Hanged Man. The BOTA Emperor sits on a cube rather than a throne. Also an esoteric symbol, the cube symbolizes both the world and the Tarot itself, as well as the Hebrew alphabet and the paths of the Tree of Life. The symbolism arises from the fact that a cube contains twelve edges, six faces, three axes, and of course a centre, adding up to twenty-two, the number of trumps, Hebrew letters, and paths. And because the Tree of Life is held to represent all creation the cube symbolizes the universe.

In readings the Emperor indicates (following the Rider pack image) the power of society, its laws and especially its authority to enforce those laws. The appearance of the trump indicates an encounter with the law. Again, the good or bad qualities depend on the context.

More personally the Emperor can signify a time of stability and order in a person's life, hopefully opening up creative energy. He also can indicate a specific person who holds great power, either objective or emotional, over the subject. This is very often the father, but it can also be a husband or lover, especially for those people who treat their lovers as substitute fathers to whom they surrender control of their lives. I have seen readings so dominated by the Emperor that all of life's possibilities become stunted and unfulfilled.

As a card of personal qualities, the Emperor can indicate the ability to defend one's territory, to create firm boundaries and vigorously maintain them. He symbolizes a rationalist approach to issues, one that values analysis and measurement over emotion and intuition.

Like the Empress reversed, the Emperor, when upside down, receives those elements complementary to his qualities when he is the right way up. He is, in Waite's terms, 'benevolence and compassion'; new life in a stony desert. But the pendulum can swing too far. The reversed Emperor can signify immaturity, and the inability to make harsh decisions and carry them through.

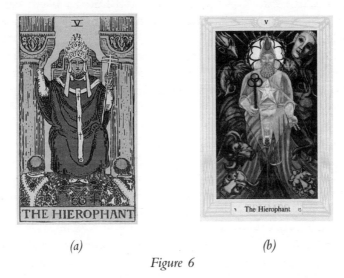

(a)   (b)

Figure 6

THE HIEROPHANT

In most Tarot decks trump 5 is called either the Pope or the High Priest, terms which connect it by name as well as picture to trump 2, the archetype of inner truth. Waite wrote that he rejected 'Pope' because the title suggested a very specific example of the trump's general idea. The name 'Hierophant' belonged to the high priest of the Greek Eleusinian mysteries. Now, Waite describes his card as symbolizing the 'outer way' of churches and dogma. But his use of the mystery term suggests another interpretation, one more favoured by those who see the Tarot as a secret doctrine of occult practices rather than a more general embodiment of human patterns. This interpretation is dramatically portrayed in the picture of the Hierophant from Aleister Crowley's *Book of Thoth*, drawn by Frieda Harris. Here the trump signifies initiation into a secret doctrine, such as the various orders and lodges which flourished around the turn of the century and which have undergone a revival in England and America. The Order of the Golden Dawn, to which Waite and Crowley at one time both belonged, possibly originated the term 'Hierophant' for trump 5.

These two meanings, 'outer way' and 'secret doctrine', appear contradictory on the most elementary level. In reality they are very similar. Whether the two acolytes are being admitted to the Church or to an occult society, they are still entering a doctrine, with a set of beliefs which they must learn and accept before they can gain entrance. There is of course a fundamental difference between say, the catechism and the rituals of the Golden Dawn. For both, however, the trump indicates an education and a tradition. Therefore, if we see the first line as describing the development of the personality then the Hierophant, coming after the natural world and society, indicates the intellectual tradition of the person's particular society, and his or her education in that tradition.

Following Waite's interpretation (and thinking specifically of the Western pope) we can see the Hierophant as a companion to the Emperor. The word 'pope' means 'father', and like the Roman Emperor the Pope is seen as a wise father guiding his children. Together, they share responsibility for humanity, the one providing physical needs, the other guiding spiritual growth. In one of the earliest treatises urging separation of Church and State, Dante argued that the two functions must not be combined for fear of corruption. However, he never questioned the idea that the Church is responsible for our souls.

Today, many people do not understand the basic idea of a priesthood. Our democratic age rejects the notions of an intermediary between an individual and God. Note, however, that the Hierophant can also symbolize the 'dictatorship of the proletariat' or any other elite leading the masses where they cannot go themselves. Originally the special function of the priests was evident; they spoke to the gods through the oracles, an often terrifying practice, and most people quite happily let someone else do it for them. When Christianity rejected such graphic and immediate connection to God, the idea of the priest became, like the Emperor, more abstract. Basically it depends on the notion that most people do not really care much about God. The average person is happiest following worldly pursuits, money, family and politics. There are, however, certain people who, by temperament, feel very directly the spirit that runs through all our lives. Called to the priesthood by their own inner awareness, these people can speak to God for us. More important, they can speak to *us*, interpreting God's law so we may live proper lives, and eventually, after death, receive our reward of returning to God. After the resurrection we ourselves will dwell in sight of God. In life, however, we need the priests to guide us.

So runs the argument. Even if we agree with the principle, in practice it tends to break down. People become priests for all sorts of reasons – ambition, family pressure, etc. – while those who do feel a genuine calling to communicate with God may show very little talent for communicating with people. Moreover, like the social institutions of the Emperor, the religious institutions of the Hierophant can easily become corrupted by the authority given them, so that the priests see their power as an end in itself, prizing obedience above enlightenment. Obviously, the position of defending a doctrine will attract doctrinaire people.

Perhaps, however, we reject the idea of a guiding priesthood for a more subtle reason. Ever since the Reformation a notion that has gained greater and greater force in the West is that of the individual's ultimate responsibility for him or herself. The whole idea of an outer doctrine, a code of rules and beliefs accepted on faith, depends on the assumption that most people prefer to have someone else tell them what to do and think. This may very well be true. To really discover God inside yourself you must undergo some uncomfortable confrontations with your own psyche. Similarly, to decide for yourself what is the moral thing to do in all situations might require a constant agony of choice. Nevertheless, many people today simply cannot accept either society or a Church bearing the ultimate responsibility for their lives.

Perhaps the interpretation of the Hierophant as representing secret doctrines suits our age better. For then the doctrine does not tell us what to do, but instead gives us direction to begin working on ourselves. And the Tarot, as we saw with the Magician, sets itself against all Churches by leading us to personal salvation in this life. For Crowley the Hierophant represents initiation as the means through which the individual becomes united with the universe.

The form and doctrine of the initiation change with each world age; having lasted nearly two thousand years, the current Piscean Age is coming to a close, so that the Hierophant is due to change, as will all strictly human relationships. Crowley comments that only the future can tell us what the new 'current of initiation' will be. But the basic quality of initiation as a merging with the cosmos always remains the same.

In the BOTA version of the Hierophant (as in the Rider pack) the crossed keys at the Hierophant's feet are gold and silver, representing the outer and inner ways, the sun and moon, the Magician and the High Priestess, which the doctrine teaches us to combine. In the Rider pack card both keys are gold, indicating that the dark side is hidden from those who follow the outer doctrine.

In the Waite-Smith imagery no veil blocks the entrance to the Church, as in the temple of the High Priestess. But the pillars are a dull grey. Those who enter here may receive protection from personal choice, but they will not pierce the secrets of duality. The unconscious remains closed. In many Tarot decks, the High Priestess holds not a scroll but a small book, locked. And the keys of the Hierophant do not fit that tantalizing lock.

Still, we must not think that the outer doctrine of religion serves no purpose to the seeker. Like the general education, of which it is a particular example, it gives the individual a firm tradition in which to root his or her personal development. The modern Western phenomenon of a kind of eclectic mysticism, drawing inspiration from all religions, is an extremely unusual development. This is based, possibly, on global awareness plus the view of religion as a psychological state divorced from science and history. Thus we see religion as an experience rather than an explanation of the universe and accept that all religious experiences are valid, whatever contradictions they show on the surface. While this idea opens great possibilities, many people have noted its potential shallowness. The fact is, throughout the centuries, the great mystics have always spoken from deep within a tradition. The Kabbalists were thoroughly Jewish, Thomas à Kempis a complete Christian, and the Sufis bowed to Mecca with all other orthodox Muslims. In its best aspect the Hierophant (as outer doctrine) can give us a place to start in creating a personal awareness of God.

One further aspect of the card's symbolism deserves special attention. The position of the three people (that is, a large figure presiding over two smaller ones on either side) introduces a motif that repeats itself, like the two pillars of the High Priestess, throughout the Major Arcana, and is resolved in Judgement and the world. The very next two cards after trump 5 repeat the motif, with the angel over the Lovers, and the charioteer of the Chariot over the black and white sphinxes.

We can see this trio as an emblem of the idea of a triad, such as the Christian trinity, or the triune picture of the mind: the id/ego/super-ego of Freud, or the conscious/unconscious/superconscious of the three lines of the Major Arcana. To understand the meaning of the image we must return to the High Priestess. She sits between two pillars symbolizing the dualities of life. She herself signifies one side, the Magician the other. The Hierophant initiates two acolytes into his church. We see, therefore, that the Hierophant and the Lovers and the Chariot all represent attempts to mediate between the opposing poles of life and find some way, not to resolve them, but simply to hold them in balance. A religious doctrine, with its moral codes and explanations for life's most basic questions, does just that. If we surrender ourselves to a Church the contradictions of life all become answered; but not resolved.

In reading the card signifies Churches, doctrines, and education in general. Psychologically it can indicate orthodoxy, conformity to society's ideas and codes of behaviour, as well as, more subtly, a surrender of responsibility. The Emperor symbolized the rules themselves and their official enforcers; the Hierophant indicates our own inner sense of obedience. Reversed, the card means unorthodoxy, especially mental – forming original ideas. It can also, however, mean gullibility and this idea suggests another virtue of the card when it is the right way up. A society builds its intellectual tradition over hundreds of years. Those who accept that tradition receive from it a standard by which to judge new ideas and information. Those who reject it must find their own ways and can easily get lost in superficial ideas. There are many people who, having given up the dogma forced on them as children, fall into some new dogma, a cult or some extremist political group, just as rigid and perhaps more shallow. Having rejected tradition they have not really rejected the Hierophant. They have not accepted the responsibility of truly finding their own way.

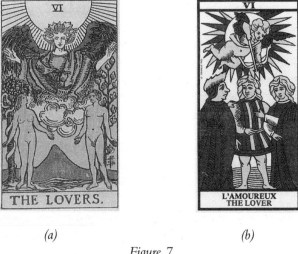

(a)   (b)

Figure 7

THE LOVERS

Of the various changes Arthur Waite and Pamela Smith made in traditional Tarot designs the card of the Lovers remains the most dramatic. Where the Tarot de Marseilles (on the right, above) shows a young man struck by Cupid's arrow and forced to choose between two women, the Rider pack shows a mature man and a single woman presided over by an angel. Further, while most decks indicate only a social situation, the Rider pack image clearly suggests the Garden of Eden, or rather, a new Garden of Eden, with the trees bringing enlightenment rather than the Fall.

The earlier version of trump 6 sometimes bears the title 'The Choice', and in divinatory readings means an important choice between two desires. Because one woman is fair and the other dark, a symbolism traditional in Europe where darkness always indicates evil and women in general indicate temptation, the choice was seen as between something respectable but perhaps dull, and something greatly desired but morally improper. The card can refer to a minor choice or even to a major crisis in a person's life. We see this ancient symbolism today in the various novels and films of middle-aged, middle-class men tempted to give up their loved but rather boring wives for a younger 'wilder' woman.

The choice can, in fact, extend to a person's whole life. Even those people who never question the boundaries of their middle class respectability have made a choice as much as the life-long criminal. And there are many people who outwardly live socially acceptable lives yet inwardly fight constant torments of desire, fighting urges to adultery, or violence, or simply a desire to leave home and become a wandering tramp.

On the esoteric level the choice between the light and dark woman indicates the choice between the outer path (symbolized in the Rider pack by the Hierophant), where your life is laid out for you, and the inner path of the occultist, which can lead to a con-frontation with your hidden desires. The Church labelled magicians as devil worshippers, and in Christian allegories the dark woman usually stood for Satan.

These meanings all see the choice between light and dark in the widest possible terms. In the context of the first line of trumps we can see it in a much more specific way, that of the first real choice a person makes independently of his or her parents. Until the sexual urge rouses itself most people are content to act out their parents' expectations for them. The sexual urge, however, points us where *it* wants to go. As a result we begin to break away in other areas as well. It is very rare that the partners our parents would choose for us are the ones we would choose for ourselves. If the difference is too extreme, or the parents too controlling, then the person can face a painful choice.

Paul Douglas has commented that the darkhaired woman, who appears much older, is the boy's mother, and the choice is whether to stay under her protection or strike out on his own. Those who believe, with Freud, that a boy's first desire is directed towards his mother will see here a classic Oedipal dilemma. One part of the personality wishes to maintain the hidden fantasy life of a union with the mother, while another wishes to find a true love in the reality of the boy's own generation. But we do not have to accept the Freudian doctrine to see the wider implications of this choice.

Whether or not the boy secretly desires his mother the life lived under the parents' protection is safe and comfortable. But he (or she, for girls basically face the same questions, though sometimes in different forms) can never become a true individual without making a break. And nothing indicates this more strongly than sexuality.

Therefore, the traditional version of trump 6 represents adolescence. Not only does sexuality emerge at this time but also intellectual and moral independence. Cards 3, 4 and 5 represented us as shaped by the great forces of nature, society, and parents. In card 6 the individual emerges, a true personality with its own ideas and purposes, able to make important choices based, not on parental orders, but on its own assessment of desires and responsibilities.

These meanings belong to the card's traditional structure. In designing his own version of the Lovers Waite addressed a different question. What functions do sex and love ultimately serve in a person's life? And what deep meanings can we find in the powerful drama of two people joining their hearts and bodies? Waite called his picture, 'the card of human love, here exhibited as part of the way, the truth, and the life'.

The sexual drive leads us away from isolation. It pushes us to form vital relationships with other people, and finally opens the way to love. Through love we not only achieve a unity with someone else, but we are given a glimpse of the greater meanings and deeper significance of life. In love we give up part of that ego control which isolates us not only from other people but from life itself. Therefore the angel appears above the man's and woman's heads, a vision unobtainable to each person individually, but glimpsed by both of them together.

Religion, philosophy, and art have always seized on the symbolism of male and female as representing duality. We have already seen this idea reflected in the Magician and the High Priestess, as well as the Empress and the Emperor. The symbolism here is reinforced by the fact that the Tree of Life, with its Magician like flames, stands behind the man, while the Tree of Knowledge, entwined with the serpent (symbol not of evil but of unconscious wisdom) stands behind the woman. The angel unites these two principles. In traditional teachings men and women are held to contain, within their bodies, separate life principles. Through physical love these principles join together.

Occultists, however, have always recognized both these elements within the self. Today we hear many people say that everyone contains both male and female qualities; usually, however, they are referring to vague ideas of social behaviour, such as aggression and gentleness. When male and female were seen as opposite in their deepest natures the occultist view was much more radical. One way of describing the goal of the Major Arcana is to say it brings out and unites the male and female principles. Therefore, in many decks, the dancer in the World is an hermaphrodite.

According to Kabbalists and Hermetic philosophers all humanity (and indeed, even the Deity) was originally hermaphroditic. Thus, on the outer level, each of us is only half a person and only through love can we find a sense of unity.

We find this same idea in Plato, but with an interesting variation. One of the Platonic myths states that humans were originally double creatures, but of three kinds: male-female, male-male, and female-female. Believing that humans possessed too much power Zeus split them with a thunderbolt, and now each one of us is looking for his or her other half. In contrast to the Jewish and Christian myths Plato's story gives equal reality to homosexuals. It reminds us of the danger in the too easy symbolism of male and female as ultimate opposites. The Magician and the High Priestess are mixed very subtly in each of us. And the angel can be evoked by any two lovers. It is not the roles that matter, but the reality of the union.

In the usual Christian interpretation of Genesis Eve bears the greater guilt, not only because she ate first, but because her sensuality tempted Adam to fall. Man supposedly was ruled by reason and woman by desire. This split led some Christians to declare that women had no souls. The whole myth of the Fall, however, with its emphasis on disobedience and punishment, is really meant to serve a repressive morality. Physical passions were seen as dangerous to society and therefore had to be controlled. As Joseph Campbell points out in *The Masks of God*, the ancient goddess religion of Palestine contained the same drama of a serpent, a Tree of Life, and an apple. But in the old story the initiate was given the apple by the goddess to allow him to enter paradise, rather than it being the cause of his expulsion. The ancient Hebrews reversed the myth, partly as a way of branding the old religion as evil, but also because they, like the Babylonians, considered the old ways 'monstrous'.

The Tarot, however, is a path of liberation. The fear that Jahweh expresses, that human beings 'will become like us', is precisely the Tarot's purpose – to fully bring out the divine spark in us and unite it with our conscious selves, to end the duality of God and human and make them one. Therefore, though it keeps much of the same symbolism as Genesis, the Rider pack Lovers subtly reverses the meaning.

Notice that while the man looks at the woman the woman looks at the angel. If the male is indeed reason, then rationality can only reach beyond its limits through the medium of passion. By its nature reason controls and contains, while passion tends to break down all limits. Our tradition has set the body and the rational mind at odds with each other. The Tarot teaches us that we must unite them (a single mountain rises between the two lovers) and that it is not the controlling power of reason that raises the senses to a higher level, but, rather, the other way around.

We can see this in direct psychological terms. Most people are bound within their egos or the masks they present to the world. But if they can surrender to sexual passion, they can, at least for a moment, transcend their isolation. Those who cannot release their egos, even for an instant, misuse sex, and are misused by it. Sex becomes a means of gaining power over someone else, but it never satisfies. When a person rejects the body's desire to release itself with another person the result is depression. The angel has been denied.

At the same time the passions alone cannot bring us to the angel. They need to be guided by the reason as much as the reason needs the passions to set it free. Those who simply go wherever their desires lead them are often thrown from one experience to another.

Paul Foster Case names the angel as Raphael, who presides over the super-conscious. This brings us back to the triune mind; here we learn that the three levels of the mind are not separate and iso-lated, like the three storeys of a house, but that the super-conscious is actually a product of the conscious and unconscious joined together. The pathway lies through the unconscious because that is where we find the true energy of life. In fact, the super-conscious can be described as the energy of the unconscious brought out and transformed to a higher state. Part of that transformation lies in consciousness giving the energy form, direction, and meaning.

If in the triangular motif the two figures below represent the dualities of life, while the larger figure above symbolizes a mediating force between them, then in trump 6 the mediator is sexual love. When we surrender to it we experience a glimpse of something greater than ourselves. Only a glimpse, and only for a moment; true liberation requires finally a great deal more than passion. But love can help us see the path, and know a little of the joy that waits for us at the end of it. A number of mystics, notably Saint Teresa, have described union with God in terms of sexual ecstasy.

The divinatory meanings for the Waite-Smith image are straightforward. They refer to the importance of love in a person's life and to a specific lover; very often to marriage or a long relationship. The card implies that the particular relationship has been or will prove to be very valuable to the person, leading him or her to a new understanding of life. If some specific problem is being considered in the reading then the Lovers indicates help in some way, either practically through the lover's assistance, or through emotional support. But this is not always true. The Lovers, in the position of the past, especially in relation to cards indicating a refusal to look at the present situation, can indicate a crippling nostalgia for a past love.

The earlier cards all represented archetypes. When we reversed them we added the missing elements. But here the individual has advanced and now the reversed meaning shows weakness and blocks. It is first of all a destructive love, particularly in a bad marriage. It can refer to romantic or sexual problems that dominate a person's life, either from difficulties with a specific person, or because the person finds love simply a great problem. Because the Waite-Smith picture indicates a mature love, and the traditional image shows the process of adolescent choice, either version reversed indicates romantic immaturity; the prolonged adolescence that keeps some people involved in childish fantasies long after their bodies have fully matured.

Figure 8

THE CHARIOT

The earlier versions of this card, which showed the Chariot pulled by two horses rather than two sphinxes, derives from a number of historical and mythological sources. Primarily it comes out of the processions given in Rome and other places for a conquering hero, when his chariot carried him through the streets that were filled with cheering citizens. The custom apparently answers some deep psychic need for group participation. We still practise it today, two thousand years later, in the parades given to presidents, generals, and astronauts, with open limousines replacing the chariot.

The Chariot implies more than a great victory. To drive a two horse vehicle at speed requires total control over the animals; the activity serves as a perfect vehicle for the powerful will. Plato, in the *Phaedrus*, refers to the mind as a chariot drawn by a black and white horse, the exact image of the Tarot.

A certain Hindu myth tells of Shiva destroying a triple city of the demons. To do so he requires that all creation be subordinated to his will. The gods make a chariot for Shiva, using not only themselves but the heavens and the Earth as materials. The sun and moon become the wheels and the winds the horses. (The symbol on the front of the Tarot Chariot, like a nut and bolt, or a wheel and axle, is called the lingam and yoni, standing for Shiva, the masculine principle, and Parvati, the feminine principle, united in a single figure.) Through the myth's images we learn that spiritual victory over evil comes when we can focus all of nature, as well as the unconscious energy embodied in Shiva himself, through the conscious will.

These two fables show two different aspects of the idea of will. The story of Shiva speaks of a true victory, in which the spirit has found a focus to release its total force. But the *Phaedrus* gives us an image of the triumphant ego, which controls rather than resolves the basic conflicts of life. Those Tarot commentators who see the cards as a group of separate images, each one contributing some vital lesson to our spiritual understanding, tend to give the Chariot its wider meaning. They point out that the Kabbalistic title for the number 7, with all its mystic connotations, is 'Victory'.

In many places, particularly India, the horse became associated with death and funerals. When the rising patriarchy abolished the ritual sacrifice of the king, a horse was killed instead. The horse sacrifice became the most holy, associated with immortality. Even today, horses are used to pull the coffins of great leaders. (A bizarre junction of two aspects of the Chariot was seen in the death of John Kennedy. He was killed in his limousine during a parade, and then a horse – who rebelled against his trainer's control – pulled his coffin in the state funeral.) These connections suggest the idea of the soul's victory over mortality.

When we look at the cards sequentially we see that 7 is only the victory of the first line of the Major Arcana. It crowns that line's process of maturation, but by necessity it cannot address the great areas of the unconscious and super-conscious. Seen this way the Chariot shows us the developed ego; the lessons of the early cards have been absorbed, the adolescent period of searching and self-creation has been passed, and now we see the mature adult, successful in life, admired by others, confident and content with himself, able to control feelings, and above all, to direct the will.

Like the Magician the Charioteer carries a magic wand. Unlike the Magician he does not raise it above his head to heaven. His power is subordinate to his will. His hands hold no reins. His strong character alone controls the opposing forces in life.

The lingam and yoni indicate his mature sexuality which is under his control. Thus he is not the victim of his emotions and his sexuality contributes to a satisfying life. The glowing square on his chest, a symbol of vibrant nature, links him to the sensual world of the Empress, but the eight pointed star on his crown shows his mental energy directing his passions (symbolists consider the eight pointed star as halfway between the square of the material world and the circle of the spiritual). His chariot looms larger than the town behind indicating that his will is more powerful than the rules of society. However, the fact that his chariot is not in motion indicates that he is not a rebel. The wheels of the chariot rest on water, showing that he draws energy from the unconscious, though the chariot itself, resting on land, separates him from a direct contact with that great force.

We have mentioned the sexual symbolism of the lingam and yoni. While Hindu myth connects horses to death, Freudian dream symbolism connects them to the sexual energy of the libido. By controlling the horses (or sphinxes) the Charioteer controls his instinctive desires.

Various magic signs adorn his body. His skirt bears symbols of ceremonial magic, his belt shows the sign and planets. The two lunar faces on his shoulders are named 'Urin and Thummim', the supposed shoulder plates of the High Priest in Jerusalem and which therefore suggest the Hierophant. At the same time the lunar plates refer to the High Priestess. Note also that the cloth at the back of the chariot suggests the High Priestess's veil; he has set the mystery of the unconscious behind him.

We see, therefore, in the Chariot's symbolism all the previous cards of the first line. The wand and symbols indicate the Magician, the water, sphinxes, and veil symbolize the High Priestess, the stars on his canopy recall the Empress's crowns, the city symbolizes the Emperor, the shoulder plates symbolize the Hierophant, and the lingam and yoni symbolize the Lovers. All these forces contribute to the outer personality.

And yet – observe the Chariot with its stone-like qualities. Observe the charioteer himself merging into his stone vehicle. The mind that subordinates all things to conscious will runs the risk of becoming rigid, cut off from the very forces it has learned to control. Observe also that the black and white sphinxes are not reconciled to each other. They look in opposite directions. The charioteer's will holds them together in a tense balance. If that will should fail, the Chariot and its rider will be torn apart.

Paul Douglas has compared the Chariot to Jung's idea of the 'persona'. As we grow up we create a kind of mask to deal with the outside world. If we have dealt successfully with the various challenges of life, then the different aspects symbolized by the other cards will become integrated into this ego-mask. But we can too easily confuse this successful persona with the true self, even to the point that if we try to discard the mask we will fear its loss as a kind of death. This is why the second line of the Major Arcana, which deals precisely with the release of the self from its outer masks, bears Death as its next to last card.

So far we have considered the Chariot as an emblem of personal maturity. But the idea of human will extends beyond the individual. With its images of the mind subduing and utilizing the forces of life the Chariot is a perfect symbol for civilization, which creates order out of the chaos of nature by using the natural world as the raw materials for its agriculture and cities. One of the chief Kabbalistic connotations for the card extends this idea. By its connection with the Hebrew letter 'Iain' the Chariot carries the quality of 'speech'. Speech has always seemed to humans to represent the rational mind and its dominance over nature. As far as we know only humans possess language (though chimpanzees have shown themselves capable of learning human sign language, and whales and dolphins may possess developed languages of their own) and we may say that speech separates us from the animal. Adam gained control over the beasts in Eden by speaking their names. Most important, humans use language to transmit the information that allows civilization to continue.

However, just as the ego is limited, so is speech. First of all, speech restricts our experience of reality. By forming a description of the world, by giving everything a label, we erect a barrier between ourselves and experience. When we look at a tree, we do not feel the impact of a living organism; rather, we think 'tree' and move on. The label has replaced the thing itself. Also, by relying too much on this rational quality of language we ignore experiences that cannot be expressed in words. We have already seen how the High Priestess signifies intuitive wisdom beyond language. Certain experiences, especially mystical union with spirit, cannot be described. Language can only hint at them with metaphors and fables. People who rely totally on speech have even gone so far as to insist that non-verbal experiences, or experiences which cannot be measured by psychological tests, do not exist. This is simply because they cannot be scientifically described. Such dogmatism receives its perfect symbol in the charioteer's merging with his stone wagon.

So far we have considered every symbol in the picture except, perhaps, the most obvious one: the two sphinxes. Waite borrowed this innovation from Eliphas Levi, the great pioneer of Kabbalistic Tarot. Like the two pillars of the High Priestess, or the black and white horses they replace, the sphinxes signify the dualities and contradictions of life. Once again, we see the triangular motif. Here the mediating force is will-power.

The use of sphinxes instead of horses suggests several deeper meanings. The sphinx in Greek legend was a riddler, presenting the mystery of life to the people of Thebes. The myth tells us that the sphinx seized the young men of the city and asked them the following riddle: 'What creature walks on four legs in the morning, two legs at noon, and three legs in the evening?' Those who could not answer were devoured. Now, the answer is 'man' who crawls as a baby, walks upright as an adult, and uses a cane in old age. The implication is clear. If you do not understand your basic humanity, with its strengths and weaknesses, then life will destroy you. The Chariot symbolizes maturity, accepting the limits of life, plus the faculty of speech, that is, rational understanding, which is used to define existence and therefore to control it.

But a further meaning lurks here. The man who answered the sphinx's riddle was Oedipus, who arrived in Thebes after killing his father. Freud's emphasis on incest has diverted attention from the deeper message of the Oedipus story. Oedipus was the perfect image of the successful man. Not only did he save Thebes from a menace and become king of the city but he did so by his understanding of life. He knew what man was. Yet he did not know himself. His own inner reality remained closed to him until the gods forced him to confront it. And the gods *did* force him. If the oracles had not spoken first to his father and then to him, Oedipus would never have done the things he did. Therefore, though he understood the outer meaning of man's life he did not understand either who he really was, or his relation to the gods who controlled his life. And these two subjects are precisely the concerns of the second and third lines of the Major Arcana. In the second we go beyond the ego to find the true self. In the third we deal openly with the archetypal forces of existence and reach at last a full integration of those dualities which the charioteer was able to dominate but never reconcile.

The divinatory meanings of the Chariot derive from its powerful will. In a reading the card signifies that the person is successfully controlling some situation through the force of his or her personality. The card implies that a situation contains some contradictions and that these have not been brought together but simply held under control. This is not to stress too highly the negative undertones of the card. When it is the right way up the Chariot basically means success; the personality in charge of the world around it. If it appears as the outcome in a reading dealing with problems then it indicates victory.

Reversed, the card's inherent contradictions gain greater force. The Chariot upside down implies that the approach of will-power has proven unsuccessful, and the situation has got out of control. Unless the person can find some other approach to the difficulties, he or she faces disaster. Will-power alone cannot always sustain us. Like Oedipus we must sometimes learn to give way to the gods.

CHAPTER FIVE

TURNING INWARDS

THE SEARCH FOR SELF-KNOWLEDGE

With the second line of the Major Arcana we move from the outer world and its challenges to the inner self. The contradictions concealed in the Chariot's powerful image must now be faced openly. The mask of ego must die.

Dramatic as it sounds this situation is actually very common, at least in the need if not the fulfilment. Self-questioning and searching have long been seen as features of middle age. When people are young they are concerned mainly with victory over the forces of life, finding a partner and achieving success. When success has been found, however, people may wonder about the value of it. The question, 'Who am I beneath all my possessions, beneath all the images I present to other people?' takes on more and more importance. Today, many younger people are not waiting for middle-age and success to ask these things. A characteristic of our time is the desire for life to have a sense of meaning, of inner essence. And more and more people are deciding that the first place to look for such meaning is within themselves.

This idea, in fact, is only a half-truth. The Magician teaches us that, as physical beings, we find reality only in connection with the outer world; the inner truth of the High Priestess is a potential and must be manifested through the consciousness of the Magician. But as long as our masks and habits and defences close us off from self-knowledge so that we never know *why* we act, then all the things we do remain meaningless. The flow between the Magician and the High Priestess needs to be free for life to possess value.

Because the line basically reverses the emphasis of the first seven cards, many of the cards appear as mirror images to the ones above them. The sexual polarity of trumps 1 and 2 become turned around in Strength and the Hermit, while the principle of light and dark, outer and inner, remain in the same positions. The Wheel of Fortune turns away from the natural and mindless world of the Empress to a vision of inner mysteries. At the end of the line Temperance shows us a new kind of victory. The Chariot's force has been replaced by balance and calm. Where the charioteer's stone chariot removed him from direct contact with the earth and the river, the angel of Temperance stands with one foot on land, one in water, showing the personality in harmony with itself and life.

Another theme appears in the second line. So far the cards have presented a series of lessons to us, things we must learn about life to become mature and successful in the outer world. But enlightenment is a deeply personal experience. It cannot be studied or even pondered but only lived. The series of outer lessons culminate in the Wheel of Fortune which shows us a vision of the world and ourselves which must be answered. The Hanged Man, however, shows something else entirely. Here we see, not a lesson, but the image of enlightenment itself, the outer personality turned upside down by a very real and personal experience.

In between these two cards, and at the exact centre of the whole Major Arcana, lies Justice, carefully balancing the scales between inner and outer, past and future, rationality and intuition, knowledge and experience.

Figure 9

STRENGTH

Waite's change of the Lovers was the most obvious of his Tarot alterations; his switch of Strength with Justice remains the most controversial. He himself gives no real reason for the change. 'For reasons which satisfy myself, this card has been interchanged with that of Justice, which is usually numbered eight. As the variation carries nothing which will signify to the reader there is no cause for explanation.' The reasons are certainly more than personal. Paul Foster Case placed Strength as 8 and Justice as 11. Aleister Crowley kept their original numbers, but assigned them the Hebrew letters that would go with switching the cards. Both probably followed the Order of the Golden Dawn, whose secret Tarot deck also switched the two cards.

This connection to a secret order suggests the idea of initiation. Now, the Golden Dawn, of course, did not originate the practice of initiation, though it claimed to receive its specific rituals directly from spirit instructors. Initiation goes back thousands of years and is seen all over the world, from Egyptian temples to the Australian desert. It represents a special means of psychological transformation – the very subject of the Tarot's middle line. By referring Justice and the cards around it to this ancient idea we gain a wider under-standing of the Tarot as an experience.

It is worth considering the implications of the old arrangement of trumps. The image of Justice suggests weighing your life in the balance. The second line takes us away from the outer achievements of the first and into the self. Thus Justice in the first position would mean an assessment of what your life has meant to you, followed by a decision to search inward for greater meaning. Obviously, this fits very nicely. But if Justice comes first then all these things occur rationally; the assessment arises as a conscious reaction to dissatis-faction. How much more powerful this assessment appears when it arises from within, forced on us by the powerful vision of the Wheel of Fortune. The double-edged sword of Justice implies action, a response to the knowledge gained in the assessment. The idea of response leads directly to the Hanged Man. If Justice came first then the Hermit would follow it. As a seeker of wisdom, the Hermit would also represent a valid response to Justice. But again, if we allow that wisdom to come before Justice, then the Hanged Man shows a response from deep inside.

Now consider Strength in both places. The picture shows a woman taming a lion. Briefly, the image suggests the energy of the unconscious released and calmed, 'tamed' by the direction of con-scious understanding. Such an idea would easily belong in the mid-dle position. We would then describe the card as the central test of the whole line. And certainly the peacefulness and great reversal of the Hanged Man would follow Strength perfectly.

But we can also see Strength as the qualities vital for beginning the line. The search inward cannot be accomplished by the ego. We need to confront feelings and desires long hidden from our con-scious thoughts. If we attempt to transform ourselves by a wholly rational process we create another kind of persona. Something very like this in fact happens quite often. Many people feel a lack of spontaneity in their lives. They look around them or read books on psychology, and observe, with a certain jealousy, or even shame at their own repressions, the characteristics of spontaneous people. And then, rather than follow the fearful process of releasing their hidden fears and desires, they carefully imitate spontaneity. They have extended the Chariot to a new domain.

By making Strength number 8 we set it against the Chariot, as a different kind of power, not the ego's will, but the inner Strength to confront yourself calmly and without fear. The mysteries can be brought out because we have found the Strength to face them. The lion signifies all the feelings, fears, desires, and confusions suppressed by the ego in its attempt to control life. The charioteer drew upon his inner feelings as a source of energy, but was always careful to direct that energy where he consciously decided it should go. Strength allows the inner passions to emerge, as the first step in going beyond the ego.

On a very simple level we can see this emergence of suppressed feelings in the person who allows him or herself to act 'childishly', to weep or scream; in short, to do all those things that previously seemed foolish or embarrassing. On a deeper level the lion symbolizes the whole force of personality, usually smoothed over by the demands of civilized life. Strength releases this energy in order to use it as a kind of fuel, propelling us along the inner path of the Hermit. This purpose can only be accomplished because the lion is 'tamed' at the same time that it is released. Strength opens up the personality like Pandora opening her box. It does so, however, with a sense of peace, a love of life itself, and a great confidence in the final result. Unless we truly believe that the process of self-discovery is a joyous one we will never follow it through.

The symbolism of the pictures and numbers reinforces the comparison of Strength and the Chariot. The Chariot shows a man and Strength shows a woman. Traditionally, of course, these represent rationality and emotion, aggression and surrender. Also traditionally, the Chariot's number 7 belongs to 'male' magic, the number 8 to 'female'. This symbolism arises from anatomy. The male body contains seven openings (counting the nose as one), the female eight. Also, the male body possesses seven points, the arms and legs, the head, the centre, and the penis. The female possesses eight, the breasts replacing the penis.

What do we mean by male and female magic? Esoteric theory considers sexual energy as a manifestation of the energy principles underlying the entire universe; male and female being similar to the positive and negative poles of electro-magnetism. Through manipulation of this bipolar energy, 'magic' power results. The occultist considers these principles a science, no more, and no less, mysterious than the modern scientist's manipulation of atomic energy. We can describe the Rider pack Lovers as a schematic energy diagram. Therefore, the Chariot and Strength belong together esoterically as the practical manifestation of the principles symbolized in the Magician and the High Priestess.

Psychologically they also embody two kinds of power. Our society emphasizes the 'masculine' force of control; conquest, dominating the world through reason and will. But the 'feminine' qualities of intuition and spontaneous emotion are far from weakness. To release your deepest emotions with love and faith requires great courage as well as strength.

The Fool comes in here. Only by a kind of psychic leap can we move from the conscious to the unconscious. And only a fool would make such a jump, for why give up success, control? The gods forced Oedipus; what inner needs will force the rest of us?

Strength's position, as first in the line, links the card to the Magician, as does the infinity sign, another reference to 8, above her head. The reversal of sex indicates a joining of aspects from both the male and female archetypes. The Magician's active involvement with life has been modified by the inner peace implied in the High Priestess.

The woman's sensual figure, her blonde hair, and the flower belt linking her to the lion, connect the card to the Empress as well. The Empress represents natural instincts and passion; again we see the image of emotional energy, the 'animal desires' as some Tarot commentators call it, released and tamed. Waite describes the flower belt as a second infinity sign, with one loop around the woman's waist, the other around the lion's neck. We can describe Strength as the Magician united with the Empress; that is, the Magician's power of consciousness and direction has mingled with the Empress's sensuality, giving it a sense of purpose and leading to the Hermit. Notice that for the first line 1 plus 3 equals 4, the Emperor. For the second line 1 plus 3 becomes multiplied by 2; the inner truth of the High Priestess.

Another aspect of the trump carries this unity of 1 and 3 still further. The Hebrew letter given by Case and others to Strength is Teth. Teth refers Kebbalistically to 'snake'; but the Hebrew for snake also means 'magic'. All over the world people have made this connection; from the snakes on Hermes's magic wand to the kundalini power of Tantric occultism in India and Tibet. And the snake, in kundalini and elsewhere, stands for sexuality. The Tarot, as we know from the serpent twined around the Tree of Life behind the woman on the Lovers, considers sexuality to be a force towards enlightenment. If, esoterically, Strength stands for the actual practice of sexual magic, psychologically it refers again to releasing that energy bound up in our strongest feelings. When we compare Strength with the Devil we will see that the release here is actually a partial one. The lion is controlled and directed rather than allowed to take the self wherever it wants to go.

In alchemy the lion stands for gold, the sun, and sulphur. Sulphur is a lower element and gold (in alchemy) the highest. The process by which sulphur becomes gold is precisely the process of transforming the lower self. And the design of Temperance, the last card of the line, with its liquid poured from one cup to another, depicts the alchemical goal of blending the opposites into a new and more meaningful existence.

Those who find life a matter of strict control, who see the unconscious as a 'moral sewer' of repressions (as Jung characterized the narrow Freudian view), and find the passions a torment, will see the lion as natural forces which the rational mind must overcome. Some older Tarot decks, including the Visconti, showed Heracles killing the Nemean lion. The passions conquered by reason. But the lion also stood for Christ, the radiant power of God. Those who allow the unconscious energy within themselves to emerge, guiding it with love and a faith in life, will discover that the energy is not a destructive beast but the same spirit force drawn down through the lightning rod of the Magician.

In readings the card of Strength indicates the ability to face life, and particularly some difficult problem or time of change, with hope and eagerness. It shows a person strong from within, experiencing life passionately yet peacefully, without being controlled or carried away by those passions. The card represents the finding of the strength to begin or continue some difficult project, despite fear and emotional strain.

If Strength appears in connection with the Chariot it can signify an alternative to force and will-power, especially, of course, if the

Chariot is reversed. The two cards can also symbolize complementary sides, the best configuration being Strength in the position of the inner self, and the Chariot in the position of the outer (the vertical and horizontal lines of a cross). Then we see a person who acts powerfully but with a sense of calm.

Strength reversed indicates first of all weakness. The courage to face life fails and the person feels overwhelmed and pessimistic. It signifies also a torment from within. The bestial side of the lion breaks away from the unity of spirit and sensuality. The passions become the enemy, threatening to destroy the conscious personality and the life it has built up for itself.

Figure 10

THE HERMIT

Like the six-pointed star within the Hermit's lantern, the idea of the Hermit goes in two directions; one inner, one outer. Primarily, the card means a withdrawal from the outer world for the purpose of activating the unconscious mind. We see this process symbolized in the downward pointing 'water' triangle, as the alchemists called it. But the Hermit also signifies a teacher who will show us how to begin this process, and will help us find our way. The upward pointing 'fire' triangle symbolizes this special guide, who might be an occult teacher, a therapist, our own dreams, or even a spirit guide evoked from within the self.

The image of the Hermit occupied a special place in the medieval imagination. Living in the woods or the desert, totally withdrawn from all the normal concerns of humanity, the hermit presented an alternative to the Church. The European version of a yogi ascetic, he demonstrated the possibility of approaching God through personal experience. People often looked upon the hermits as living saints, and attributed magic powers to them, in the way that yoga disciples will tell wonderful stories about their masters.

Though the hermit withdrew from society he or she★ did not withdraw from humanity. Among other functions, they gave shelter and sometimes blessings to travellers. Countless stories, especially the Grail legends, depict the hermit who acts as a giver of wisdom to the knight on a spiritual quest. Again, we see the Hermit's double image: example and guide.

The Hermit image has persisted long after the special practice has died away. The transcendental philosopher Ralph Waldo Emerson travelled days through remote Scotland to find the cabin of Thomas Carlyle. Emerson's friend, Henry David Thoreau, himself lived in a cabin at Walden Pond to find a sense of himself and of nature. He then wrote about it as an example to others. Nietzsche's *Dus Sprach Zarathustra* enshrined the Hermit's image; the book begins with Zarathustra's return after achieving personal transformation. And today, countless people have given themselves to Eastern gurus in the hope that these hermit-like teachers can transform their lives.

For those who cannot find an actual guide the psyche will often provide one. Jung and his followers have described their patients' many dreams of wise old men guiding them on mysterious journeys into the psyche. In many cases dream analysis discovered that the dream guide actually stood for the therapist. The unconscious can recognize a Hermit teacher before the conscious mind can.

The great thirteenth-century Kabbalist, Abraham Abulafia, described three levels of Kabbalah. The first was doctrine; that

★ Women often became hermits and the medieval hatred of women sometimes became a veneration of a particular woman who had supposedly conquered the evil of her sex.

which can be learned from texts. The second came from the direct guidance given by a personal teacher, while the third, the most developed, was the direct experience of ecstatic union with God. These three levels connect very directly to the Tarot, not only in the three lines, but in three specific trumps which together form an isosceles triangle. The first level we see in the Hierophant; the third, directly below the Hierophant, one level removed, appears in the joyous child of card 19, the Sun. The second level, however, comes not in the card between them, the Hanged Man, but on the other end of the pattern, as the second card in the second line, the Hermit.

Doctrine and mystery both come as the end of a process; doctrine because you first must arrange your life before you can approach the study of a special way (Kabbalists often restricted certain important texts to people over thirty-five), and ecstasy because you first must pass the archetypal confrontation with darkness and mystery. A guide, however, appears at the very start of the journey, after the traveller has found the Strength to begin.

As an emblem of personal development, rather than a guide, the Hermit signifies the idea that only by withdrawing from the outer world can we awaken the inner self. Those who see the Tarot in two halves, with the Wheel of Fortune as the mid-point, view the Hermit as the period of contemplation before the Wheel of Life turns towards its second half. When we view the Tarot in lines of seven we see that this withdrawal, and the vision of the Wheel itself, are steps towards a greater goal.

We see the Hermit on a cold lonely peak. He has left the world of the senses to enter the mind. This image of the mind as stark and chill conveys only a partial truth, or rather, an illusion. The mind is rich with symbols, with joy, with the light and love of the spirit. But before we can apprehend these things we must first experience the mind as a silent alternative to the noisy world of the senses. For shamans the barren peak is often a direct reality. In places as far apart as Siberia and the American South-West shaman candidates go alone into the wilderness to seek the spirit guides who will teach them how to heal.

The Hermit signifies a transition. Through the techniques of meditation, or psychic discipline, or analysis, we allow the hidden parts of the psyche to begin to speak to us. Later we will experience a sense of rebirth, first as an angel (the eternal part of the self, beyond the ego), then later, more deeply felt, as a free child riding forth from the garden of past experience. For now, the path belongs to the image of the wise old man, alone, supported and warmed by his stiff grey cloak of contemplation.

The symbol of the lantern returns us to the Hermit as guide and teacher. He holds the light out to us, indicating his willingness to lead us and our ability to find the way if we will only use the Strength we have to follow. In some decks the Hermit conceals his lantern under his cloak, and then it symbolizes the light of the unconscious hidden under the cloak of the conscious mind. By making it visible, yet within a lantern, the Rider pack indicates that we release the light through a definite process of self-awareness, and that this process is available to anyone.

We have seen the star both as a symbol of the Hermit as teacher, and also as a light of the unconscious, beckoning us to discover its secrets. It further signifies the goal of resolving the opposites of life. The water and fire triangles traditionally represent not only two elements usually opposed, but also male and female united in a single form.

The Hermit's staff suggests a wizard's staff, and therefore the magic wand of the Magician. Whereas the Fool used the wand instinctively, the Hermit leans on it as a conscious support. It therefore symbolizes the teaching which helps open the inner awareness.

Directly below the High Priestess the Hermit relates to her principle of withdrawal, indicating again that we must in some sense leave the outer world if we wish to work on ourselves. As with Strength the second line reverses the sexual archetype. The role symbolism here teaches us is that a deliberate mental effort, based on specific techniques and teachings, takes us beyond the locked up intuition of the High Priestess's closed temple. The waters of that temple are not fully released; the veil remains in place until the lightning of the Tower, below the Hermit, tears it open. Under the influence of trump 9, however, the unconscious speaks to us from behind the veil, through symbols, dreams, and visions.

The distinction between male-female symbolism and the reality of individual people leads us to some important realizations about archetypes. We tend to see hermits and teachers as wise old *men*, even in our dreams, because our five-thousand-year-old patriarchy has so impressed this image on our minds. In earlier times, the guides were most often women, as representatives of the Great Goddess, and even in our age such women as Madame Blavatsky have served this ancient function. The fact that our dreams often choose wise old men demonstrates the very important fact that the unconscious too draws its material from the cultural background of the individual dreamer. Many people view archetypes as rigid fixed images shared by all people at all times. Rather, archetypes are tendencies for the mind to form certain *kinds* of images, such as that of a guide, and the specific form an image takes will depend very much on a person's cultural background and experience. Medieval Grail initiations and Australian desert rites follow the same archetypal pattern; it underlies them like a grid. Yet the outer form of that pattern varies immensely.

The divinatory meanings for the Hermit derive from both its aspects. On the one hand it symbolizes a withdrawal from outer concerns. The person may physically remove himself, but this is not really necessary. What matters is the inner transfer of attention from 'getting and spending' as Wordsworth called our worldly activities, to a person's inner needs. It therefore requires an emotional withdrawal from other people and from activities once thought to be all-important. The card carries within it a sense of deliberate purpose, of withdrawing to work on self-development. In connection with this sense of purpose and with the picture of an old man the card symbolizes maturity, and a knowledge of what really matters in a person's life.

The card can also signify assistance from a definite guide, sometimes as indicated above, a psychic guide from within, but more often a real person who will help you in your self-discoveries. Sometimes we do not ourselves recognize that such a guide exists for us. If the Hermit appears in a Tarot reading it may be wise to look carefully at the people around you. If you are involved in helping others find understanding then the Hermit can symbolize you in your role as guide and teacher.

When we reverse the card we corrupt the idea of withdrawal. In the same way that the High Priestess reversed can mean a fear of life, the Hermit reversed can indicate a fear of other people. If we withdraw from society as a retreat then the fact of withdrawal becomes more and more dominant, leading to phobias and paranoia. As with other trumps the negative and positive aspects of the Hermit depend on the context. The Hermit reversed can sometimes simply mean that at this moment the person needs to become involved with other people.

Because the card, when the right way up, suggests maturity the Hermit reversed can sometimes indicate a Peter Pan attitude to life. The person hangs on to basically meaningless activities, or else imitates childlike enthusiasm (like the imitation of spontaneity) as a way of avoiding the responsibilities of doing something with his or her life. I first encountered this interpretation for the Hermit reversed in a reading given by a man in New York to a friend of mine; I have since found it useful in many situations. Interestingly, I met the man through another friend who looked on the reader as a personal guide in her spiritual development.

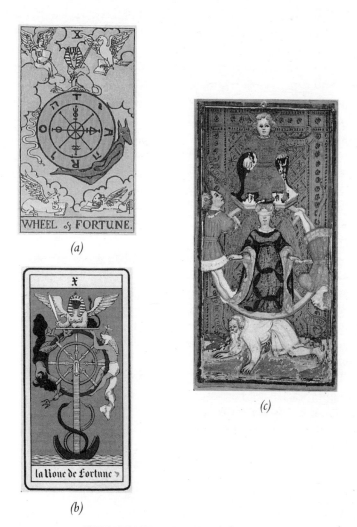

(a)

(b)

(c)

THE WHEEL OF FORTUNE

Like certain other trump cards (most notably Death) the Wheel of
Fortune derives from a medieval homily. The Church considered
pride the greatest of sins, for in pride you set yourself before Christ.
One lesson against pride was the idea of a great king falling from
power. In many versions of the King Arthur legend, the king
dreams or sees before him on the eve of his final battle, a vision of

a rich and powerful king seated on top of a wheel. All of a sudden the goddess Fortuna turns the wheel and the king gets crushed at the bottom. Sobered, Arthur realizes that no matter how much secular power we accrue, our fate rests always in God's hands. The Visconti cards, on the right, above, enshrines this practical sermon.

Now, we might consider this neat morale fable to be far removed from the powerful and mysterious symbols staring at us from the Waite-Smith card, on the top left, and the Oswald Wirth version on the bottom left. But Fortuna and her shining hoop have a curious history. First of all, the medieval image derives from a much earlier time, when Fortuna represented the Great Goddess, and the crushed king was a real event. Every year, at mid-winter, the priestesses sacrificed the king; by imitating the death of the year they humbled themselves to the Goddess's power, and by choosing a new king they subtly suggested to her that she might once more create spring out of winter – an event by no means automatic to people who did not believe in 'natural laws' such as gravity. Thus, the Wheel originally symbolized both the mystery of nature and the human ability to take part in that mystery through a ritual sacrifice. Notice that the card comes directly below the Empress, the emblem of the Great Mother herself.

By the Middle Ages the Wheel had lost its original meaning; this did not mean that it had lost its power to suggest the mystery of life. In Thomas Malory's version of the King Arthur story we find the suggestion that the Wheel symbolizes the random turnings of 'luck'. Why do some people get rich and others poor? Why should a powerful king fall, and a formerly weak one rise to power? Who, or what, controls the turning wheel of life? Malory suggests that luck, seemingly meaningless ups and downs, is in reality fate; that is, the destiny God has chosen for each individual, based on reasons only God can understand. Because we cannot understand those reasons we say that the events of people's lives arise out of luck, but it all belongs to God's plan.

With the Wheel, therefore, we come to the great question of how and why anything happens at all in the universe. What makes the sun shine? Burning elements, yes, but what makes them burn? How did atomatic energy come into existence? Why should spring follow winter, after all? Why, and how, does gravity work? Going further, we find that fate is also an illusion, a dodge to cover up the fact that we, with our limited vision, cannot see the inner connection between all things. 'Oh well,' we say, 'it's fate', a meaningless statement because we cannot understand the meaning. Things do not just happen, they are made to happen. The power to shape events, to give life and form and purpose to the universe, belongs, Malory tells us, to the Holy Ghost, dwelling in the physical world as a presence within the Holy Grail (the Ace of Cups) in the same way that the Shekinah physically dwelt within the veiled sanctuary of the temple at Jerusalem.

We come then to the truth that both the random events of life and the so-called 'laws' of the physical universe are mysteries leading us to an awareness of the spirit force drawn down by the upraised arm of the Magician and manifested in the natural world of the Empress. A great many mystics and shamans have said that their visions showed them how all things connect, how everything fits together, because the spirit unites the entire universe. Possibly we would all see and understand this grand scheme of life, if it were not for the fact that we do not live long enough. Our short lives narrow our vision to such a miniscule portion of the world that life appears meaningless.

Now, this idea of the Wheel as the mystery of fate, with its hidden meaning, fits very well the modern Waite-Smith version of the card, especially when we consider it as halfway to the final trump. If we place the Rider pack Wheel beside the World we see immediately the link between them. In one we have a wheel filled with symbols; in the other we find a wreath of victory, and inside it a dancer who embodies the truth behind the symbols. Even more striking, we find the same four animals on each card in the corners, except that the mythological beings of card 10 have been transformed into something real and alive in the World. Thus, at the halfway point, we receive a vision of the inner meaning of life; at the end that vision has become real, embodied in our own being.

In India, the king also lost his life each year to the Goddess. When the patriarchal Aryans ended this practice the image of the turning wheel of the year became an even more powerful symbol of the new religion. The ever-turning Wheel of Life came to signify the laws of karma, leading you to reincarnate in one body after another. Now, karma is in a way simply another explanation for the mystery of fate. By the actions you take in one life, you build up a certain destiny for yourself in the next, so that if you commit a great many evil deeds you create in your immortal self a kind of psychic need for punishment. When the time comes for your next incarnation you inevitably choose a low caste or diseased body. (This simple psychological explanation of karma is perhaps based more on Buddhism than Hinduism.)

Again, our limited understanding prevents us from directly experiencing the truth behind the wheel of Fate, or karma. When Buddha attained enlightenment he remembered every moment of every one of his past lives. Indeed, the memory was the enlightenment. By gaining full knowledge he was able to perceive that all those lives were only forms created by his desires. When he ended his desires he 'got off the Wheel'. We could say that enlightenment means (or includes, at any rate) piercing through the outer events to the spirit which dwells within them, that is, finding the Holy Ghost within the Wheel of Fortune.

It is significant that King Arthur experiences the Wheel of Fortune as a vision in a dream. Because whether we see it as the halfway point of the Major Arcana, or simply one of the steps to completing the second line, the wheel is indeed a vision given to us by the unconscious. The Hermit has turned away from the outer world. As a result the unconscious shows him a vision of life as a turning wheel filled with symbols.

The Wheel of Life does not become visible until we step away from it. When we are involved in it we see only the events immediately before and behind us; the daily concerns our egos find so important. When we withdraw we see the whole pattern. Psychologically we can view this vision as an assessment a person makes of where his or her life has gone and where it is going. On a deeper level, the vision remains mysterious and symbolic. We can see what we have made of our particular lives, but fate remains a mystery.

The symbols on the Wheel all possess meaning; they help us to understand the truth within the visions. Nevertheless, we do not experience the full living force. The light of the unconscious remains veiled.

It is significant also that Malory connects the Wheel of Fortune to the Holy Grail. For the Grail symbols, which are also the symbols of the Minor Arcana, go back probably almost as far as the yearly regal sacrifice. When the candidate for initiation into the ancient European mysteries was given his 'vision' of the inner secrets of the cult it was most likely the four symbols of the cup, the sword, the lance, and the pentacle, that were shown to him with great mystic ceremony. And the basic tools of the ritual magic, laid on the Magician's table, are the same four symbols and also the suits of the Minor Arcana.

Though we do not see the four symbols directly on trump 10 we do see two of their many analogues. The four creatures on the corners of the card derive from the vision of Ezekiel 1:10. They appear also in Revelations 4:7. Originally, these four figures represented the four 'fixed' signs of Babylonian astrology: Leo, Scorpio, Aquarius and Taurus. The early Christians identified them with the four evangelists, which is why we see them holding books. Sometimes called the 'guardians of heaven', they also came to symbolize the four basic elements of ancient and medieval science. From the right-hand corner anti-clockwise they are fire, water, air, and earth, and these elements belong as well to Wands, Cups, Swords, and Pentacles. As the fixed signs, the four beasts evoke the zodiac as a whole. A circular plane created by the Sun's apparent motion through the year, the zodiac forms the Great Wheel of the visible universe.

The other connection with the four elements comes in the four letter name of God on the Wheel's rim. Beginning at the upper right-hand corner, and again reading anti-clockwise, the letters are, Yod, Heh, Vav, Heh. Because this name appears in the Torah without vowels (the four letters are all consonants) it is unpronounceable; therefore God's 'true' name remains a secret. For at least two thousand years Jews and Christians have seen this name as magical. Mystics meditate on it (Abulafia's ecstatic third level of Kabbalah was reached through working with God's name) and magicians manipulate it. For Kabbalists the four letters are the very symbol of the world's mysteries. The process of the universe's creation was held to have occurred in four stages, corresponding to the four letters. And of course, the letters also connect with the four elements, the Grail symbols, and the Minor Arcana.

The Roman letters interspersed between the Hebrew are an anagram. Read clockwise from the top, they spell 'TARO'; read anti-clockwise they form 'TORA' (remember, the High Priestess's scroll). We can also find the words 'ROTA', Latin for 'wheel', 'ORAT', Latin for 'speaks' and 'ATOR', an Egyptian goddess (also spelled 'Hathor'). Paul Foster Case, following MacGregor Mathers, founder of the Golden Dawn, has formed the sentence 'ROTA TARO ORAT TORA ATOR'. This translates as, 'The Wheel of Taro speaks the Law of Ator'. Case calls this the 'law of letters'; since Ator became best known in Egypt as a goddess of the dead, it is actually the 'law' of eternal life, concealed in the natural world. Though the body dies, the soul continues. Case also points out that the Hebrew number values of the letters of 'TARO' add up to 691, and that this, added to 26, the number value for the four-letter name of God (called 'Tetragrammaton') makes 697. Those digits add up to 22, the number of letters in the Hebrew alphabet and of the trumps in the Major Arcana. And of course 22 returns us to 4.

The four symbols on the spokes are alchemical. From the top, read in a clockwise direction, they are Mercury, sulphur, water, and salt, and refer to the alchemical goal of line two, that is, transformation. Water is the symbol for dissolution, that is, dissolving the ego to release the true self that has become immersed in habits, fears, and defences. We will see just what this means when we consider Death and Temperance.

The idea of death and rebirth is also symbolized in the creatures adorning the Wheel. The snake represents Set, the Egyptian god of evil, and legendary bringer of death into the universe. It is he who kills Osiris, god of life. It is very likely that this legend, like the Wheel itself, originated in the practice in pre-history of killing the god-king, especially when we consider that Set was once a hero god, and that the snake was sacred to the Goddess who would have received the sacrifice. The snake follows the Wheel down; the jack-al-headed man going up is Anubis, guide to the dead souls, and therefore giver of new life. Now, according to some legends Anubis is Set's son, and so we see that only death can bring new life, and when we fear death we are seeing only a partial truth. Psychologically, only the death of the outer self can release the life energy within.

The sphinx on top of the Wheel represents Horus, Osiris's son, and god of resurrection. Life has triumphed over death. But the sphinx, as we saw in the Chariot, also signifies the mystery of life. The Chariot controlled life with a strong ego. Now the sphinx has risen above the wheel. If we allow the unconscious to speak we will sense some great secret to life, more important than the endless round of apparently meaningless events.

Set, the snake, was also called god of darkness. Again, to see darkness as 'evil' is an illusion, and indeed, the fear of darkness, like the fear of death, belongs to the ego. The ego loves the light just as the unconscious loves the dark. In light everything is simple and straightforward; the ego can occupy itself with the sense impressions from the outer world. When darkness comes the unconscious begins to stir. That is why children see monsters at night. One reason we make the outer self so strong is so we will not face demons every time the lights go out.

Those, however, who wish to go beyond the Chariot must face those terrors. Snakes and water, darkness and dissolution are all symbols of death, that is, death of the body and death of the ego. But life exists before and after the individual personality, which, of course, is only a bubble on the surface of our selves. Life is powerful, chaotic, surging with energy. Give way to it and Horus, the god of resurrection, will bring new life out of the chaos. The Wheel turns up as well as down.

The Wirth version of the Wheel of Fortune proclaims this idea even more strongly. The Wheel rests on a boat in water. Dissolution, chaos, emerge as the essential reality underlying the physical universe. All the forms of existence, the great variety of things and events, are simply momentary creations out of that powerful energy that fills the cosmos. In Hindu myth Shiva periodically destroys the entire universe, when the outer forms, like the ego, have grown weary and dull, by releasing the basic energy from which the universe originally emerged.

The number 10 suggests 0. The Fool is nothing and has no personality. But the Fool, like the number 0, is also everything, because he feels directly that energy of life, that sea surging beneath the boat. On the Rider pack Wheel of Fortune the centre of the Wheel bears no symbol. When we come to the still centre of existence, without ego or fear, all the outer forms vanish. We can understand this intuitively, but to really experience it we must allow ourselves to descend into that dark sea, to let the personality die, dissolve, and give way to the new life emerging out of darkness.

In divinatory readings the Wheel of Fortune signifies some change in the circumstances of a person's life. The person would likely not understand what has caused this change; there might be no direct reason that anyone can see, and in fact the person is likely not to be responsible in any normal sense of the word. A large corporation buys the company a man works for, and he becomes redundant. A love affair ends, not because the people have made any 'mistakes' in their treatment of each other, but simply because life continues. The Wheel turns.

The important thing about change is the reaction. Do we accept the new situation and adapt to it? Do we use it as an opportunity and find some meaning and value in it? If the wheel appears the right way up it signifies adaptation. In its strongest sense it can indicate the ability to pierce through the mystery of events to find a greater understanding of life. The end of a love affair, despite its pain, can give greater self-knowledge.

Reversed, the card signifies a struggle against events, usually doomed because the change has happened and life will always win against the personality that tries to oppose it. If the person concerned, however, has always reacted passively to whatever life has done to him or her, then the wheel reversed can signify a more important change than simply a new set of circumstances. It can open the way to a new awareness of responsibility for your own life.

Figure 12

JUSTICE

The image of this trump derives from the Greek Titaness Themis, who appears, with her blindfold and scales, on court house frescoes throughout the Western world. The legal Justitia, to give her her Latin name, was blindfolded to demonstrate that the law does not discriminate and applies to weak and powerful alike. The principle of *social* justice, however, properly belongs to the Emperor, directly above Justice. Card 11 indicates that the psychic laws of Justice, by which we advance according to our ability to understand the past, depends on seeing the truth about ourselves and about life. The Tarot Justitia, therefore, wears no blindfold.

So far, we have spoken of the second line as a process of withdrawal from outer concerns to awaken the inner vision of ourselves and of life. But a vision of the underlying nature of things is meaningless if it does not produce an active response. We must always act (the Magician principle) on the wisdom received from the inner self (the High Priestess principle). Not just the perfectly balanced scales but all the images on the card point to an equilibrium between understanding and action. The figure, a woman, appears androgynous; though she sits firmly on her stone bench she looks poised to stand; one foot points outward from her robe, the other remains hidden. The sword, an emblem of action, points straight upward, indicating both resolve and the idea that wisdom is like a sword piercing through the illusion of events to find the inner meaning. Two-edged, the sword signifies choice. Life requires us to make decisions; at the same time each decision, once made, cannot be revoked. It becomes part of us. We are formed by the actions we have taken in the past; we form our future selves by the actions we take now.

The scales also represent the perfect balance of past and future. Past and future balanced, not in time, but in the clear sight of Justice staring out at you from the exact centre of the Major Arcana.

Throughout the first half of the Major Arcana, when a person involves himself in the outer world, he suffers from the illusion that he is living life on the active principle. This is because we confuse doing things with action. As we turn inwards we assume we turn away from action; and indeed the process of line two cannot be accomplished without a pause in our outer lives, or at least a shift in attention. But real action, as opposed to pointless movement, always brings meaning and value to our lives; such action comes out of understanding. Otherwise, we remain truly passive, machines being pushed from one event to the next with no understanding of what causes us to do the things we do. The true purpose of line two is not to abandon the active principle but to awaken it.

The imagery of trump 11 combines the Magician and the High Priestess more completely than ever before. First of all, the digits of number 11 add up to 2, but the number also signifies a higher version of 1 (as well as a lesser version of 21). The woman seated before two pillars with a veil between them suggests the High Priestess, but her red robe, and her posture, one arm up, one arm down, implies the Magician. True action arises from self-knowledge; wisdom arises out of action. In life, as in the picture, the Magician and the High Priestess are inextricably combined, like a male and female snake twined around each other (symbol of the kundalini as well as the caduceus of Hermes), or the double helix of DNA. The colour of the veil is purple, emblem of inner wisdom; background, crown, hair, and scales are all yellow, signifying mental force. Wisdom does not arise spontaneously. We must think about our lives if we wish to understand them. But all our thinking goes nowhere unless it develops out of a clear vision of the truth.

On the microcosmic level of personal psychology the Wheel of Fortune represented a vision of a person's life; the events, who you are, what you've made of yourself. Justice indicates an understanding of that vision. The way to understanding lies in responsibility. As long as we believe that our past lives just happen, that we do not bring our own selves into existence through every thing we do, then the past remains a mystery, and the future an endlessly turning wheel, empty of meaning. But when we accept that every event in our lives has helped to form our characters, and that in the future we will continue to create ourselves through our actions, then the sword of wisdom cuts through the mystery.

Further, by accepting responsibility for ourselves we paradoxically free ourselves from the past. Like Buddha remembering all his lives, we can only get loose from the past by becoming conscious of it. Otherwise we constantly repeat past behaviour. This is why Justice belongs in the centre of our lives. The ego may be only a persona, a kind of mask, but that mask can control us as long as we will not admit having forged it ourselves.

The idea of responsibility for our own life does not imply any sort of invisible control over the outer world. It does not mean, for instance, that if an earthquake destroys your house you have somehow willed this to happen, for whatever hidden reasons of your own. Understanding includes accepting the limitations of your physical existence. The universe is vast and strange, and no individual can control what happens in it.

Nor does responsibility imply anything moral. It simply means that, like it or not, whatever you do, whatever you experience, contributes to the development of your personality. Life demands that you respond to every event. Not a moral requirement, just a fact of existence.

And yet all our instincts, psychology, and religion, as well as the testimony of mystics, tells us that life contains something more, an inner core independent of that outer self thrown from one experience to another. The second line shows the outer personality dying and the inner core, the angel of Temperance, being allowed to emerge. Before such a release can happen we must accept the 'justice' of our lives; what we are we have made ourselves.

Our age sees this process of awareness as primarily psychological, best exemplified in the difficult process of psychoanalysis. Other ages have externalized the process of transformation in the dramatic rituals of initiation. There are two kinds of initiations. In many tribal societies all members were taken to special ceremonies at the onset of puberty. In pre-Christian Greece and Rome, people chose to submit themselves for initiation into the 'Mysteries' of particular gods or goddesses. These mystery initiations followed a special pattern. Having gathered his or her courage to become a neophyte the candidate first receives instruction in the teaching of the cult or mystery; during this time steps are taken, through meditation, ritual and drugs, to open the channels to the unconscious and make the person receptive. These first stages are symbolized in Strength and the Hermit. Then, in a great atmosphere of mystery and drama, the candidate is shown a vision of the cult's secret mysteries. (They are kept secret partly to protect them from unbelievers, but even more to make them effective when revealed.) In the Grail cults this vision was a dramatic procession of the Grail and its attendant symbols, carried by women weeping for a wounded king. We see an analogue of this vision in the Wheel of Fortune.

And now comes the crucial moment. The candidate must make a response. If he or she simply stands there passively waiting for the next events, then the initiation cannot continue. In the Grail cults the necessary response was most likely a question, either 'What is the meaning of these things?' or more subtly, 'Whom does the Grail serve?' By asking this question the candidate gives the cult a chance to answer, that is, to continue the initiation through the ritual death and rebirth. More important, he or she shows a recognition of being part of the process, responsible for its proper outcome. This is more difficult than it sounds. The ritual symbolizes the life, death, and rebirth of nature, as well as the body dying to release the eternal soul. To speak at such an awesome event (and remember that the initiate believed in his or her gods and goddesses in a way impossible for most of us today) required a courage at least as great as that needed to accept the truths revealed through psychological analysis and awakening.

In our time the emphasis on individualism leads us to think only of personal death and rebirth. The great initiations, on the other hand, served not only to transform the particular person, but also linked him or her to the wider mysteries of the universe. Following this lead we can see another reason why Justice belongs in the centre of the Major Arcana. We have spoken of the world as a great interplay of opposites, a constantly turning wheel of light and dark, life and death. We have also said that at the centre of the wheel is the stationary point around which the opposites endlessly revolve. The balanced scales of Justice again suggest that stationary point. When we find the centre of our lives everything comes into balance. When all the opposites, including past and future, come into balance we are able to be free within ourselves.

Many people wonder what the Tarot, or the I Ching, or astrology tell us about free will. If the cards can predict what we will do does that mean free will does not really exist? The question arises from a misunderstanding of free will itself; we think of it as something simple and independent of the past. At any moment, we think, we are free to do whatever we want. But our supposedly free choices are governed by our past actions. If we do not understand ourselves, how can we expect to make a free choice? Only by seeing and accepting the past can we free ourselves from it.

A person may ask the cards about some situation. The cards very directly outline the consequences of some decision, say, whether or not to go ahead with a love affair, or to start some new project. Let us say that the cards indicate disaster, and that the person really can see the likelihood of what the cards predict. Now the person might say, 'Well, this is likely, but my free will allows me to change the situation.' So he or she goes ahead and the situation turns out exactly as the cards predicted. The person has not really used free will at all; rather the idea of free will has served as an excuse for ignoring what he or she recognized as a valid projection. This is not a hypothetical situation; it happens again and again with Tarot readings. It is not enough just to foresee a likely outcome for us to change or prevent that event. We must understand why it is coming, and we must work on the causes within ourselves for the things we do and the ways we react. Free will certainly exists. We just do not know how to use it. The most important thing we can learn from Tarot readings is just how little we exercise our freedom.

In Tarot readings one should always pay very careful attention to the card of Justice. Its appearance indicates first of all that events have worked out in the way they were 'meant' to work out; that is, what is happening to you comes from situations and decisions in the past. You have what you deserve. Secondly it indicates a need and a possibility for seeing the truth of this outcome. The card signifies absolute honesty. At the same time it shows the possibility that your actions in the future can be changed by a lesson learned in the present situation.

We cannot become honest with ourselves without extending that honesty to our dealings with other people. In this sense the card carries the obvious meanings of Justice; honesty, fairness, correct actions, and of course, in legal and other matters, a just decision – though not necessarily the decision a person might prefer.

Reversed, the card indicates dishonesty with yourself and others. It shows an unwillingness to see the meaning of events and shows especially that you are missing some opportunity for a greater understanding of yourself and your life. On the outer level it indicates dishonesty and unfair actions or decisions. Sometimes it is others who are unfair to us. The reversed meaning can refer also to unjust legal decisions or to bad treatment from someone.

On the other hand we must not allow the suggestion of unfairness to act as an excuse for denying our own responsibility for what happens to us. Justice reversed sometimes reflects the attitude, 'It is unfair. Look how everybody treats me'. And on and on. Whether the right way up or reversed the clear eyes of Justice send us an overwhelming message. In the words of Emerson, 'Nothing can save you but yourself'.

THE HANGED MAN.

(a)

12 THE HANGED MAN

(b)

Figure 13

THE HANGED MAN

After the crisis of seeing what you have made of your life comes the peace of acceptance; after Justice, the Hanged Man. Artists, writers, and psychologists have all felt drawn to this card, with its hints of great truths in a simple design. We have already referred to the occult tradition behind the upside down posture and crossed legs. In discussing Strength we said that occultists seek to release the energy of the desires and transform it into spiritual energy. Many occultists, following the ideas of traditional yoga, have believed that one very direct way to do this is literally to stand on your head, so that gravity will pull down the energy from the genitals to the brain. Of course, only most naïve and optimistic occultist would have expected such a thing to literally happen. They may have believed that trace elements found in genital fluid will seep down and affect the brain; more to the point, the reversal of physical posture serves as a very direct symbol of the reversal of attitude and experience that comes through spiritual awakening. Where everyone else is frenzied, you will know peace. Where other people believe themselves to be free, but are actually pushed from one thing to another by forces they do not understand, you will achieve true freedom by understanding and embracing those forces.

The Hanged Man hangs on a tree shaped like the letter T. Now, this is the bottom half of an ankh, Egyptian symbol of life and is sometimes called a Tau cross. According to Case the ankh in Egypt stood for the Hebrew letter Tau, which is the letter belonging to the World. Thus, the Hanged Man lies halfway to the World. We see this as well in the fact that 12 is 21 backwards, and if you turn the Hanged Man upside down (making the man himself right side up) you will have almost the same figure as the World Dancer. When we ask, therefore, what card serves as the halfway point for the Major Arcana, the answer is not one but three – the Wheel, Justice, and the Hanged Man, symbolizing a process rather than a moment.

Notice that while the Dancer extends her arms with their magic wands the Hanged Man keeps his arms crossed behind his back. Remember also that he *is* upside down. At this stage a deep spiritual awareness can only be maintained by withdrawing from society. In the World we see that same awareness maintained amidst all the outer activities of life.

He hangs on an ankh, which makes his tree the Tree of Life. Recalling Odin sacrificing himself of Yggdrasil we can also call the gallows the World Tree. This tree begins in the underworld (the unconscious) and reaches up through the physical world (the conscious) to heaven (the super-conscious). The ideas first represented by the diagram of the Lovers have begun to actually happen. What we saw previously as concepts now becomes, after Justice, a genuine experience. The Hanged Man's number, 12, is 2 times 6, that is, the High Priestess raising the Lovers to a higher level.

Beyond all its symbolism the Hanged Man affects us because it shows a direct image of peace and understanding. The calm shows so strongly in the card because the Hanged Man has surrendered to the rhythms of life. In the old initiations surrender involved joining the rituals instead of just watching them. For many modern people it involves releasing the emotions they have locked up for years. Notice that both these things are acts; surrender to the World Tree is an actual step we take, not a passive waiting.

T. S. Eliot's poem *The Wasteland* links the idea of an individual surrender to emotions with both the barrenness of European life after World War I and the ancient Grail mysteries. The wounded Fisher King can be healed by a 'moment's surrender which an age of prudence can never retract'. Earlier in the poem the hero is told 'Fear death by drowning'. The ego sees surrender as death — dissolution in the sea of life. The person who gives this warning is a Tarot reader. Eliot's poem helped to popularize Tarot cards in the 1920s. Specifically, it made famous the Hanged Man. Actually, the Hanged Man does not appear in the poem but is important because of his absence.

Eliot claimed to know nothing of the Tarot, but only to use some images from it. If so, he understood intuitively that the Hanged Man bears a connection to water. Most Tarot Kabbalists assign the letter Mem to trump 12. Mem stood for 'seas' and thus the element of Water. Madame Sosotris warns her ego-blind client, 'Fear death by drowning.' She tells him 'I do not find the Hanged Man' but then she points to another card (not a standard title), 'The Drowned Phoenician Sailor', and says 'This is your card.'

The crossed legs represent the number 4 upside down. 4 symbolizes the earth with its four directions. By reversing his own sense of values the Hanged Man has turned the world on its head. The arms and head together form a downward pointing water triangle. The way to the super-conscious is through the unconscious. The Golden Dawn card on the right of the Rider version shows the Hanged Man suspended over water.

We therefore see 4, the world, consciousness, and 3, here representing water, or the unconscious, in the Hanged Man's body. These numbers multiplied form 12. In multiplication the original numbers become dissolved and form something greater than their sum.

The number 12, like 21, suggests both 1 and 2. The card reflects the Magician in the sense that the power drawn down by the wand has now entered the Hanged Man; we see it as the circle of light about his head. The experience of really feeling the spirit force within life is one of great power and excitement in the midst of complete calm. The number 2 suggests the High Priestess; so does the image of water. Both cards indicate a withdrawal, but where trump 2 indicated the archetype of receptivity, trump 12 shows an experience of it.

1 plus 2 equals 3. The Empress directly felt life through emotional involvement, the Hanged Man feels it through inner awareness.

In readings the Hanged Man bears the message of independence. Like the Fool, which signified doing what you sensed was best, even if other people thought it foolish, the Hanged Man indicates being who you are, even if others think you have everything backwards. It symbolizes the feeling of being deeply connected to life and can mean a peace that comes after some difficult trial.

The trump reversed indicates an inability to get free of social pressure. Rather than listen to our inner selves we do what others expect or demand of us. Our awareness of life always remains second-hand, never a direct experience but only a series of stereotypes, like the person who models his or her behaviour on the orders of parents and the actions of movie stars.

The card reversed also means fighting your inner self in some way. It can mean the person who tries to deny some basic part of himself or simply the person who cannot accept reality and who in some way or other is constantly battling life. By putting his or her ego against the world this person too never fully experiences life. None of us can know the full meaning of being alive until, like Odin, we hang ourselves on the World Tree, its roots deep beyond knowledge in the sea of experience, its branches lost among the endless stars.

(a)

(b)

Figure 14

DEATH

As much as the Lovers (directly above Death) Arthur Waite's design for trump 13 departs from standard Tarot imagery. The picture on the right, opposite, comes from the esoteric Golden Dawn Tarot, but, even so, illustrates the older, essentially social message of Death. Death strikes everyone, kings and commoners alike. This basic democracy of death was a favourite theme of medieval sermons. As an idea it goes back at least as far as the Jewish practice of burying everyone in the same style, a white shroud and a plain pine box, so that in death rich become level with the poor.

As we might guess, the great power of death leads us beyond democracy to both philosophical and psychological meanings. Death, like life, is eternal and always present. Individual forms are always dying while others come into existence. Without death to clear away the old, nothing new could find a place in the world. Many science fiction novels have shown the tyrannical society that would result if the world's leaders did not die. The liberation of Spain after the death of Franco aptly demonstrated death's importance.

When we die our flesh decays, leaving only the skeleton. That too will eventually pass but it lasts long enough to at least hint at eternity. Therefore, the skeleton in the Golden Dawn card implies that eternity triumphs over the transitory. Now, the skeleton has an occult meaning as well. All over the world the training for shamans includes methods of seeing one's own skeleton, using drugs, meditation, even scraping the skin off the face. By freeing the bone from the flesh shamans connect themselves to eternity.

Because people fear death they seek reason and value in it. The Christian religion teaches us that death liberates our souls from the sinful flesh so that we may join God in a greater life to come. Carl Jung has written of the value of believing in an afterlife. Without it, death may seem too monstrous to accept.

Other people have pointed out that death joins us to nature. The consciousness that isolates us from the world will be obliterated; though the body will decay, that only means that it is feeding other creatures. Each death brings new life. Many people find the notion of themselves being eaten horrible to contemplate. The modern practice of embalming and painting corpses so that they look alive, and then of burying them in sealed metal caskets derives from the desire to maintain the body's separateness from nature even in death.

The fact is, since we will not know what happens to our bodies once the spirit has left them, what we really fear is the destruction of the personality. It is the ego that sees itself as separate from life; because it is only a mask the ego does not wish to die. It wishes to make itself superior to the universe.

If we can accept death we will be able to live more fully. The ego never wants to release energy; it tries to hoard it against the fear of death. As a result new energy cannot get in. We see this very graphically in people's breathing when they panic. They try to gulp air in without letting any out and as a result become short of breath.

In sex too the ego hoards energy. It fights climax and surrender because at that moment the ego partly dissolves. In Elizabethan England sexual intercourse was often called 'dying'. And Death in the Tarot comes below the Lovers.

Because the ego resists the very idea of death and therefore keeps us from enjoying life we must sometimes take extreme steps to get past it. The initiation rites always led up to a simulated death and rebirth. The initiate is led to believe that he or she is actually about to die. Everything is done to make this death as real as possible so that the ego will be tricked and in fact experience that dreaded dissolution. Then, when the initiate is 'reborn' he or she experiences a new maturity and a new freedom of energy. In recent years many people have experienced something very like these rites through using psychedelic drugs. They believe they are dying and they feel themselves reborn. However, without the preparation symbolized in the Hanged Man the experience can often be deeply disturbing.

Contrary to what many people believe the card of Death does not actually refer to transformation. Rather, it shows us the precise moment at which we give up the old masks and allow the transformation to take place. Perhaps we can understand this better if we consider the Tarot's parallel in psychotherapy. By force of will (Strength) the person, with the help of the therapist-guide (the Hermit), allows knowledge to emerge of who he or she really is, and what habits or fears he or she wishes to shed (Wheel and Justice). This knowledge brings calm and a desire to change (the

Hanged Man). But then a fear sets in. 'If I give up my behaviour', the person thinks, 'maybe there will be nothing left. I will die.' We live under the ego's control for so many years we come to believe that nothing else exists. The mask is all we know. Often people will stay stuck in therapy for years because they fear release. The nothingness of the Fool terrifies them. The fact is, they are right. The 'I' created out of these lifelong behaviours will indeed die. That person will cease to exist. But something else will emerge.

The Waite image for trump 13 increases the psychological meaning of the card. The four people demonstrate different approaches to change. The king, struck down, shows the rigid ego. If life comes at us with enough power the ego may collapse; insanity can result from an inability to adjust to extreme change. The priest stands and faces Death directly; he can do so because his stiff robes and hat protect him and support him. We see here the value of a code of belief to help us past our fears of death. The Maiden symbolizes partial innocence. The ego is not rigid, yet still aware of itself, unwilling to surrender. Therefore she kneels but turns away. Only the child, representing complete innocence, faces Death with a simple offering of flowers.

Death wears black armour. We have already seen how blackness and darkness symbolize the source of life as well as its end. Black absorbs all colour; death absorbs all individual lives. The skeleton rides a white horse. White repels all colours and therefore symbolizes purity, but also nothingness. The white rose stands for the desires purified, for when the ego dies selfish and repressive needs die with it.

At the back of the card we see a sun rising between two pillars. The ego belongs to the outer world of duality, separating and categorizing experience. Through Death we feel the radiant power of Life, which knows only itself. The landscape before the pillars reminds us of the 'land of the Dead' described in all mythologies. We fear the death of our old selves because we do not know what to expect afterwards. One main function of those shamans who see their skeletons is to go ahead through the Land of the Dead and thus be able to guide the souls of others.

A river flows through the middle of the card. Rivers, as we saw with the Empress, indicate the unity of change and eternity. The fact that they lead to the sea reminds us of the formlessness and oneness of the universe. The boat, reminiscent of the Pharaohs' burial boats, symbolizes the true self carried through Death to a new life.

No matter the picture, all Tarot cards bear the number 13. Though most people consider 13 unlucky they do not know why. In our culture 13 refers to Judas, since he was the thirteenth man at the Last Supper, and therefore the number indicates Christ's (and all people's) death. Friday the thirteenth is especially unlucky because Christ died on a Friday. But we can also describe Christ as the thirteenth man. Death leads to resurrection.

In a more symbolic sense 13 is unlucky because it takes us beyond 12. 12 is something of a 'perfect' number. It combines the archetypes of 1 and 2, it symbolizes the zodiac and therefore the universe, it can be divided by 1, 2, 3, 4, and 6, more digits than any other number. 13 destroys this elegance. It can be divided by nothing but 1 and itself. Again, we can go beyond the negative aspects of the symbolism. Precisely because it ruins the perfection of 12, 13 signifies a new creation; death breaks up old forms and makes way for the new.

13 is also considered unlucky because it suggests the frightening half-light of the Moon. A year contains roughly 13 lunations (the Moon goes around the Earth in 29.5 days). As well as being associated with darkness and mystery, the Moon goes through its own death and rebirth every month. Christ's three days of death underground suggests a borrowing from earlier lunar figures, for the Moon disappears for three days between the final sliver of waning and the first return in the waxing crescent. Because of the link between the menstrual cycle and the Moon, worship of the Moon in the ancient world belonged primarily to women. Many people believe that the medieval witches were really an underground survival of Pagan Moon worship. This is another reason why our Christian (and patriarchal) cultures consider 13 unlucky. It signifies witchcraft, and subversive women following the Moon in secret rituals.

The number 13 adds up to 4, the Emperor. Through Death we overcome our outer 'social' selves. Since 13 is a higher form of 3 the card also recalls the Empress, and reminds us again that in nature life and death are inseparable.

In divinatory readings Death signifies a time of change. Often, it indicates a fear of change. In its most positive aspect it shows a clearing away of old habits and rigidness to allow a new life to emerge. In its most negative aspect it indicates a crippling fear of physical death. This fear goes deeper than many people realize, and often a reading with many positive indications will end badly because of Death in the position of fears.

The trump reversed indicates being stuck in old habits. Waite talks of, 'inertia, sleep, lethargy' in life. This sense of a sluggish, boring life masks the sometimes desperate battle of the ego to avoid change. The card always indicates that Death, with its subsequent rebirth, is not only a possibility, but also in a sense, a necessity. The moment has come to die. By drowning us in lethargy, the ego prevents awareness of this fact from coming to consciousness. Inertia, boredom and depression often conceal inner terrors.

TEMPERANCE

The Chariot symbolized the successful construction of an ego able to deal victoriously with life. As time goes by this ego becomes rigid; slowly behaviour becomes less a response to reality and more and more a string of habits. The purpose of the second line of the Major Arcana is to free us from this artificial personality, and at the same time give us a glimpse of the greater truths within the universe. Temperance, appearing below the Chariot, shows a person whose behaviour is once again connected to the real world but in a way more meaningful than ever before. For if the child relates directly to life it does so without consciousness, and as consciousness grows so does the ego. Temperance indicates the ability to combine spontaneity with knowledge.

The term 'temperance' means moderation. For most people this means self control. The Tarot Temperance, however, does not go to extremes simply because extremes are not necessary. Not an artificial inhibition according to a moral code, but exactly the opposite; a true and proper response to all situations as they arise.

The word 'temperance' derives from the Latin 'temperare' which means 'to mix' or 'to combine properly'. The person who has released his or her inner self is characterized not only by moderation but by an ability to combine the different sides of life. Many people can only deal with life by parcelling it off into sections. They create one personality for business and another for their private lives; both are false. They consider certain moments and situations to be 'serious' and others to be 'fun' and are careful never to smile at a serious subject. The people they love are often not the people whom they find sexually attractive. All these separations derive from the inability to take life as it comes, moment by moment. Temperance combines the elements of life. In reality it combines the elements of the personality, so that the person and the outer world will flow together naturally.

(a)

(b)

(c)

Figure 15

The trump displays the signs of combination all through the picture. When we look at the Waite-Smith image on the left we see first of all the water being poured from one cup to another; the elements of life flowing together. Notice that the lower cup is not directly below the upper, so that the picture shows a physical impossibility. To other people the Temperate person's ability to handle all life's problems with joy appears magical.

The Rider pact Temperance presents both cups as magical. In the Wirth picture on the right the upper one is silver, indicating a flow from the Moon, that is, the unconscious, to the Sun, consciousness. The second line began with a withdrawal from the world to find the inner self; the time has now come to return to the normal activities of life.

The road especially signifies return. We have gone down into the self and now we are making our way back to involvement with the outer world, enriched. Notice that the two pillars of the earlier cards have become two mountains. Abstract ideas are becoming reality; Temperance is a card of behaviour, not concepts.

The angel stands with one foot on land, one foot in water. As the water represents the unconscious so the land symbolizes the 'real world' of events and the other people. The Temperate personality, acting from an inner sense of life, links the two realms. The water also indicates potentiality, that is, the possibilities of life, while the land symbolizes manifestation or actuality. The Temperate person, through his or her actions, brings into reality the wonders sensed by the Hanged Man.

The BOTA Temperance (see Fig. 15b) shows water being poured on a lion, and a torch dripping flames on an eagle. Leo symbolizes fire (the Magician), while the eagle, the 'higher' form of Scorpio, stands for water (the High Priestess). The angel is mixing the basic duality, inseparably combining the different sides of life that previously appeared hopelessly alien to each other. Now, the eagle stands for the higher Scorpio because Scorpio represents the energy of the unconscious. As the lower form, the scorpion, this energy shows itself primarily as sexuality, the 'animal desires' of the undeveloped personality. When the energy has been transformed by channelling it through awareness it becomes the eagle of spirituality. Strength showed this energy brought out in the form of the lion; in the BOTA Temperance we see the process completed, the eagle and the lion combined.

The angel resembles the Greek goddess Iris, whose sign was the rainbow; a rainbow appears on the BOTA card and iris flowers on the Rider pack version. Rainbows appear as a sign of peace after a storm, which reminds us that Temperance shows the personality released by the fearful experience of Death. The rainbow comes from water yet shines as light across the sky, an emblem of the inner self, which once seemed dark, chaotic, fearful, brought out and joy-ously transformed into the promise of new life. In Jewish and Christian tradition the rainbow is a sign of renewal after the Flood. The Flood, like Shiva's destruction of the universe, stands psycho-logically for the death of old patterns, which do not reflect the truth and joy of life and which lead people into 'evil' – behaviour destructive to themselves and to others.

As Zeus's messenger Iris travelled to the underworld to fill her golden cup with water from the River Styx. The Greeks believed that dead souls travelled across the Styx to the land of the dead. Only a descent into the underworld of the self can renew life.

Religiously the angel symbolizes the immortal soul liberated by death. If you look closely below the collar you will see God's name worked into the fabric of the gown. In Christian tradition the soul will become joined with God after the resurrection. The triangle within the square indicates that the Spirit rises from within the material body.

Psychologically the angel indicates the energy of life which emerges after the ego's Death. The triangle now shows that this energy works within the square of ordinary activities. We do not need to perform miracles to sense our connection with the immor-tal universe. We need only be ourselves.

Remember that the Tetragrammaton appeared on the Wheel as a mystery of fate. Here the name has become part of us. We become 'masters' of our fate when we learn to deal with life as it comes and not according to routines of habits and defences.

The divinatory meanings, like the card's ideas, begin with mod-eration, balance in all things and taking the middle path. The card means right action, doing the correct thing in whatever situation arises. Very often this means doing nothing. The intemperate person always needs to be doing something, but very often a situation requires a person to simply wait. The card will sometimes appear as an antidote to cards of recklessness and hysteria.

Temperance signifies mixing disparate elements together, blending activities and feelings to produce a sense of harmony and peace. Because it means balancing and combining the different sides of life Temperance carries a special significance for the Minor Arcana. If a reading shows a person split between say, Wands and Cups, activity and passivity, or Cups and Pentacles, fantasy and reality, then Temperance, moderation and acting from an inner sense of life, can give a clue to bringing these things together.

Like the Fool reversed Temperance upside down indicates a wildness, going to extremes. In Temperance this is because the person lacks the inner awareness to know what is appropriate to a situation. The trump reversed can act as a warning that you have allowed your life to become fragmented and that you are sliding from one extreme to another. It can in fact indicate failure in the great task of letting old habits and fears die away into the past. On a simple level the reversed Temperance tells us to calm down and avoid extremes; in its deepest sense it sends us back to Strength to begin that long, sometimes painful, sometimes frightening, but always essentially joyous process of death and rebirth.

CHAPTER SIX

THE GREAT JOURNEY

THE GOAL OF ENLIGHTENMENT

Most people find fulfilment when they have destroyed the mask of
the persona and are able to return to the ordinary world, renewed.
However, there have always been people who have sought something greater – a complete union with the spiritual foundations of
reality. For them it is not enough to simply sense this spirit running
through their lives. They wish to know this force in full consciousness and their enlightenment, teachings and example enrich the rest
of us. For these people the achievement of the second line is a
preparation and a clearing away of obstacles.

In its truest form life is simply pure, undifferentiated energy in
which everything living exists at once. There are no forms, no
parts and pieces of eternity. Consciousness protects us from such
overwhelming experience. It breaks down the totality of life into
opposites and categories. In the Hanged Man and Temperance we
partly reach beyond these limiting illusions to a sense of life's great
power, and a sense of ourselves as part of that power. But even in
Temperance the illusion of separateness returns. The card below
Temperance is called the World because it is through experiencing
it we and the universe become one.

The line begins with a paradox, a seeming fall into the illusions
of the Devil. By pursuing the meaning of the card at this particular
place we come to a new understanding of what is involved in

liberation. At the beginning of the Major Arcana we said that darkness and light were bound up together. The dark unconscious side, however, lay hidden in the temple of the High Priestess, to be experienced only through intuition. To get beyond the veil we must first go into the darkness of the self. Many religions celebrated the passage through darkness to the land of eternal life. When the Christian Church established its religion of light it banished all evocations of darkness as evil. The common image of the Devil is simply a mixture of the Greek god Pan and various other competitors of Christ.

The Tower's meaning depends on how we view the Devil. If we see the Devil as simply illusions then the Tower shows them shattered by violent upheaval. However, if the Devil signifies release of repressed energy then the illusion shattered by the lightning is nothing less than the veil of consciousness itself.

In each line the middle three cards form a special group. For the first it was the triad of nature, society, and education; for the second it was the change, through Justice, from the outer vision of the Wheel to the inner experience of the Hanged Man. In the last line the three cards show the passage from the inner revelation of the Star back to the consciousness of the Sun. In between, filled with strangeness, lies the moon.

The Sun is not the end. Once more we descend into darkness to experience, in Judgement and the World, a total joining with the universe and the spirit that fills it. We are now able to act in the outer world while never losing that sense of vastness and wonder within. The Magician and the High Priestess united in one joyful dance.

Figure 16

THE DEVIL

Why does this grim figure of oppression appear so late in the Tarot? After achieving the balance of Temperance why fall so abruptly? The Devil bears the number 15, which reduces to 6, the Lovers, and in fact, we can say that Waite worked backwards from the Devil when he designed his radical version of the Lovers. Thus in the Rider pack the Devil, with his captured demons, appears as a perversion of trump 6. But why the 'true' card so early and the perversion so near the end?

The Devil introduces the last line. This hints that it provides some vital energy for the work of that line. Now, the line deals with archetypal forces beyond the self. Does the road to enlightenment take us through the dark world of the Devil? Remember that Dante goes through Hell before he can reach Purgatory and Paradise; and that William Blake, the occultist and poet, described the Devil as the true hero of Milton's moralist poem *Paradise Lost*.

In order to understand the esoteric value of the Devil we must first consider its more usual meanings as a force of illusion and oppression. The main illusion is materialism, a term which we usually think of as an over concern with money, but which more properly means the view that nothing exists beyond the world of the senses. The Devil perches on a block of stone similar to the Emperor's cube in the BOTA deck (See Fig. 5). But where that cube symbolized the entire universe the Devil's rectangle, half a cube indicates an incomplete knowledge.

Denying any spiritual component to life the materialist pursues only personal desires – monetary, sexual and political. Since such narrowness often leads to unhappiness the Devil has come to symbolize misery. When we look at the two figures, however, we do not observe any discomfort in their faces or posture. Notice also that the chains do not really hold them; the large loops can easily come off. The Devil's power rests in the illusion that nothing else exists. In a great many situations, from political oppression to the personal misery of a bad family life, people only become consciously unhappy when they realize that life holds other alternatives.

The Devil's posture, one hand up, one down, recalls the Magician. Where trump 1 raises a wand to heaven, bringing down spiritual power, the Devil's torch points to earth, signifying the belief that nothing exists beyond the material.

The Devil's palm bears the astrological glyph for Saturn, a planet often seen as symbolizing evil or misfortune, but more properly viewed as limitations, weaknesses or restrictions. The outspread fingers plus the number 5 in 15, recall the Hierophant's two fingers up, two down. Where the latter gesture signified that there was more to the universe than what you can see before you, the Devil's open palm indicates again that nothing exists beyond the obvious.

The Devil wears a reversed pentacle, a symbol of black magic, on his forehead. Now, the pentacle carries a great many significances. If you stand with your feet apart and your arms out you will see that the pentacle symbolizes the human body. The right way up the head is uppermost and when we reverse the pentacle the genitals are above the head. In traditional Christian teaching the power of reason, the ability to tell right from wrong, rules the desires. Therefore, the reversed pentacle indicates letting your desires overpower your judgement. The Devil's torch inflames the man's tail, and people who experience their sexual needs as both overpowering and destructive have often described it as a fire burning inside them. The card's background is black, symbolizing black magic, the inability to see the truth and depression.

Thus we see the Devil's traditional meanings: illusion, materialism, misery and sexual obsession. And yet, the card carries a great force. The Devil stares out at us intensely. Practitioners of Tantra describe the kundalini as a fire in the body, beginning at the root of the spine, the tailbone, and evoked by sexual rites.

Consider again the pentacle. The sex organs over the head. The image reminds us of the Rider pack Lovers, where the woman, symbol of the unconscious and the passions, looks to the angel. We can also recall Strength, directly above the Devil, where the lion symbolizes the animal energy raised up and tamed. We have already spoken of the occult belief that sexual and spiritual energy are actually one and the same, symbolized by Scorpio's double image of scorpion and eagle. Strange as it sounds this idea is not really so mysterious. It takes neither an occultist nor a Freudian to recognize the great power of sex in our lives. How much of popular culture, with its love songs, romantic movies, and sexual jokes and slang, is devoted to it? If, for the average person, the sex urge is so dominant, then it makes sense that the occultist should seek to tap this energy and raise it to such a level that eventually it becomes wholly transformed into the overwhelming experience of enlightenment.

A more subtle point – dreaming is always accompanied by the body's sexual arousal, an erect penis or clitoris, plus other indications. Now, a dream is the unconscious manifesting itself as images. The indication is that the unconscious is sexual in nature and that dreams are a partial transformation of that energy into a wider form. In fact, the term 'unconscious' does not really refer to the dreams and myths which reveal it to us, but rather to the great pool of energy which sustains us through life.

Our Western culture has taught us that the body and the spirit are fundamentally opposed. We assume that the monk and nun abstain from sex so as not to contaminate themselves. But we can look at celibacy in another way. By refraining from sex the celibate can turn that energy in another direction. In India, the connection between sexual and spiritual energy has always been recognized. Shiva's symbol is a phallus, while the Tantra rites call for copulation as a way of charging the body with energy. The Gnostics, a major influence on European occult ideas, practised rites very similar to Tantra. And the Gnostics, like Blake after them, considered Satan the true hero of the Garden of Eden, seeking to give Adam and Eve knowledge of their true selves.

If the way to spirit leads through the desires, then why does society repress them? And if the path to liberation has been known and mapped out for centuries why keep it a secret? The answer to these questions lies in the terrible power of sexual-spiritual energy. If raised to the higher level it frees us from the limitations of duality. However, if the power is released and not transformed it can result in obsessions, sexual crimes, violence and even the destruction of the personality. It was not simply sexual politics that led the Greek patriarchs to attack the female-dominated mysteries of ecstatic rapture. Overwhelmed by the forces released within themselves, the worshippers would whip and mutilate themselves, and sometimes rage through the countryside, tearing to pieces animals, men and even children who were not safely locked indoors. It is only the person who has been trained, who has achieved a deep level of inner peace, who has, in fact, reached the understanding the Tarot calls Temperance, who can deal safely with the forces implied in the Devil.

Actually, the Devil implies a great deal more than sexual rites and violent energy. On a wider sense it symbolizes the life energy locked up in the dark hidden areas of the self, which cannot be entered by ordinary means. It is called the Devil because for those who are not prepared to receive this energy it can manifest itself as monsters, a sense of the universe as filled with evil, or the temptation to indulge in violence. We said in the second line that the child develops a strong ego so it will no longer fear the darkness. The action of the second line gave us a glimpse of the dark waters beneath the Wheel of Life. The third line requires a complete release of unconscious energy. Such a flood can only come through entering that hidden area, with all its illusions, horrors, and desires which can so easily distract the unprepared from the final goal.

Look again at the gestures of the Hierophant (See Fig. 6) and the Devil. The priest's two fingers held down signify that there is more to life than what we see; at the same time the fingers imply that the path to that deeper knowledge is closed. The Devil's open fingers can symbolize the narrow illusion of thinking that what you see is all that exists; or it can symbolize seeing everything. Nothing hidden away. The specific gesture made by the Devil, with a gap between the two double fingers, is the gesture made by the High Priest in Jerusalem to bring down the spirit force. It survives today in the Jewish New Year celebrations as part of the 'priestly blessing'.

Paul Douglas has called trump 15 the 'dark side of the collective unconscious'. When the so-called 'black magicians' (once a title for the Devil) conjures a demon he or she is actually bringing out a force from inside the self. If the operation goes successfully the magician masters the demon, making it his or her servant. That is, the magician uses the liberated energy rather than falling a prey to it. To do this, the magician must be purified of ego desires and of fear. In short, he or she must have achieved Temperance, otherwise the demon can 'win' the encounter. The magician becomes a slave to the illusions of the Devil.

We have gone quite deeply into a radical interpretation of the Devil. The card's divinatory meanings tend to follow the more usual interpretations. We take the more obvious meanings because in a reading the card appears out of context. The Devil can indicate a narrow materialistic view of life; it can mean any form of misery or depression, especially feeling chained or imprisoned, with the illusion that no alternatives are possible. If it appears in connection with the Lovers it shows that a relationship which began with love has turned into a trap.

The Devil signifies being the slave of your desires, rather than acting the way you think is best. It can mean a controlling obsession, particularly a sexual one, where the person feels drawn to commit acts he or she finds morally repugnant. The extreme example is the sex criminal; on a much more common level many men and women find themselves powerfully attracted to people they actively dislike. The feeling of helplessness and shame which results from giving in to these desires belongs to the Devil.

Earlier we observed the calm on the faces of the chained men and women. This indicates the acceptance of a bad situation. Eventually we come to view our unhappy conditions as normal, and may even fight against change. The Devil reversed, on the other hand, indicates an attempt to break loose from some misery or bondage, either real or psychological. The person no longer accepts his or her situation and moves towards liberation. Paradoxically it is precisely at such a time that we feel our unhappiness and the limitations of our lives most strongly. Before you can slip off the chains you must become conscious of them. Therefore, people who are undergoing some process of liberation – say, leaving home, psychotherapy or a difficult divorce – often find themselves far more unhappy than when they blindly accepted their oppressed condition. Such a period can be crucial to a person's development. If one can survive it, one will emerge happier and with a more developed personality. Sometimes we can find the period of transition unbearably painful and slip back to our chains.

The Devil reversed in the position of the past often means that the change has occurred, but the feelings of sadness, of anger, of depression remain, perhaps hidden from conscious view, but still an influence. We must often deal with the devils of the past, even those we have long ago overcome in practical terms. The psyche never lets anything go; it never simply forgets about anything. The way to liberation lies in using and transforming the knowledge and energy bound up in every experience.

Figure 17

THE TOWER

Like the Devil, this trump carries a great many meanings, and the explanations given by most Tarot books indicate its surface moral lessons. The Tower is said to be the materialist conception of the universe, and the lightning the destruction that comes to a life based on purely materialist principles. Even here we find a great deal of subtlety. While it may appear that some outside force strikes down the narrow-minded person, the violence shown in the card actually derives from psychological principles. The person who lives only to satisfy the ego demands of wealth, fame, and physical pleasure, ignoring both introspection and the spiritual beauty of the universe, raises a prison around himself. We see this prison as the Tower; grey, rock-bound, with a gold crown. At the same time a pressure builds up inside the mind as the unconscious strains at its bonds. Dreams become disturbed, arguments and depression more common, and if a person represses these manifestations as well, the unconscious will often find some way to explode.

The explosion may appear as an external disaster; your friends and family turn against you, your work collapses and violence of one kind or another swirls around you. And it is true that one of the mysteries of life is the way that bad luck comes in clusters. Yet, how many of these problems result from long neglected or mishandled situations, striking us at the moment we become vulnerable? And if some problems, illness or death of people close to us, economic problems in society, even natural disasters, such as storms – or lightning bolts – appear at the same time as personal problems, such coincidence shows again that life does indeed contain more than we can see in front of us.

We should not think that the psyche, or life, brings on disaster simply to punish us. The drops of fire falling one each side of the Tower are shaped like the Hebrew letter yod, the first letter of God's name. They symbolize not anger, but grace. The universe, and the human mind will not allow us to stay forever imprisoned in our towers of illusion and repression. If we cannot free ourselves peacefully then the forces of life will arrange an explosion.

I do not mean to imply that we in any way enjoy the painful experiences that shake us loose, or that we can see the beneficial ends from such means, or even that the process always results in freedom. Very often a series of disasters or a period of violent emotions will cripple a once strong personality. The point is only that given no other outlets the unconscious will erupt all around us, and that we can use this experience to find a better balance. Some decks call this card 'The House of the Devil'; but others call it 'The House of God', reminding us that it is spiritual force which destroys our psychic prisons.

There is a deeper meaning in the linking of God's and the Devil's houses, a meaning implied even more directly in the fact that the Hebrew for 'snake' bears the same numerical value (and is therefore seen as equivalent to) the word for 'messiah'. The Devil is God's shadow. In trump 15 we saw that the person seeking unity with life must bring out the energy normally repressed by the conscious personality. By embracing the Devil, however, we endanger that calm and balance shown in Temperance. We set the psyche on a violent course leading to the explosion of the Tower. Jung described consciousness as a dam blocking free flow of the river of the unconscious. Temperance acts as a kind of sluice, letting the waters through at a controlled rate. The Tower blows away the dam completely, releasing the locked up energy as a flood.

Why take such a dangerous course? The answer is that no other way exists to finally go beyond the barrier of consciousness, or to break free from that which separates life into opposites and which cuts us off from the pure energy contained within ourselves. The veil across the temple is the conscious personality, protecting us from life itself. As mystics, shamans, and ecstatics have testified, eternity is all around us, blinding and overwhelming. The unprepared mind cannot encompass such power, and so consciousness comes to our rescue, closing off the major part of our spiritual energy, parcelling experience into time and opposing categories.

The mystics tell us as well that revelation comes as a lightning bolt which destroys the illusions of the material world in a single blinding flash, like that seen by Paul on his way to Damascus, or that which struck Buddha under the Bo tree. No matter how long the meditation, the years of prayer or occult training, the truth comes all at once or it does not come at all. Which is not to say that the preparation was meaningless. The work shown in the first two lines of the Major

Arcana serves a double purpose. Not only does it make us strong enough to withstand the lightning when it comes, it also puts us in a position to bring about the lightning. All occult practices begin with one assumption: that it is possible to call down the bolt of revelation, that a person can take definite steps to make this happen.

These steps include the teaching, the meditations, the ego death, and finally the embracing of the Devil. By releasing that energy we get past the barriers of repression and open ourselves to the lightning. For the spirit exists all the time; it is we who are blind to it. By going into the darkness of the self we open ourselves to the light.

Obviously, this is a dangerous process. The unprepared person can become trapped in the illusions of the Devil. We will see also that the release of energy carries its own dangers as the psyche tries to integrate it with the conscious awareness. The hero on the way back from the centre of the labyrinth can become lost if he has not carefully prepared himself.

The Tower comes below the High Priestess, for it shows the veil being ripped away. At the same time the lightning recalls the Magician. That energy and truth which passes through the Magician here strikes in full force. We also see trumps 1 and 2 in the two people; one in blue, the other in a red cloak. The polarity symbolized in so many of the earlier cards is here overwhelmed by the unity of existence. Count the yod drops of fire and you will find that they come to twenty-two, the number of trumps. You will find also that they are separated into ten and twelve. The Sumerians used a number system based on ten (for ten fingers) for worldly matters, but a separate system based on twelve, for the zodiac, for spiritual counting. This duality is also an illusion. Both worlds are manifestations of the same spirit fire.

The image of a destroyed tower brings to mind the tower of Babel. On a literal level that story explains why people speak so many languages, while morally it teaches us not to put our faith in human abilities (the Tower as materialism). But we can see another meaning in Babel's destruction. The lightning that struck it was God speaking directly to humanity rather than indirectly through the ordinary phenomena of the physical world.

In an instant the speech of God replaces the human speech that built the tower; revelation replaces the step by step knowledge of the senses. Remember that the descent of the spirit at Pentecost scrambles human language; people 'speak in tongues' or make animal noises. And the shamans in their trances speak the languages of the beasts and birds. Human language is an aspect of culture and a limitation of consciousness. Many linguists, notably Benjamin Whorf, have demonstrated that our languages restrict our ability to perceive reality, like a filter over the universe. And truth, the mystics tell us, cannot be expressed in words.

The Tower's 16 reduces to 7, the Chariot, linked by Case and others to human speech. The speech of God of the Tower destroys in a moment all the careful constructions of culture, language and consciousness. In so doing it returns us to the chaos of the sea beneath the Wheel of Fortune and the Pool of water behind the veil of the Priestess.

In some ways the Tower is the most complex of all the trumps; its more subtle meanings are at odds with its obvious ones. Like the Devil its divinatory meanings usually derive from the obvious. It usually refers to a period of violent upheaval (either literally or psychologically), the destruction of long established situations, the break-up of relationships in anger or even violence.

Because the card carries such furious significance many people recoil at the sight of it. The reaction raises the vital question of how to regard the Tarot's more fearful images. We must learn to use all experience, the Tower as well as the Lovers. When the Tower appears it is necessary to remember that it can lead to freedom; the explosions are clearing away some situation that has built up intolerable pressure. They can lead to new beginnings.

To say that the Tower's appearance usually signifies difficult experience is not to insist that the deeper meanings will never arise. The card can mean a flash of enlightenment, particularly if such enlightenment replaces a limited view of life. Only the reader's intuition and experience, as well as the hints from the other cards, can indicate the specific meaning.

The Tower reversed indicates a modified version of the card's meaning when the right way up. The violence and storm are still there but milder. At the same time the reversed trump carries the extra meaning of 'imprisonment', to use Waite's term. This paradox becomes resolved when we consider that when the right way up the Tower liberates. When reversed, then, the card means that we do not allow ourselves to undergo the full experience. By keeping a tight control on our reactions we lessen the pain; we also do not release all the repressed material. Within ourselves the painful experience continues, never having gone its full course. By shielding the Tower from the lightning we become its prisoners.

Figure 18

THE STAR

After the storm, peace. The person who undergoes emotional upheaval finds afterward a sense of calm and emptiness. Lay the cards out for someone who has never seen them and the Star will hardly need interpretation. Everything in it speaks of wholeness, openness, and healing.

It is worth comparing the Star with Temperance, where we also see a figure pouring water and holding two cups, with one foot on land and one in water. Both cards come after a crisis, but where Temperance is controlled the Star is free. Not clothed, but naked. Not standing stiffly, but supple and relaxed. And finally, where Temperance pours the water back and forth, blending but at the same time conserving, the Star maiden pours it out freely, confident that life will continually supply her with new energy. The picture suggests all those mythical chalices that could never be emptied.

The Tower's release of energy ripped away the veil of consciousness. Here in the Star we are behind the veil. The pool of water, small though it is, represents the unconscious; that same water we saw concealed behind the pillars of the High Priestess. Now this universal life energy has been stirred up by the act of pouring the person's own life waters into it.

The water being poured onto land indicates that the energy freed by the Tower is directed outwards as well as inwards; it links the unconscious with the outer reality of the physical world. One way to describe the streams of water is as the archetypes of myth, the images through which the unconscious expresses itself. The unconscious is a whole, without shape or division, but it emerges into awareness through the separate streams of mythology. With the Star we have gone beyond myth to its source as formless energy; as light coming out of darkness. The transformation of darkness into light is the unconscious, the hidden vastness within us, changed into the ecstatic awareness of super-consciousness.

One stream of water flows back into the pool, signifying that all archetypes blend back into the formless truth. The value of the archetype lies only in its power to arouse the inner self and to connect us to the source. The maiden's foot does not penetrate the water. The collective unconscious has not been entered, but only stirred up.

The bird on the right is an ibis, a symbol of the Egyptian god Thoth, who was considered the inventor of all arts, from poetry to pottery. Literally he taught the first artists their techniques, but on a more symbolic level, we can say that all creative action stems originally from the pool of unformed energy. It is one function of being a physical creature that we take this energy and use it to make poems, paintings and tapestries. All these human creations are symbolized in those several streams of water. Every act of creation objectifies spiritual energy in the thing created. At the same time no work exhausts the artist's inspiration as long as he or she remains connected to the inner sources. Therefore, the one stream returns to the pool, just as each work gives its creator new inspiration.

The Star appears below the Empress and the Wheel. In the Empress we saw the natural world glorified in the passions. But the

Empress was heavily clothed to indicate that she expresses her emotion through things outside herself – nature, lovers and children. In the Star we see the inner self joyfully experiencing itself. The Star maiden combines the two female archetypes, the inner sensitivity of the High Priestess brought out and expressed with the passion of the Empress.

In the Wheel of Fortune we saw a vision of the universe in mysterious symbols. Here the Tower has taken us beyond visions. In the Star we directly experience the unconscious, rather than its images.

As trump 17 the Star goes beyond 7, with the Star releasing the life force that the Chariot controlled and directed. 1 plus 7 equals 8, and we can see that the Star is Strength raised to a higher level, with the lion of desire no longer simply tamed, but transformed into light and joy.

The stars on the card are all eight pointed which is another reference to Strength. Since an eight pointed star can be formed by placing one square over another with the points alternating, the octogram is sometimes thought of as halfway between the square and the circle. The square stands for matter and the circle for spirit. Human beings are the link between the spirit and the physical world; our ability to both feel the truth, and to act, makes us vehicles through which the truth can manifest itself.

The Church used to describe humans as halfway between the animals and the angels. Usually a moral interpretation was given; people could follow their desires or their reason. But we can use this metaphor to say that human awareness and action connect the physical world to the 'angels'.

Despite all the suggestions of manifestations the Star is not really a card of action, but of inner calm. In contrast to Temperance and the Moon, the Star shows no road leading back from the pool to the mountains of outer reality. Though the streams and the ibis imply the uses of creative energy, the experience of the Star is one of peace. For the moment, the journey can wait.

In divinatory readings the card expresses hope, a sense of healing and wholeness, especially after emotional storms. Very often the Star and the Tower suggest each other even when only one actually appears. Trump 17 indicates the unconscious activated, but in a very benign way.

Reversed, we close ourselves off from the card's calm and hope, experiencing weakness, impotence, and fear. This deep insecurity can sometimes mask itself as arrogance. If the Star indicates the human as a link between the spirit and the outer world then the card reversed symbolizes the channels closed, and when the waters of life are dammed up inside, the outside can only become tired and depressed.

Figure 19

THE MOON

The true task of the third line is not revelation but bringing that inner ecstasy back to consciousness. The Star contained no road back. It shows us dwelling in the glories of darkness transformed into light. To use that light we must pass through distortion and fear.

The Star experience lies beyond words or even form, though it implies forms emerging with the streams of water. In the Moon we see this process happening, as visions, myths and images. The Moon is the card of the imagination as it moulds the energy of the Star into shapes that the consciousness can comprehend.

Myths are always distorted. They can never really say what they want, they can only appeal to things deep within the self. The Star stirred up the waters; as we return to outer awareness those waters give forth their creatures. Remember that the Star and the Sun give off their own light, but the Moon reflects the hidden light of the Sun. The imagination distorts because it is reflecting inner experience to the outer mind.

As the world's mythologies demonstrate the collective unconscious contains monsters as well as heroes, fear as well as joy. This is one reason why we cover our sensitivity to life with the protective layer of ego consciousness, so we will no longer fear the dark and the distorting shadows of the Moon.

The Moon's eerie half-light has always brought out strange feelings in people and animals. One word for madness, 'lunacy', derives from 'luna', Latin for moon, and in the Middle Ages people believed that the souls of the insane had flown off to the moon. Today, too, many doctors and police have observed the prevalence of suicides and other signs of disturbed emotions during the full moon. Something about the moon excites fear and strangeness, just as the sun relaxes and consoles us. The Tarot Sun comes after the Moon; simplicity can only be appreciated after a journey through the lunar strangeness.

The dog and the wolf represent the 'animal self' roused by the Moon, just as a full moon can set both creatures howling all night long. The Emperor, directly above trump 18, showed us learning the rules of society so well that they become automatic. With the last line we go beyond this 'super ego' repression; in the process the 'id' wildness comes to the surface. A werewolf howling under a full moon is a vivid metaphor of the power of the unconscious to bring out something primitive and non-human in the most respectable people.

As 18 the Moon relates to 8. Strength saw the animal nature tamed, and channelled through the Hermit. Here no such direction is given; as we come back from the Star the beast returns in all its wildness. Only when the Star energy is fully integrated in the World will the animal self be wholly transformed. Notice that in Strength the woman, the human side, controls the lion. Even in the Devil the demons appear clearly human. But there are no people on trump 18. In that half-light our sense of ourselves as human breaks down.

We sense something of the Moon's wildness in the aftermath of a nightmare, when we feel strange within ourselves. The wild sensations are not the result of the nightmare; it is more the other way around. We said earlier that dreams are transformations of unconscious energy into images. A burst of energy which is too great for the dream mechanisms to peacefully assimilate can result in both a nightmare and the feeling when you wake up of the body being charged with wild energy.

Madness is also accompanied by uncontrolled sensations in the body. Very often lunacy takes the form of transformation into an animal. People will crawl on all fours, naked, howling at the moon. A sudden release of unconscious energy has disintegrated the personality. In the Tarot this very dangerous moment happens only after long preparation, with all the normal ego problems left behind. The Shaman too experiences a transformation into a beast. Shamans will leap about and speak as animals during their trances. But the shaman, like the occultist, has prepared himself with years of preparation. He is also armed with the knowledge of what to expect, handed down from the generations of shamans who have gone before. Remember that the Moon's number adds up to 9, the Hermit. The teacher-guide of that card is not visible, for we must face the Moon alone, but the guidance given beforehand can help us find our way.

If the animals symbolize the savage in man, the crayfish is something very different. In one of his most vivid phrases Waite calls it 'that which lies deeper than the savage beast'. It symbolizes the most universal fears within the collective unconscious, experienced in visions as nameless demons. The emergence of such terrors is a well known occurrence to people who expose their lunar side through such methods as deep meditation or drugs. They are also seen as monsters encountered by shamans on their trance journeys. The arousal of these fears, often experienced as creatures emerging from water or pools of oily liquid, can produce unreasoning panic. Yet these images belong to our inner world; we cannot reach the Sun without passing them.

The crayfish half emerges from the water. Waite tells us it never comes completely onto land but always falls back again. The deepest terrors are the ones that never fully take shape. We feel something inside, but we can never see just what it is. At the same time the half emerging crayfish suggests that in the journey back to consciousness the deep perceptions of the Star become distorted because we cannot bring it all back. For this reason too the Moon is disturbing, because the peace and wonder of the Star have become partially destroyed and lost.

And yet, despite the wildness, the fearful excitement, the cool light can calm as well. The Moon is said to increase on the 'side of mercy', a reference to the pillar of mercy on the Kabbalistic Tree of Life. Even more striking, the drops of light falling on the animals' heads are, again, yods; the first letter of God's name and symbols of grace. If, through preparation and simple courage, we accept the wild things brought out by the deepest imagination, then the Moon brings peace, the terrors subside, and the imagination leads us back, enriched, with its wonders. Waite writes, 'Peace, be still; and there shall come a calm upon the waters.' The crayfish sinks back, the waters settle. The road remains.

The road leads through two towers, suggesting a gateway into unknown areas. The gateway is a very common symbol among mystics and shamans, seen also in many myths. Sometimes a circular pattern, like the mandala, or some physical formation, like a cave (very often compared to the vagina), the gateway allows us to leave the ordinary world to enter the strangeness of the mind.

The Tarot's two towers carry another meaning, as the last complete manifestation of that duality we first saw in the pillars of the High Priestess's temple. If the revelation of the Tower is not integrated with ordinary life then a new and more acute duality may result. At the same time, the very fact of having heard the speech of God totally changes our relation to the question of opposites. Previously duality was seen as basic to life, but we now know that in fact reality combines all things; where before the veil kept us from passing between the two pillars, here we have already passed through. We are looking at the two towers of consciousness from the other side. The task is not to pierce through to the inner truth but to take back that truth.

In all this we have looked at the Moon primarily in terms of its disturbing aspects. But as we saw with Death and the number 13, the Moon also suggests the power and mystery of women's fertility. Menstruation (the word 'menses' relates to 'month' and 'moon') is miraculous, because menstruating women bleed copiously yet do not die. Further, many women find themselves more emotional, but also more psychic when menstruating. Fearing this power, men have created disturbing myths and taboos around menstruation. But power does not have to be destructive or even frightening. If respected, this lunar psychic awakening enriches life.

In divinatory readings the Moon indicates an excitement of the unconscious. We begin to experience strange emotions, dreams, fears, even hallucinations. We find ourselves more intuitive, more psychic. If the card appears the right way up then the person will allow this to happen. When accepted, the imagination enriches life. But if the card appears reversed, it shows a struggle against the experience. This struggle leads to fear and often very disturbed emotions as the person does not allow the Moon's calming side to emerge.

Like the High Priestess the Moon indicates turning away from outer concerns and becoming introspective. It can indicate giving up some specific activity or simply a period of withdrawal. In many cultures women withdrew from the general society during menstruation. This allowed them to pay attention to that inner lunar state, and experience the powerful Moon stirrings in a safe environment. In Tarot readings the Moon does not have to symbolize literal menstruation or withdrawal from the world. Instead, for men as well as women, it can indicate a psychic awakening and the need to pay attention to it. However, while the High Priestess symbolizes quiet intuition, the Moon is excited, stimulating images from the unconscious. Again, the Moon reversed signifies a disturbance. The person does not wish to turn away from the solar side, and may try to fight off the Moon by a great deal of activity. The Moon, however, will not be denied, and the fears can get stronger the more we fight it. The psyche, operating under its own laws for its own reasons, has turned to the Moon. If we allow ourselves to experience it the fears will turn to wonders and the gateways open to adventure.

(a)   *(b)*

Figure 20

THE SUN

Like the Hanged Man above it the Sun is both a joyful release after
the test shown in the previous card and a preparation for the death
and rebirth in the two cards following. Justice required action as a
response to the knowledge gained about ourselves. As a result the
Hanged Man is passive. The Moon requires passive surrender, since
there is no way we can control the visions rising under its influence.
Therefore, the Sun shows an active, energized state. By accepting
the Moon's fearful images we bring the energy outside ourselves,
giving all of life a radiance.

Under the Sun everything becomes simple, joyous and physical.
The light of the unconscious brought into daily life. The two children in the Oswald Wirth version above the more common image
for the trump, are sometimes called the eternal self and the mortal
body. Holding hands, they have joined together. The two figures
with the Sun above them returns us to the triangular motif first
seen in the Hierophant two lines above. Here the joy and simplicity of the Sun does not mediate between the inner and outer poles
of life but joins them together.

We are all children, in the way that sun religions speak of us all as holy children of our father, the sun. If you look at the bodies, in the picture, especially the female, you will see that they are adults. The successful passage from the Tower has given them a childlike simplicity.

The Tarot shows this passage in its various stages, giving the impression of the passage of time. Sometimes, however, perhaps most often, it happens all at once, the blinding revelation of the Tower, the inner radiance of the Star, and the acute fear of the Moon, all joined in a single instant of transformation. And the aftermath is joy, a sense of all life and all the world being filled with a wondrous light.

Among all people enlightenment bears the same characteristics, whatever the cultural interpretation through mythology, doctrine, psychological theory, etc. Enlightenment is an experience, not an idea. The person feels struck by a burst of light, sometimes coloured, like the yod drops in the Wirth card. Suddenly the world is seen or felt, as spiritual and eternal, rather than the day to day existence of drudgery and confusion. The person feels totally alive with a childlike joy that, in fact, most children probably never know, for the sunstruck person has gone beyond the child's fear of darkness by travelling through it.

In its journey across the world the sun sees everything, and so represents knowledge. Gods associated with the sun, like Apollo, are said to know everything that happens. The sunstruck person feels a sense of wisdom, of seeing everything with total clarity. He or she is 'lucid', a word which means clear and direct, but which literally means 'filled with light'.

It is interesting that Apollo, god of light, was born from Leto, goddess of night, and that his major shrine, the oracle at Delphi, belonged originally to goddesses of darkness. Even under Apollo's direction the wisdom and light of the oracle operated out of darkness. It was Apollo who forced Oedipus to discover the mystery within himself.

The spring sun brings forth life out of the dead winter ground. In many places it was believed that the sun impregnates not only the soil, but all women. When the biological means of reproduction was discovered the role of the sun was not dropped but made more subtle. People now saw the soul – the atman or true self – as sunlight contained within the embryo. Buddhist myth states that Gautama, in his mother's womb, was all light so that her belly shone like a translucent screen over a powerful lamp. Zoroaster too blazed so powerfully in his mother's womb that the neighbours ran with buckets, thinking the house had caught fire.

The Gnostics carried this idea further, believing that the Fall had broken up the godhead into the bits and pieces of existence. Most important, the light had become imprisoned (rather than simply contained) in individual bodies. In was each person's duty, through the Gnostic rites, to release the light within his body so that unity could be restored. The Kabbalist Isaac Luria preached a similar doctrine. The Tree of Life, or Adam Kadmon, the unity of existence, had been shattered because the god light was too powerful for it. Again, the light became separated and imprisoned, so that it was the responsibility of each person to aid in 'tikkun', that is, restoration of the light to unity.

These doctrines derive from the Sun experience common to all cultures. The sunstruck person sees everything, each person, each animal, all the plants and rocks, even the very air, alive, and holy, united through the light that fills all existence. And yet, the Sun is not the World. With trump 19 we perceive the universe as unified and alive. 21 embodies those feelings.

The usual drawing for the Sun shows the children within a garden, often standing in a circle. Douglas calls this the 'inner garden of the soul', a feeling of purity and holiness, a new Garden of Eden. When we liberate and transform the energy locked inside us we find that the Garden of Eden was never really lost, but has always existed within us.

The Rider pack shows its single child riding out of a garden. For Waite the Sun experience was essentially a burst of freedom. It was a breaking loose, a wonderful liberation from ordinary restricted consciousness to openness and freedom.

The grey, stone wall in the picture represents the past life, bound by a narrow perception of reality. The super-consciousness of the Sun is characterized by feeling a part of the whole world rather than an isolated individual. We can perhaps combine the two images for the trump by saying that once you realize that the

Garden of Eden exists within you, you are free to leave it, taking it with you always as you create a new life.

The number 19 suggests a higher level of 9. The light contained in the Hermit's lantern, the wisdom of his teachings, here bursts forth as Abulafia's ecstatic third level of Kabbalah. We said of the Hermit that the old man and the bleak mountain were illusions required because the inner self could only be reached through withdrawal. Here the truth has emerged and the robed stiff Hermit is transformed into a gloriously open child. The other half of 19 is 1. The Magician force joined to the Hermit wisdom is super-consciousness. The energy of life united with its meaning and purpose.

1 plus 9 equals 10, the Wheel of Fortune whose vision was of something outside us that we tried to comprehend. Here we see life in a visionary way from inside ourselves. And in this kind of vision there are no mysteries and no symbols, only the universe, filled with light.

The Sun's divinatory meanings are as simple and direct as the wondrous children in the pictures. The card signifies joy, happiness, and a great sense of the beauty of life. In its deepest sense it means looking at the world in a wholly new way, seeing all life united in joy and light. Above all it is a card of optimism, energy and wonder.

Reversed, the good things do not become lost but confused, as if the sun had become clouded over. Life is still giving the person a time of simple happiness, but it cannot be seen so clearly. The person is no longer lucid and must work to realize the joy which is the great gift of the Sun.

Figure 21

JUDGEMENT

Under the Sun we see all of life as filled with spiritual light. This awareness of eternal truth frees us from all illusion and fear so that now we feel, like a call from deep inside, the urge to dissolve ourselves completely into the spirit and wondrous life contained in every being.

This call comes from both inside and outside us, for one of the effects of the Sun was to break down the artificial barrier between inner experience and the outer world. We feel the call in our deepest selves as if the very cells of the body were filled with a shout of joy. At the same time, we recognize that the call comes from some force greater than any individual life.

This idea of Judgement as a call to rise to a more meaningful existence has its analogues in more ordinary situations. Sometimes in life a person can come to a crossroads (notice the cross in the banner) where a decision is required on whether to make some great change. And sometimes it can seem as if something within the person has already decided and the only choice left to the conscious self is to follow with the appropriate action. The old ways of believing and thinking, the old situations, have died without ourselves even noticing.

Most versions of the trump show only the angel and the figures rising up. The Rider pack adds a range of mountains in the background. Waite calls them the 'mountains of abstract thought'. The term implies eternal truth beyond the limited knowledge available to us through ordinary means.

One of the basic features of morality is the inability to know anything in an absolute sense. We are bound by our short lives and by the fact that all knowledge comes to our minds through the medium of the senses. In modern physics we learn that scientific investigation can never form an exact picture of reality because the observer is always a part of the universe that he or she is observing. In the same way, each person's thoughts about and perceptions of life are influenced by that person's past experience. 'Abstract thought' implies, like the Platonic ideals, a sense of the absolute.

We reach this 'abstraction' by making one last descent into the waters of nothingness in order to rise up liberated from all partial knowledge. Death, directly above, showed a dissolution. There the ego was dying and the trump emphasized the fear of letting go. Here all illusions of isolation are dissolved, and the emphasis rests not on the death but on the resurrection.

We call the card Judgement because, like Justice, it involves coming to terms with past experience as a part of going beyond it. With Justice the experience and the response were personal, based on your actions in the past. Here a force greater than yourself is leading and calling you, and the Judgement is not simply on the meaning of your own life but on the true nature of existence, and the way in which you and all beings are a part of it.

At times in this book we have referred to the Hebrew letters assigned to the different trumps. Usually we have followed the system in which the Fool is Aleph. There is another system, where the Magician receives Aleph, and in that system Judgement bears the letter Resh. Resh means 'head' and refers, like Waite's mountains, to the true mind awakened by the call. Resh also suggests Rosh Hashanah, the Jewish New Year, literally 'head of the year'. Now, Rosh Hashanah is not the start of the calendar, like the secular New Year, but represents, in fact, the anniversary of creation. Similarly, Judgement indicates not a change of circumstances but a new consciousness, one directly acquainted with the truth through a merging of yourself with the forces of life.

The Wheel of Fortune, with its invisible laws of psychic cause and effect, was 10; Judgement is 20, 10 multiplied by 2. Through the workings of the last line we reveal the High Priestess's hidden wisdom so that now we understand the inner mysteries concealed in the Wheel.

The cross in the banner indicates a meeting of opposites, a joining of all the things that had been separated. It symbolizes a meeting of two kinds of time; the ordinary time we perceive with our senses and by which we live from day to day, and eternity, the spiritual perception of life. These two times are symbolized by the horizontal and vertical lines of the cross. Their meeting in the centre indicates that the higher self does not abandon its old activities but goes about them in a new way.

The card above Judgement is the Lovers and, in the Rider pack, also shows an angel. There, however, the angel was a glimpse of a greater truth experienced through the medium of love. Here the angel leans down from the cloud to call to us. In the traditional version of the Sun we saw the final example of that triangular motif begun in trumps 5 and 6. Here we see a child between the two people. The poles of life have come together to form a new reality, in the way that every child is both a combination of its parents and something completely new.

The child in front stands with his back to us. The new existence is a mystery, with no way for us to know what it will be like until we experience it. The child's hidden face also implies that we do not really know ourselves, and that we cannot until we hear and respond to the call. Virtually all mythologies contain stories of the hero separated from his parents and raised as an ordinary child, with other people, and very often the child himself, knowing nothing of his true identity. King Arthur, Moses, Theseus, and Christ all follow this pattern. We see this same idea in many science fiction stories, where the hero awakes in a strange place with no memory; his search for his true identity leads him to discover great powers within himself. Very often he finds himself in the centre of either a powerful plot or at the very workings of nature. We have all 'forgotten' our true identities and have become separated from our 'parents'. And when we find or create our true selves, we will find ourselves at the centre of the universe. For the centre is everywhere.

Most decks show only the three people in the foreground. Waite's addition of three more people, all facing us, suggests that while Judgement leads to the unknown, there is still an awareness (also symbolized as well by the mountains) of the ways in which the unknown life will develop.

The extra people imply another, very vital point. By showing a whole group rising the trump reminds us that there is no personal liberation. Each human being is part of the human race and therefore responsible for the development of the race as a whole. No one can be truly free while someone else is enslaved. Buddha was said to have come back as a boddhisatva because he understood that he could not liberate himself until he had liberated all humanity. At the same time, any single liberation liberates everybody. This is because any person's attainment of Judgement and the World alter the circumstances of everybody's life. Gautama's Buddahood and the resurrection of Christ are seen as events that have totally changed the world. Lest we think this idea applies only to such godlike prophets as Buddha and Christ, we might recall the Talmudic saying (quoted at the end of the film *Schindler's List*) 'He who saves one life, it is as if he has saved the entire world.'

In the divinatory readings the card of Judgement carries a special significance. Whatever else is going on around you, there is a push, a call from within, to make some important change. The change can refer to something mundane and immediate, or to an entire shift in the way a person looks at life – depending on the other cards, and the subject of the reading. The important thing is the call. In effect, the person has already changed; the old situations, the old self, have already died. It is simply a matter of recognizing it.

Judgement reversed can indicate that the person wishes to answer the call but does not know what to do. More often it shows someone trying to deny the call, usually from a fear of the unknown. There may, in fact, be a great many rational reasons why the person should not follow the suggested change: lack of money, lack of preparation or responsibilities. Judgement, the right way up or reversed, indicates that all the objections are excuses. When the card is upside down the excuses become dominant; the person

remains standing in the grave. The word Judgement implies that the
reality of life has changed. The only choice is to follow.

Figure 22

THE WORLD

What can we say of an understanding, a freedom and rapture
beyond words? The unconscious known consciously, the outer self
unified with the forces of life, knowledge that is not knowledge at
all but a constant ecstatic dance of being – they are all true and yet
not true.

We have already observed a great deal about this card and its
images. The number as well as the two wands unify the Magician
and the High Priestess. We saw the World foreshadowed as well in
the Wheel of Fortune, and reflected how the symbols of that trump
are now living realities. One way or another, the Wheel has come
up for virtually every card in the last line. The purpose of this line
can be described as that of uniting ourselves with all those things
seen in trump 10 as external vision, that is, fate, the workings of
life, the elements of existence. When the unity is achieved the symbols vanish, dissolved into a dancing spirit.

We saw the World in the Hanged Man, by number and picture.
Trump 12 maintained its bliss through complete inactivity. But even

the World Tree is an illusion created by the mind's need to grasp onto something. When we have dissolved our isolated selves into that water lying beneath the Hanged Man's glowing face we learn that true unity lies in movement.

Everything in the universe moves, the Earth around the sun, the sun within the galaxy, the galaxies in clusters, all cycling around each other. There is no centre, no place where we can say, 'Here it all began, here it all stops.' Yet the centre exists, everywhere, for in a dance the dancer does not move around any arbitrary point in space, but rather the dance carries its own sense of unity focused around a constantly moving, constantly peaceful centre. Nothing and everything all at once.

And so we return to the Fool. Innocence and emptiness, united with wisdom. As we said at the beginning, of all the Major Arcana cards, only these two are moving. The oval wreath suggests the number 0, with all its symbolism. It implies as well the cosmic egg, the archetype of emergence; all things exist in potential and all potentials are realized. The self is everywhere in all things. The sashes at the top and bottom of the wreath are tied into infinity signs, indicating that the self is not enclosed but open to the universe.

The sashes are red, the colour of the root chakra in Kundalini symbolism. The dancer has not lost her physical being, her root in material, sexual reality. Instead, the energy is constantly flowing, transformed and renewed. The green of the wreath symbolizes the natural world raised up rather than abandoned. Green is also the colour of love and healing, radiating wholeness to everyone, even those who are not consciously aware of it. Purple (the banner) is the colour of divinity and blue (the sky) the colour of communication. When we know that divinity is not something out there, but within ourselves, then our very presence communicates this truth to those around us.

One of the World's analogues is Shiva, Lord of the Cosmic Dance. He too dances with the arms out, one foot down and the other raised, the head balanced and the expression calm. The right foot of both figures is 'planted' in the physical world, while the raised left leg symbolizes the soul's release. When we become most joined to life, at that moment we realize our freedom. The face is neither sad nor joyful but at peace, free in its emptiness. The arms are open to all experience.

Dancing Shiva is often depicted as an hermaphrodite, one half of the body of Shiva, the other Parvati his female side. The esoteric tradition describes the World dancer as hermaphroditic, the dual sexual organs concealed by the banner, as if to say that the unity they represent lies beyond our knowing. In discussing the Lovers we referred to the widespread belief that all people were originally hermaphrodites. The dancer expresses and unites all the different sides of being.

The same feeling that leads us to a 'memory' of primeval hermaphroditism has taken people a step further to the image of the entire universe having once been a single human being. We find this belief among the Gnostics, in Blake, in German, Indian, and other mythologies, and in great detail in the Kabbalah. There the figure bears the name 'Adam Kadmon' and is said to be the original creation emanating from the unknowable God. Rather than a physical being, Adam Kadmon, also hermaphroditic, was described as pure light. Only when the figure broke up into the separate parts of the universe did the light become 'imprisoned' in matter. It is a fascinating fact that the contemporary scientific theories of cosmogony describe the universe as originally one particle. At the moment that the particle broke up it was all pure light; only later, as the pieces became more isolated did some of that energy condense into matter, following Einstein's famous formulation, $E=mc^2$.

The myths consider the break-up of primeval Man an irreversible event. Occultists, however, believe in the possibility of restoration. By following the process outlined in the Major Arcana we become united with life and so ourselves become Adam Kadmon and Shiva-Parvati.

Adam Kadmon is linked to the Tree of Life, with its ten Sephiroth, or points of emanation. We have already seen the connection between this figure and the Tarot through the Tree's 22 paths. The World Dancer, by her posture, is an exact representation of the Tree of Life's most common form. The Tree is drawn in the following way:

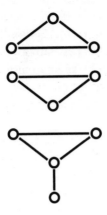

Figure 23

Very simplified, the top triangle is super-consciousness, the middle is consciousness, the bottom the unconscious, and the final point, the root of the Tree, is the manifestation of all these principles in the physical world.

In the Dancer the top triangle is the crown of the head and the points of the shoulders, the middle triangle is the hands and the genitals, the bottom triangle is the crossed leg and right foot. At the same time it is all one body. By contemplating the dancer we learn that the unconscious, conscious and super-conscious are not separate parts or even separate stages of being, but are all one. But what about the tenth Sephira, the root of the Tree? We find it not in the body but in all the universe, the wonderful ground of being in which we move.

Descriptions, metaphors, even contemplation can only hint at the wonders embodied in trump 21. When the card comes up in divination these wonders become further reduced to the ordinary situations with which most readings concern themselves. The card means success, achievement, satisfaction. To greater or lesser degree it indicates a unification of the person's inner sense of being with his or her outer activities.

Reversed, the trump indicates stagnation, the movement and growth slowed down to the point of being stopped. Or so it seems. In fact, the freedom and rapture of the World exist always in potential to be released when the person feels ready to begin, once more, the dance of life.

These are the meanings of the World in divination. Its true meanings are unknowable. They are a goal, a hope, an intuition. The way to that goal, the steps and music of the dance, lies in the living images of the Major Arcana.

PART TWO

THE MINOR ARCANA

INTRODUCTION

THE RIDER PACK

In 1910 the Rider Company of London published a new Tarot deck, designed by the well-known occultist Arthur Edward Waite, and drawn by a lesser-known psychic artist named Pamela Colman Smith. Waite himself apparently did not expect a wide public for these new cards; like all his works, his book on the Tarot speaks primarily to people already involved in the occult tradition. And yet the Rider pack, as the deck came to be called, is now known all over the world – in its original version, in pirate editions, in thinly disguised 'new' Tarots, in several different sizes published by US Games Systems Inc., the deck's American publisher, in illustrations for novels, books on psychology, comic books and television shows. The outstanding popularity of this particular esoteric Tarot over hundreds of other traditional and modern decks derives largely from one aspect of the cards that Waite himself seems hardly to have noticed – the drawings of Pamela Colman Smith which revolutionized the Minor Arcana.

In his apologia for his deck Waite took great pains to defend certain changes he made in the design and number of the cards in the Major Arcana. However, most newcomers to Tarot, comparing the Rider pack to say, the more traditional Marseilles deck will have to look quite closely before they observe most of these changes. They will immediately see the difference in the Minor cards. In virtually every deck designed before the Rider pack the 'pip' cards, numbers 1-10 of the four suits, bear geometric patterns containing the number of swords, or wands, or cups, or coins. In this they resemble ordinary playing cards. In most decks these patterns are plain and repetitious. The elaborate Crowley deck stands out as the exception (painted by Lady Frieda Harris, the 'Thoth' cards actually appeared several decades after the Rider pack). The Waite-Smith deck, however, has an illustration on every card.

Primarily concerned with the more esoteric Major cards, Waite apparently did not realize how this rich variety of scenes would captivate the average viewer seeking to experiment with Tarot. In a way, their very newness adds to their charm. Where the Major Arcana strikes us with the ancientness as well as the complexity of its symbolism, the Minor cards, having no pictorial tradition, appear to us as scenes taken directly from life, or in some cases, fantasy.

The fact that Smith drew these scenes in a pseudo-medieval style seems not to bother most people. They find the liveliness more important. Almost all the Major cards show a figure sitting or standing; only the Fool and the World move. In fact, they dance. But in the Minor cards, all the scenes show something *happening*, rather like a frame from a movie.

The contrast is no accident. The Major cards depict archetypal forces rather than real people. The Fool and the World Dancer move, because only they fully embody these principles. But the Minor cards show aspects of life as people actually live it. In these four suits, and more especially in the combinations they form when we lay them out in readings, we find a panorama of experience, constantly showing us new insights into the wonders of human nature and this magical world.

Precisely because it shows ordinary life rather than a formal system the Rider pack does not appeal to many occultists. While a great many subsequent decks have copied, with small or large variations, the Rider pack, other decks, including ones we might characterize as 'most serious', such as the Crowley or the Builders of the Adytum deck, have returned to the use of patterns for the pip cards. They do so because their creators concerned themselves with the Tarot as a system of organizing and structuring esoteric practices, both as a tool and as a living force. The Tarot, for them, forms a vital link to mystical systems.

The most important of these links is that connecting the four suits to the four worlds described in the Kabbalah. Kabbalists view the universe as existing in four stages, the closest to us (and the furthest from direct union with God) being the ordinary material world, called Assiyah, the 'World of Action'. For greater understanding the medieval theosophists described each world as embodied in a Tree of Life, a diagram of cosmic law. Now, the structure of the Tree does not change in the different worlds. Each tree contains ten Sephiroth, or archetypes of emanation. (For the Tree's most common pattern, see the Ten of Pentacles.) And here, of course, the Tarot comes in. Because the four suits each contain ten pip cards, we can place the cards on the Sephiroth to give us a concrete aid in meditation. And because the Sephiroth represent archetypal forces, most occultists prefer abstract designs to emblemize them. For them, a scene of people doing something, such as three women dancing, or a group of boys fighting, only distracts from the eternal symbolism.

Some occultists go further, believing that the geometric patterns on the cards carry a psychic power all their own, and that by looking deeply at these patterns in their special colours, we can produce certain distinct effects within the brain.

Many people who are not especially esotericists will still prefer the older decks to any of the modern interpretations, including the geometric ones. For them, the sense of a tradition, of meanings developed over centuries, carries a power no revised edition can equal. In readings they look to the ancient formulas and find the Rider pack's detailed scenes a distraction. Often the more psychic readers will use the older cards, finding that the very abstractness of the pip cards helps trigger clairvoyant awareness.

For most of us, however, the repetitious patterns sharply limit the insights available from either studying the cards alone or using them in readings. Once we have memorized the formulas attached to each card we find it difficult to go further. In this book I have attempted to create what I call a 'humanistic' Tarot, derived not just from esoteric truths, but also from the insights of modern post-Jungian psychology to give a rounded picture of who we are, how we act, and what forces shape and direct us. In such a Tarot the goal is not fixed meanings, but rather a *method* by which each person can gain a greater insight into life. While the analysis of each card will come partly from its use in readings, with right side up and reversed meanings, the analysis will show primarily how that card adds to our knowledge of human experience.

Because the Rider pack shows such vivid scenes the formulas or commentaries belonging to each card serve only as starting points. We can ponder the pictures themselves, and how they combine with the pictures around them. In a way the pictures and each person's imagination (and experience) act as a partnership. In every reading, or in each meditation or reflection, we can look at each card as a fresh experience. Just as the more esoteric decks work best for occult discipline, and the older decks for fortune-telling, so the Rider serves those of us who use the cards primarily for awareness of self and of the world around us.

The Smith pictures attract people through their cartoon-like action. They hold us over years because of the very real meanings contained in their pictures. How did Pamela Smith do it? As far as we know, she created her pictures with no tradition to assist her. In Part One of this book I stated my opinion that Waite probably did not dictate the designs as he clearly did with the Major cards. His own book gives no account of their origins; nor does he defend the radical change, as he does his changes in the Major cards. His interpretations, moreover, do not utilize the new pictures to any great extent. Though he briefly describes each picture his explanations are usually formulae and catch phrases ('desire, will, determination, project'), no different in substance from those meanings attached to earlier decks.

Some writers have claimed (though I have not found any evidence for this in Waite's own writings) that Smith drew the pictures as four comic book-like stories, one for each suit. The quality of the suit determined the character of the story, in which the court cards formed a family and the pips events happening to them. The so-called Moroccan Tarot, based very closely on the Rider pack, follows this system. This story explanation for the pictures begs the question. The important question remains the relation of the picture to the meaning.

I suspect Waite gave Smith the formulas he wished illustrated, perhaps consulted with her on the picture, and then Smith's artistic instincts took over, at times working with the surface symbolism and at times operating beyond the level of conscious choice. (Modern research has indicated that Smith drew inspiration from an obscure early Tarot, known as the Sola-Busca. Several of the Minor cards show similar scenes to the Rider, in particular the Three of Swords and the Ten of Wands). Waite's formulas derive from various sources. Waite himself speaks at times of contradictory meanings, as if he had consulted different fortune-tellers. His arrangement of the court cards also shows the influence of the Order of the Golden Dawn, a secret society of mystic magicians, to which Waite and Smith (like Crowley and Paul Foster Case, designer of the BOTA deck) at one time belonged.

In many cases, of course, the pictures are very simple and directly related to the meanings they were meant to illustrate. The Four of Pentacles, for example, shows the image of a miser, someone 'cleaving' to the 'surety of possessions'. But is it coincidence or plan that these four pentacles cover the crown of the head, the heart and throat, and the soles of the feet, thereby leading to deeper interpretations than simple greed? And in many cases, the picture touches something in us beyond the meaning officially connected to it. Look at the Six of Swords, supposedly a 'journey by water'. The dreamlike silence, the sadness implicit in the picture suggest the mythical journey of dead souls across the River Styx.

I do not mean to describe Waite as bland, or insensitive to the pictures in his own deck. Sometimes his comments, especially on the pictures, increase our understanding beyond the simple list of meanings. In that Six of Swords he observes that 'the freight is light', and this, along with Eden Gray's comment, 'The swords do not weigh down the boat', leads us to contemplate the image of a spiritual or emotional journey in which we carry our memories and sorrows with us. In the Two of Wands Waite gives two opposed meanings and then says that the picture 'gives a clue' to their resolution. At other times, however, the meaning given contradicts the picture, as in the Two of Swords, where a powerful image of isolation and defence supposedly illustrates 'friendship'.

Since the Rider pack quite a few Tarot designers have attempted to include a scene on every card. Just about all have paid tribute to Pamela Smith's images, some extremely closely, while others have imaginatively transformed the Rider pictures. Nothing compels them to use these images; they carry no authority of ancient tradition, as do the Major cards. Their authority derives from creative achievement. These crudely drawn pictures, awkward, often out of all proportion or perspective, based on sentimental ideas of the Middle Ages, somehow have led thousands of people into an understanding not just of the cards but of themselves. In one stroke Pamela Smith created a new tradition.

THE FOUR SUITS

However much the depiction of the individual cards broke with previous practice, Waite stayed close to earlier decks in his arrangement of the suits and their emblems – with one exception. Where older decks, going all the way back to the fifteenth-century Visconti-Sforza deck, used Wands (or Staves), Cups, Swords, and Coins (or discs), the Rider pack substituted Pentacles – five pointed stars enclosed in gold discs – for the final suit. Waite was following the Order of the Golden Dawn when he made this change. He used their substitution of Pentacles for coins for two reasons. First, he wanted his fourth suit to represent the full range of the physical world, not simply the narrow materialism of money and business. Second, he wanted the four suits to carry the four basic tools of ritual magic. In reality the two reasons are one. Waite knew that magicians used these objects partly because they symbolized in concrete form the various aspects of the physical/spiritual universe.

The association of these four emblems with both magical practice and the spiritual truth underlying life goes back at least as far as the Middle Ages, where we find their equivalents in the symbolic objects carried by the Grail maidens. Waite himself knew these objects from his experience in magical Orders. The Rider pack also depicts them as lying on the table before the Magician in the Major Arcana.

In the Tarot, as in magic, the four emblems stand for the world itself and for human nature, as well as the act of creation (both the creation of specific *things*, and the continuous creation of evolution). Their place on the Magician's table signifies that he or she has become a master of the physical world. In one sense mastery means the real powers over nature that many people see in magic. Those who use the Tarot as an esoteric discipline sometimes maintain that meditation and ritual with the Minor Arcana will give the adept control over the forces of nature. In Charles William's Tarot novel, *The Greater Trumps,* he carries this idea to dramatic extremes when the hero raises a hurricane by flapping together the cards associated with wind. In psychological terms 'mastery' of the Minor Arcana means understanding, in ourselves and in the world around us, all those experiences and forces depicted in the cards. A 'master' means a person who has control over his or her life – who is master over him or herself.

Such a goal is a great deal harder to achieve than many people might think. It means really knowing who we are, on unconscious levels as well as conscious. It means knowing why we act the way we do, knowing our true desires instead of the muddled ideas most people have of their goals in life. It means knowing the connections between seemingly random experiences. The Tarot can at least help us increase our understanding in all these things. How far each person goes depends on, among other things, that person's relationship to the cards.

The number four has figured very strongly in human attempts to understand existence. Because our bodies suggest this number (front and back, right and left sides) we tend to organize our perceptions of the ever shifting world by breaking things down into fours. The view of the year as four seasons comes also from the two solstices and the two equinoxes. (Cultures without astronomical awareness will often divide the year into the two basic seasons of summer and winter, or sometimes into three seasons.)

The zodiac contains twelve constellations, three times four. Therefore we find the signs of astrology divided into four groups of three. One 'fixed' sign in each group gives us the four 'strong points' of heaven. We see these four represented in the Major Arcana on the cards of the World and the Wheel of Fortune as the four beasts shown in the cards' four corners. (The very shape of the cards, and for that matter most Western houses, demonstrates our four-sided bias. The ancient Chinese used circular playing cards.) The four creatures symbolize the zodiac, but they derive most directly from Ezekiel's vision in the Old Testament, later repeated in Revelation.

Of all the four symbolisms the two that pertain most directly to the Minor Arcana are the four elements of medieval alchemy and the four letters of God's name in Hebrew, the tetragrammaton. Our modern concept of the atomic elements derives from an earlier idea (originating in ancient Greece) that all things in nature are formed out of four basic constituents: fire, water, air, and earth. We find this idea not just in Europe but also in cultures as diverse as China and North America. The elements sometimes change; sometimes the numbers change also, from four to five, adding 'ether' or Spirit to the four elements of nature (just as many cultures add the 'centre' as a fifth direction). The basic concept, however, remains the same – that everything can be reduced to its basic parts, that the world combines these basic qualities in an infinity of ways.

Today, we carry this idea much further, reducing all matter to sub-atomic particles (throwing out the idea of Spirit altogether, except in certain rarefied theories of contemporary physics) and looking upon the mediaeval 'elements' as very elaborate chemical combinations. However, we are mistaken if we think that the old system can no longer teach us anything. For one thing that characterizes the old view – and indeed the views of virtually all cultures before the modern West – is the non-separation of physical, spiritual, moral, and psychological theories and values. For us the element of, say, helium, carries very little if any spiritual meaning. For the mediaeval thinkers the element Fire suggested a whole range of associations. Obviously we would be wrong to reject the great achievements of knowledge we call modern science. But neither should we reject the insights from earlier times.

In the Tarot we see the four elements as Fire-Wands (Staves), Water-Cups, Air-Swords, Earth-Pentacles (Coins). Different writers sometimes give variations on this listing, most often switching Wands and Pentacles, on the grounds that sticks grow out of the earth, and coins are forged in a fire. I have chosen to stay with the more common listing because of the wider associations of fire and earth. Fire is not simply a human tool, but a great force in nature, seen most powerfully in the sun which brings the staves out of the ground. Earth stands not only for the soil, but traditionally for the entire material universe of which Coins represent a small part and Pentacles a much wider part.

If we wish to see the world in terms of five rather than four including Spirit centre, then the Major Arcana stands for Ether, the fifth element. The fact that we set it apart from the four Minor elements symbolizes the intuition that Spirit somehow exists on a different level from the ordinary world. At the same time the fact that we mix all five together for readings helps us see that in reality Spirit and all the elements of matter constantly work together. Working with the Tarot helps us understand the dynamic ways in which Spirit gives meaning and unity to the material world. A true understanding of this relationship, in practice as well as theory, forms a great step towards that 'mastery' described earlier.

Many people will know the imagery of the four elements from astrology, with its four 'triplicities': Fire – Aries, Leo, Sagittarius; Water – Cancer, Scorpio, Pisces; Air – Gemini Libra, Aquarius; Earth – Taurus, Virgo, Capricorn. Jungian psychology also utilizes the four elements, linking them to basic ways of experiencing the world. Fire stands for Intuition, Water for Feeling, Air for Thinking, and Earth for Sensation.

In astrology and Jungian thought the elements stand for types and characteristics. In the Tarot we see these types reflected in the court cards. The suits as a whole show activities and qualities of life rather than individual psychology. In other words, if Wands dominate in a reading we do not say that the person is a 'fiery' character, but rather that she or he is currently going through many Fire experiences. We study the four suits separately to learn just what we mean by Fire or Water or Air or Earth experience. We study them together in readings to learn how life in reality embraces and combines all the elements together.

As a brief summary, Wands/Fire stand for action, movement, optimism, adventure, struggle, business in the sense of the activity of commerce rather than the things sold, beginnings. Cups/Water stand for reflection, quiet experiences, love, friendship, joy, fantasy, passivity. Swords/Air stand for conflict, angry or disturbed emotions, sadness, but also for mental activity, wisdom, the use of intellect to understand the truth. Pentacles/Earth stand for nature, money, work, routine activities, stable relationships, business in the sense of things made and sold. Also, because Pentacles are magic signs, they stand for the magic of nature and the wonder of ordinary life, not always perceived, but often hidden under the surface.

Drawing on another well-known symbolic system Wands and Swords represent 'yang' or 'active' situations, while Cups and Pentacles stand for 'yin' or 'passive' ones. We can also substitute, with reference to the Major Arcana, Magician for yang and High Priestess for yin. Whatever the terminology, these distinctions become clearer in the imagery. Both wands and swords are used for striking; cups, on the other hand, fulfil their function by receiving and holding water; while pentacles, as either magic signs or money, can influence the world without physically moving. Similarly, fire and air are constantly shifting, while water and earth tend more to inertia.

A little reflection, as well as a look at the pictures, will show how these separate categories actually blend together in reality. Both Wands and Pentacles deal with business, both Wands and Swords indicate conflict. Cups and Wands tend towards happy, positive experiences, while Pentacles and Swords often represent the more difficult sides of life. At the same time, Cups and Swords cover the general range of emotions, while Pentacles and Wands depict the more physical activities. Rather than showing rigid separations the cards tend toward combinations and the blurring of all distinctions.

In Part One I wrote that the study of Tarot readings teaches us above all that no quality is good or bad except within the context of an actual situation. We learn also from readings that no situation, quality, or personal characteristic exists in isolation, but only in combination with others. In a reading we look first at the individual cards in their individual positions, but we understand what the reading tells us when we see how the cards blend together into a whole pattern. Similarly, we study the cards individually but we understand them fully only when we see them working.

The different elements represent not only different experiences but also different approaches to life. One reason to study the suits as a whole is to see the advantages and problems of each approach. For each suit we will look at a 'problem' and a 'Way to Spirit'. As an example, the problem of Cups is passivity, the Way to Spirit is love.

Through the different images we see how the Cups experiences bring out these qualities.

In arranging the cards I have followed Waite's example in moving from the King down to the Ace, rather than the other way round. Here too Waite was following the example of the Golden Dawn, which saw Spirit as metaphorically descending into the physical world, so that we count down from the higher numbers. Because kings (as traditional symbols rather than political reality) bear a responsibility for maintaining society, and because the king gives an image of maturity, the four Kings all symbolize the most socially-minded stable version of the suit. The Aces, on the other hand, signify unity and perfection. Therefore, the Aces stand for the elements in their purest form. The Ace of Wands stands for Fire itself and all that it means, while the other thirteen Wands cards depict some specific example of Fire, either in a situation (cards 2 – 10) or as a personality type (the court cards).

In the Rider pack we see each Ace held in a hand coming out of a cloud. This symbol, seen also in other decks, teaches us that each element can lead us to spiritual mystery. It also teaches us that all experience is a gift, from a source we cannot consciously know, unless we follow the deep spiritual journey shown in the Major Arcana. For this reason I have ended each suit with the Ace.

THE TETRAGRAMMATON

Besides the four elements we should look at the other symbol implied by the four suits, that of God's name. We find these four letters, Yod-Heh-Vav-Heh, arranged in the Wheel of Fortune, the tenth card of the Major Arcana. In European letters we write them as YHVH, or sometimes IHVH. Because the Bible gives no vowels for the name we cannot actually pronounce it; it therefore symbolizes God's unknowable nature, the essential separation between God and man that characterizes Western religion. Writers have assigned the names Jehovah or Jah or Yahweh to those letters, but this leads to confusion. When we consult the writings of the Kabbalists we discover that the letters do not form a 'name' in the human sense of a label that stands for a person, but rather they depict a formula. And that formula describes the process of creation.

The tetragrammaton and the four elements do not really form two separate systems, but in fact one unified symbol. Each of the elements belongs to a letter, Yod-Fire, Heh-Water, Vav-Air, Heh-Earth,* and when we apply God's name to the elements we complete the meaning of their symbolic differences.

The process goes as follows: Yod, or Fire, symbolizes the start of any enterprise, the first creative spark, the energy needed to begin. In mythic terms the Yod indicates the divine spark emerging from the unknowable God. In psychological terms it stands for the impulse to begin some specific project, or new way of life. The first Heh, Water, symbolizes the actual beginning as the spark is 'received' into a pattern. Mythically, this refers to God's Fire touching the 'Waters of the deep', that is, the chaos before God began to order the universe. Psychologically we understand that our plans and hopes remain formless, vague, until the Fire energy enters into them and starts us actually doing something. At the same time, restless Wands energy cannot benefit us unless we give it a definite purpose .

The third letter, Vav, connected to Air, symbolizes the development of the plan, the directed purposeful movement that makes everything take shape. In its holy sense, it means the stage of creation in which God gave the world its underlying form. Air stands for intellect, and psychologically Vav indicates the mental process of going from a goal to an actual plan which will bring the project into reality.

Finally, the second Heh, Earth, stands for the finished creation, the thing itself. In religious terms it means matter, the physical universe, that which God created through the process of the other letters. In human terms it means the completion of the goal.

Let us take the example of a poem. It cannot begin without an impulse towards poetry and a desire to express something. At the same time this desire goes nowhere unless we can choose a particular subject. In a sense the subject 'receives' the impulse to write. Still, the poem will never emerge until we work on it, using

* These links come from Tarot tradition. Some Kabbalists use a slightly different order.

intellect and the writing of several drafts to solve the problems of imagery, rhythm, and so on. Finally, the process ends when we can hold the actual poem in our hands and pass it on to others. A little thought will show that the same development holds true for any action, from building a house to brewing beer to making love.

Clearly the last element, Earth, stands somewhat apart from the others. The mathematician and occultist, P. D. Ouspensky, has drawn this relationship in the following diagram:

Figure 24

A look at the Hebrew letters will also help us understand the symbolism. Reading right to left they are:

Notice how the Yod, the Fire letter, hardly has any shape at all, but resembles rather a point, the flash of a first impulse. Observe too that the two Hehs vaguely resemble upside down cups, or beakers. The first one 'receives' the impulse, the second receives the entire process and gives it a physical form. Finally, observe how the third letter, Vav, extends the first letter, Yod. The intellect, Air, takes the Fire energy and gives it a definite direction.

It may seem at first that the fourth element, Earth, can exist by itself. However, in order for us to find any meaning in our possessions we must understand the creative processes that brought them into being. When we look at the 'problems' relating to each suit, we see that each arises only when we remove the suit from its relationship to the others. Or, in other words, when we lean too much in one direction in life. Earth's problem of materialism, is counteracted through adding Cups, for emotional appreciation. The way in which one suit is added to another will be discussed in the section on Readings.

Just as each suit has special qualities, so does each number or Court position. For each cards we can see the meaning as a combination of the number and the suit. There are various numerological systems describing the values of numbers. Rather than drawing on any particular one, the meanings given here derive from the qualities of the cards themselves.

King – social responsibility, power, success
Queen – deep appreciation of the suit; creativity
Knight – action, responsibility to others
Page – exploration, study
10 – completion, the need to go beyond
9 – compromises, struggle
8 – movement
7 – victory
6 – communication
5 – loss, conflict
4 – structure
3 – full expression of the element
2 – union
Ace – basic quality, root

In some situations the suit and the number support each other, in some they conflict, sometimes even producing the opposite of the number's meaning. For example, the unifying theme of Eight is movement. Since Fire also means movement, Wands express this theme very directly. Swords, however, stress conflict. Instead of someone on the move, the Eight of Swords shows a woman whose movement is *restricted*. The issue remains movement, but now the opposition becomes the focus.

THE GATE CARDS

If the Rider Minor cards serve us primarily as a commentary on ordinary life, they do not ignore or cut us off from deeper perceptions. On the contrary, the philosophical bias of the cards leads us always in the direction of 'hidden forces' giving shape and meaning to ordinary experience. A truly realistic view of the world (as opposed to the narrow materialist ideology commonly thought of as 'realism') will recognize the spiritual energy always present within the constantly shifting patterns of the world. Much of mainstream science is currently moving away from the notion that such forces as electro-magnetism are static and mechanical, and towards the image of them as dynamic and constantly creative.

The Rider pack greatly encourages such awareness. We see it celebrated in the Ten of Cups; we see it most directly in the Aces, where each element is shown as a gift.

But the Rider pack does more than *teach us* this awareness. Certain cards, taken in the right way, can help produce it. Earlier, we considered the occult view that looking at geometric patterns will create effects in the brain. In a similar way joining ourselves meditatively to particular cards in the four suits will bring experiences reaching beyond the cards' specific meanings.

I call these cards Gates, because of the way in which they open a path from the ordinary world to the inner level of archetypal experiences. Each suit contains at least one of these cards, the Pentacles containing the most. They all share certain characteristics: complex, often contradictory, meanings, and a myth-like Strangeness which no allegorical interpretation can completely penetrate. By choosing certain cards to fulfil this function I do not mean to imply that no others will do so, but only that in my experience these cards in particular do act in this way.

Sometimes the Strangeness of a Gate will lie on the surface, but in other cards it only becomes apparent after we have analysed the card intellectually. The latter cases demonstrate a very important point - that outer and inner perceptions do not oppose each other, but rather bring each other out. The best approach to a Gate card begins with a knowledge of the card's literal and symbolic meanings. When we have taken those as far as they will go we will arrive at the path of Strangeness that lies beyond them.

The Tarot demonstrates many things, some very unexpected. These things emerge through interpretation of the Tarot's images, through joining ourselves to those images in meditation, and through seeing the combinations formed in readings. Taken separately, the cards of the Minor Arcana present us with a grand panorama of human experiences. Together, and in union with the archetypal Major cards, they draw us into ever wider knowledge of the changing wonder of life.

CHAPTER SEVEN

WANDS

In one way or another, human beings have taken virtually all of nature as symbols for the spiritual essence of life. Of all these symbols fire stands out as the most powerful. We speak of the 'divine spark' in the soul, of someone being 'on fire with an idea', and when someone has become bitter or disillusioned we say, 'the fire has gone out of him'. When God banished Adam and Eve from the Garden of Eden and its Tree of Life He set a cherub with a flaming sword to guard the entrance. By their Fall the first humans had alienated themselves from the heavenly fire. When yogis, through meditation and exercise cause the kundalini, or spiritual force, to rise, they experience this rising as a great heat moving up the spine. And shamans the world over demonstrate their spiritual power by becoming masters of fire, dancing in flames or holding hot coals in their mouths.

Fire stands for the vital life essence that animates our bodies. Without it we become corpses. Michelangelo's famous painting of creation shows a spark leaping from God's finger to Adam's. We describe the chemical changes of food in our stomachs as the body 'burning fuel'. Fire symbolizes the very energy of existence. Because it rises, constantly leaping upwards, fire stands for optimism, confidence, hope. To give human beings a touch of immortality and make them immune to Zeus's threats of annihilation, Prometheus gave them fire. People have always understood that fire was spiritual. Evidence in caves and from archaeological digs indicates that when our earliest ancestors discovered how to control fire, they used it for rituals long before they thought to cook food or make tools.

Because the Minor Arcana deals primarily with the outer range of experience Wands tend to show the way the inner fire shows itself in ordinary life. Besides the specific knowledge gained, a study of the Minor Arcana shows how mundane experience derives from a spiritual base.

Wands, then, stand first of all for movement. Whether they win or lose Wands constantly struggle, not so much because of the actual problems or goals, but just for the love of conflict, of the chance to use all that energy. In business Wands stand for commerce and competition; in love they symbolize romance, proposals, the act of winning a lover rather than the emotion of love itself. Wands lead us to approach life with action and eagerness.

When Wands succeed too greatly, as with the King, or the figure in Two, then a melancholy can grip them, for the rewards of success can tie them down. At other times, as in the Nine or Ten, they allow the habit of fighting or of taking on all problems, to blind them to more peaceful alternatives.

Mostly, however, the Wands' influence shows us people winning their battles. Through Wands we find the Way to Spirit in movement, action, living for the joy of living. They find their most powerful expression in the Four, dancing out of the walled city to celebrate the lifegiving power of the Sun.

And yet, for all that vitalizing energy expressed in the Sun's power to literally bring life out of the ground, fire also destroys. If not controlled and directed, that energy burns up the world. Therefore we see all the Wands court cards standing or sitting in a desert. Despite their optimism and eagerness Wands need the softening influence of Cups, for without water the summer sun brings only a drought. From Cups, then, comes a sense of depth and the ability to feel as well as act. From Swords we get a sense of planning and direction for all the energy. From Swords also comes an awareness of sorrow and pain to balance the Wand's optimism and conquering spirit. And from Pentacles comes a sense of being rooted in the real world, an ability to enjoy life as well as to overcome it.

Figure 25

KING

In readings, the court cards of each suit traditionally represent people who will influence the subject's life. While this is often the case, they can also symbolize the subject him or herself. Taken by themselves, that is, outside the context of specific readings, the sixteen court cards provide a greater range of human character. Either in a reading or by itself as an object of study any specific court card indicates a person having or expressing those qualities signified by that card.

A King (or a Knight or a Page) does not necessarily mean a man, nor a Queen a woman. Rather, they show qualities and attitudes traditionally symbolized by those figures. The particular social functions of a king, or a queen, or a knight, suggest certain experiences and responsibilities. The cards symbolize these as often as they stand for age or sex.

We should also avoid the idea that a card might symbolize an individual person throughout life, in the sense of saying about someone, 'She's the Queen of Wands', and thinking that sums up her life. A person might go through a Queen of Swords phase one month, and move to a Knight of Cups the next. Or experience both at once, in different aspects of her life at that time.

A king is a ruler, responsible for the welfare of society. In the Rider pack all four Kings wear what Waite calls 'a cap of maintenance' underneath their crowns. Traditionally the king bears responsibility for maintaining his people. Therefore, all the Kings represent both success (for the king, after all, is supreme) and social responsibility.

The King of Wands translates these qualities into Wands terms. He indicates a strong-minded person, able to dominate others by strength of will. His power derives from a firm belief in his own rightness. He *knows* the truth; he *knows* his method is best. He considers it only natural for others to follow him.

At the same time he shows the Wands energy controlled and turned into useful projects, or long-term careers. The adventurous Wands nature can make such a person uncomfortable in this role. He leans forward on his throne, as if he would like to leap up and go to seek new experience.

He is naturally honest, seeing no reason or value in lies. He is positive and optimistic for much the same reason; the Wands energy burns so strongly in him he does not understand why anyone would express negative attitudes.

Such a strong personality can tend towards intolerance, unable to understand weakness or despair because he has not experienced these things himself. This impatient side of the King might bear the motto, 'If I can do it you can'. Once, in a reading, I saw a very nice expression of what people used to call 'the generation gap': the King of Wands and the Fool, both of them energetic, yet one the essence of responsibility, the other the pure image of instinct and freedom.

Two symbols dominate the card: the lion, emblem of Leo, and the salamander, a legendary lizard believed to inhabit fire. They represent the mundane and the spiritual, for while Leo indicates the personality traits belonging to Fire, the salamander was a favourite symbol of the alchemists. At his best the King is master of the creative Fire. His sense of social commitment has tamed it and put it to use. Notice that the salamanders on his robe are shown with their tails in their mouths. The closed circle means maturity and completion. Compare this image with the knight's shirt, where the tails and mouths do not meet.

REVERSED

When we reverse a card we alter in some way its prime meaning, as if the original impact had become blocked or rechannelled, or, in some cases, liberated. Some Tarot commentators prefer to discount reversed meanings, and it is true that in meditation or creativity we usually consider all cards as right side up. But in readings or study reversed meanings do more than double the possible meanings in the deck. By showing us the card from a different angle they give us a wider understanding of what the card really means.

In a reading, if a court card refers to a specific person (by physical type, say, rather than the card's qualities), then reversed indicates that person disturbed or blocked, or maybe having a bad influence on the subject. If, on the other hand, we look at the qualities in the card then reversed shows those qualities altered.

Right side up the King shows us someone powerful and commanding, yet often intolerant of other people's weaknesses. Reversed we see that natural fire after it has encountered obstacles and defeats that might make a less forceful person cynical or frightened. Because he is the King of Wands he does not lose his force but becomes instead tempered, more understanding of others and at the same time harsher in his attitude to life, which no longer appears such an easy contest. Waite's formula here is very apt: 'Good but severe, austere yet tolerant'.

Figure 26

QUEEN

The Queen represents the yin, or receptive qualities of each element. She shows an appreciation of that element rather than the King's social use of it. This does not mean that the Queens indicate weakness, or even inaction, but rather the element translated into feeling and understanding.

Once again, we need not apply these qualities only to women. If, in a reading, we see the Queen as identifying a person by physical type alone, then the Queen naturally means a woman. But if we wish to apply the symbolic qualities to someone, then any court card can signify a woman or a man. And apart from readings the Queen of Wands stands for a particular appreciation of life.

In contrast with the King's eagerness and impatience, the Queen sits on her throne as if planted there. Her crown is flowering, her dress is sunshine. Alone of all the Queens she sits with her legs apart, signifying sexual energy. She shows a Fire appreciation of life, warm, passionate, very solidly in the world. Like the King, she is honest and sincere, seeing no purpose in deceit or nastiness. More sensitive than the King she allows herself to love both life and other people, seeing control or dominance as of no more value than cynicism.

A black cat guards her throne. In Christian folklore the Devil gave a black cat to a witch to guard her from attack. The meaning here is less melodramatic. Sometimes if a person loves life, the world appears to respond by protecting that person from harm and send her or him joyous experiences. We cannot understand the way in which this happens without reaching the complex and inner knowledge of the universe symbolized by the last cards of the Major Arcana. Nevertheless it can happen, and the black cat shows this response by nature to someone who approaches it with fiery joy.

REVERSED

As with the King the upside down Queen shows the reaction of such a person to opposition and sorrow. The basic good nature and positive attitudes of the Queen, as well as her energy, make her invaluable in a crisis or disaster. We can see her as the kind of person who will take over the running of someone's house when they have had a crisis and at the same time offer advice, consultation, emotional support, all these things coming from a natural impulse rather than any sense of duty.

At the same time this good nature demands that life respond in a positive way. Too much disaster or too much opposition from life (and the weakness of such a person can be a tendency to think of life as 'unfair'), and a nasty streak can emerge. She can become deceitful, jealous, unfaithful, or somewhat bitter.

Figure 27

KNIGHT

The Knights translate the quality of each suit into movement. The energy we saw as accomplishment in the King, and awareness in the Queen, here bursts forth at an earlier stage. In the Knights we see the ways in which each element is put to use. At the same time, the Knights lack the sureness and stability of the Kings and Queens.

Because Fire itself symbolizes movement, the Knight of Wands shows this quality in the extreme. He represents eagerness, action, movement for its own sake, adventure and travel. Without some grounding influence all this excitement can dissipate itself as he tries to fly in every direction at once. Allied to a sense of purpose and aided by some Air–like influence of planning, the Knight of Wands can provide the energy and self-confidence for great achievement.

Notice that on his shirt the salamanders' tails do not touch their mouths, symbolizing incomplete action, unformed plans. In contrast to the King, the Knight has only begun his adventures.

REVERSED

Picture the young Knight. Unlike the experienced warrior he seeks battle at every opportunity, needing to prove his courage and strength, to himself and to others. And yet he is easily thrown from his horse. Untried, all that Wands and Knight eagerness carries a certain fragile quality. Opposition confuses him, even brings his great projects crashing down around him. Expecting everything to fall before him, he may find himself in basic disharmony with people or situations around him. His actions are interrupted as he finds his basic good nature at odds with people and situations. In a reading, therefore, the reversed Knight symbolizes confusion, disrupted projects, breakdown, and disharmony.

Figure 28

PAGE

The Pages represent the quality of each suit in its simplest state, enjoying itself for itself in a lighter, more youthful, way than the mature Queen. Physically, Pages refer to children. In relation to adults they indicate a moment when a person experiences some aspect of life just for itself, free of external pressures. As children, the Pages very often symbolize beginnings, study, reflection, the qualities of the young student.

Because Wands symbolize beginning, the Page of Wands especially indicates the start of projects, and in particular an announcement to the world, and to ourselves, that we are ready to begin either a 'project' (this can refer to a relationship as well as practical plans) or a new phase of life. On a simpler level the Page can represent a messenger, message or information. In emotional situations the Page's simple eagerness implies a faithful friend or lover.

REVERSED

Quieter than the Knight, the Page is not thrown so wildly by problems but instead becomes confused and indecisive. His eagerness to start is disrupted by complexities and outright Opposition, leaving him afraid or unable to declare himself. Because his basic qualities are simplicity and faithfulness (notice that many of the salamanders on his suit are complete, signifying not finished projects as with the King, but rather a simple wholeness in the self), when indecisive he can become unstable and weak. A person indicated by this card needs either to get away from complexity or to develop the maturity to deal with it. Continued indecision can only lead to the resolve and self-confidence degenerating further.

Figure 29

TEN

Because they are so involved in movement and action the Wands invite problems. Constantly in conflict they almost attract enemies and difficulty. This comes partly from the lack of purpose and plan, but also from Wands' secret enjoyment of any contest.

The Ten shows us, on the surface, an image of a person burdened and oppressed by life, and especially by responsibility. His Wands eagerness has involved him in so many situations that now, paradoxically, that very energy is weighed down with commitments and problems. He wants to be free to travel, to seek adventure and new involvements; but instead he finds himself, like the suburban career man, caught in a net of endless responsibilities – financial, family, work that he himself has created. He did not plan this; it has grown up around him.

We see here the great Wands problem. The Fire energy acts without thinking, takes on new problems simply for the challenge. But these situations and responsibilities do not go away when the person becomes bored and wants to go on to something new. They remain and can swamp the fire that seemed to conquer them.

In emotional situations the card shows us the person who takes on himself or herself all the weight of a relationship. Whatever problems arise, conflicts and dissatisfaction, he or she tries to smooth them over. With bent back she or he struggles to keep the relationship going, while the other person(s) may not even recognize what is happening.

In both the practical and the emotional situation the person has taken the burdens on her or himself. He or she has made the situation and needs to realize that other approaches are still possible. In such situations the burdens may not be wholly real, or at least may be avoided; they may in fact serve as an excuse to avoid doing anything really constructive such as breaking away from a bad situation.

REVERSED

Like many cards, especially when reversed, more than one meaning is possible. In a reading we can determine the best meaning (though sometimes more than one meaning will apply, as with a choice) partly through the other cards, and partly through an intuition that can only develop with practice. In study this variety of meanings demonstrates the fact that a situation can change 'in many ways.

Most simply the Ten of Wands reversed indicates that the burdens have increased in weight and number to the point where the person may collapse from them, physically or emotionally. At the same time it can mean that the person has thrown off the burdens (perhaps because they have become too much to bear). From here the situation branches again. Does he or she throw down the sticks because of a realization that he or she can use the energy to better purpose? Or does the person only rebel against the responsibilities without really doing anything constructive? A woman I once read for described it as a question of throwing the sticks behind or before us. If behind, we attempt a new direction. If before, it means we will pick them up again and continue trudging on the same road.

Figure 29

NINE

The Nines show how the suits deal with problems and the compromises they demand. Fire implies great strength, physical power, mental alertness. Emotionally, however, this predilection to fighting can trap Wands in patterns of conflicts. In the Nine we see again the image of someone who has faced a lot of opposition, from others and from life; rather than take it on himself, however, he has fought back. The act of fighting has developed his strength so that the picture shows someone muscular and keen-eyed. The Wands behind him can represent his resources in life, or else his problems looming up behind him. Either way, he is ready for the next fight.

Notice, however, his rigid posture, the stiffness and the raised shoulder. Notice also the bandage around his head, indicating a psychic wound. The battler is not a whole person. Whether by necessity or habit he has closed off awareness of life beyond conflict, and now looks only for the next fight, while his eyes see only the enemy, sometimes even after the enemy has surrendered.

REVERSED

Again, alternatives. First, the defence fails. The obstacles and problems grow too great for his strength to hold them back. The other meaning, however, is that of looking for some different approach.

We should not assume the card always advises us to give up fighting. To abandon defensiveness means taking a great risk, for what happens if the problems we have kept at bay for so long rush up at us? Context is everything and sometimes the context demands those powerful shoulders and sharp eyes. And yet, observe how much energy the person uses up simply keeping himself tense and ready for battle. In specific readings the true implications of this card can only become clear through seeing it combine with other cards.

Figure 31

EIGHT

Fire implies swiftness and movement. Though this movement sometimes lacks direction we see here the image of a journey reaching an end, or things completed. When the Fire finds its goal, the projects and situations come to a satisfactory end. The Wands have come to earth. Therefore, the image on this card implies the addition of Pentacles grounding to Wands energy.

Romantically Waite calls them the 'arrows of love'. We can see this especially as meaning action taken in a love affair, seduction, or proposals made and accepted.

REVERSED

Turned around the image becomes one of continuance, of nothing coming to an end, especially when an end is desired. A situation or attitude simply goes on and on, with no conclusion in sight. If such a situation cannot be avoided, then it is good to recognize it and accept it, rather than let it bring frustration or disappointment. On the other hand, sometimes we ourselves can bring about this up-in-the-air quality by expecting a situation to remain unresolved. One of the most important positions in a reading is that called 'hopes and fears'; very often it turns out to be a self-fulfilling prophecy.

The arrows of love, when reversed, become arrows of jealousy and argument. The jealousy may derive from uncertainty and confusion, both in our feelings and in those of the other person.

Figure 32

SEVEN

Like the Nine, this a cards of conflict, but here we see the battle itself, and the effect is exhilarating. With their natural strength and positiveness Wands expect to win and usually do. Through active conflict the figure in this card rises above any depression into the clear intoxicating air. In a way this card shows a background to the Nine. We become defensive and committed to fighting through an earlier experience of winning, staying on top. While the fight goes on we enjoy it. People under Wands' influence need to know they are alive, they need that charge of adrenalin to show them that the Fire still runs through them. Only later does the habit of constant battle close them in.

REVERSED

As implied in the picture the person is using the excitement of con-flict to rise above uncertainty and depression. Reversed indicates sinking into anxiety, indecision, embarrassment. Right side up he was not so much in control of his life as staying on top of it. Here he can no longer put off the contradictions. Above all, the card warns against indecision, suggesting that if a person can come to a clear course of action the natural Wands self-confidence will return to overcome the anxieties and outer problems.

Figure 33

SIX

As the Wands progress down to the Ace they become stronger. The emphasis shifts from problems to joy, from defensiveness to optimism until, with the Ace, we become unified with the live-giving Fire. The Six marks a turning point. In the Golden Dawn system the card bears the title 'Victory', and we see, in fact, a victory parade, the hero crowned with a wreath and surrounded by his followers. However, he has not yet reached his destination. (A fiction, of course; he could just as easily be coming home. I am following Waite's lead on this.) He is assuming victory. Optimism produces the very success it desires and expects.

Often, though certainly not always, it requires only a true belief in ourselves to find the energy to accomplish what we want. More, such belief will inspire others to follow us. Sixes deal with communication and gifts. Here it is the Fire belief in life that Wands give to the people around them.

REVERSED

True optimism creates victory. False optimism, covering our doubts with bluster or illusion, leads to fear and weakness. The attitude shown in the card right side up cannot be faked, for when it does not work it becomes the opposite: defeatism, a sense that enemies will overwhelm us, or that life or specific people will betray us in some way. This attitude too often becomes a self-fulfilling prophecy, for suspicion can produce betrayal.

Figure 34

FIVE

Again conflict, but on a lighter level. It is in the nature of Wands to see life as battle, but in its best sense battle becomes an exciting struggle, eagerly sought after. The Fives in general show some difficulty or loss, but the element of Fire translates problems into competition, seen as a way in which people communicate with society and with each other. The young people are fighting, but not to hurt each other. Like children playing knights they bang their sticks together without really hitting anyone. They seek not to destroy but only to compete for the sheer joy of action.

REVERSED

The exciting competition right side up implies a sense of rules and fair play, for without understood agreements struggle as a game becomes impossible. Reversed, the card indicates that the rules are being abandoned, that in fact the battle has taken on a more serious, a nastier tone. The sense of play changes to bitterness or disillusionment as people seek actually to hurt or ruin each other. The Fire attitude to life, especially when not extended by Swords awareness and wisdom, demands that life respond in a positive way and not show its crueller side. The Five reversed brings to mind again that phrase 'the fire has gone out'.

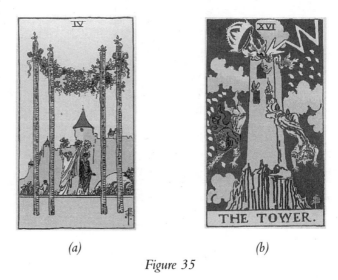

(a)   *(b)*

Figure 35

FOUR

The number four, with its image of the square, implies stasis or solidity. The irrepressible Wands energy, however, require no protective fences as does, say, Pentacles. It will not be contained, and so we see people marching out ecstatically to the simplest of structures, trusting in the sun to burn off any clouds of trouble. The card represents a domestic environment filled with Fire optimism, eagerness, and celebration. As in the Six we see people following the dancers. Unlike that card, however, where the soldiers followed the charismatic leader, the people here are swept along by joy.

They are leaving a walled city for the open bower. In other words, their spirit and courage carry them from a defensive situation to an open one. We can contrast this image with that of the Tower, shown on the right. The two figures in that Major card are dressed very similarly (even to blue and red robes) to the two in the Four of Wands. In its less esoteric meanings the Tower shows the explosion that results when people allow a repressive or miserable situation to build up to an intolerable level. In the Four of Wands optimism and love of freedom carry the people, together, out of their walled city before it becomes a Tower-like prison.

REVERSED

Waite calls this card unchanged upside down. The joy is so powerful it cannot be blocked. We can add, however, that the reversed Four might indicate, like the Sun in the Major Arcana, that the happiness in the environment is not so obvious. As with the family in the Ten of Pentacles, the people symbolized here may need to learn to appreciate what they have. Another possibility: the happiness in the person's environment is just as strong, but unorthodox, at least in terms of other people's attitudes and expectations.

Figure 36

THREE

The number three, because it joins one and two in a new reality (see the Empress in the Major Arcana) indicates combinations and achievements. In each suit it shows that element in its maturity. With Wands this becomes accomplishment. The figure is shown strong, but at rest, unthreatened. The young competitors of Five have achieved success especially in business, career, etc., though the card implies emotional maturity as well. The Wands eagerness does not vanish, but here he sends his ships out to explore new areas while himself stays behind. Conversely we also can look on the boats as returning, bringing back to daily life the results of some exploration or new experiencing. In contrast to the Knight the image suggests keeping a solid basis in what we have already accomplished while we continue to open new areas and interests in ourselves. Sometimes in readings this can mean maintaining a primary commitment to existing relationships while still looking for new friends or lovers.

Some Tarot cards acquire special meanings that apply only to specific situations. For a person troubled or struggling with the past the Three of Wands can indicate becoming at peace with his or her memories. They become like boats sailing past on a wide river and then out to sea. The setting sun, a symbol of contentment, lights up the river, symbol of a person's emotional life, with a warm golden light.

In the Three of Wands we see the first of the Gate cards (the suit of Wands, with its emphasis on action, contains fewer of these inner cards than any of the other suits). Metaphysically the sea has always evoked in people a sense of the vastness and mystery of the universe, while rivers symbolize the experience of the ego dissolving into that great Sea. The boats represent that part of us which explores deep experience, while the man expresses the importance of rooting ourselves in ordinary reality before we attempt such metaphysical journeys. This schematic explanation gives only an intellectual shadow of the card's true meanings. That meaning lies in the experience of merging with the picture until the boats carry us into the unknown areas of the self. Significantly it is the addition of Water and Earth in the form of the sea and the rock which direct the images to Fire's greatest potential. Nevertheless, the special quality of this Gate, that of exploring the unknown, belongs to Fire.

REVERSED

Several meanings reflect the complex nature of the card right side up. On the one hand it can mean the failure of some 'exploration' or project (either practical or emotional) due to 'storms', that is, problems greater than we had hoped for or expected. But it can also mean becoming involved in our environment after a time of detachment and reflection. The image right side up carries a certain isolation as he looks down at the world. Finally, it can indicate being disturbed by memories.

Figure 37

TWO

Again a card of success, even greater than the Three, for here a man stands in a castle and holds the world in his hands. Yet the card does not carry the same contentment as the Three. He is bored; his accomplishments have only served to wall him in (a situation very unpleasant to Fire), and the world he holds is a very small one. Waite compares his weariness to that of Alexander, who supposedly wept after he had conquered the known world because he then could think of nothing else to do with his life (his death shortly afterwards no doubt gave this legend an extra boost).

Waite's comment suggests that the Wands love of battle and challenge can leave one with no real satisfaction in actual accomplishments when the fight has been won. Comparison with the Four (as well as the Ten) is obvious. There several people dance together, out from a walled city. Here one person stands alone, walled in by his own success.

Here we find one of Waite's best formulas: 'Surprise, wonder, enchantment, trouble, and fear'. All these terms together describe someone jumping directly into new experience. When we leave behind safe situations and past success to enter the unknown, we liberate so much emotion and energy that we cannot avoid either the wonder and enchantment or the fear that goes with it. The card speaks very strongly to people who have lived for a long time in some unpleasant or unsatisfying situation, and finally decide to make a change all at once.

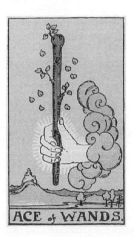

Figure 38

ACE

A gift of strength, of power, of great sexual energy, of the love of living. The leaves burst out so abundantly that they fall off to become yods, the first letter of God's name. The yods' presence in all the Aces but that of Pentacles indicates that we receive these primal experiences as a gift from life. We cannot cause or produce them by any normal means; they come to us as hands emerging from clouds. Only by reaching the high states of awareness shown in the later cards of the Major Arcana can we understand the sources of these bursts of elemental energy. In ordinary situations it is enough to experience and appreciate them.

At the beginning of some situation, no card could signal a better start. It gives eagerness and strength. At the same time, the card teaches humility, for it reminds us that ultimately we have done nothing morally to deserve the optimism and greater energy that sometimes allows us to overwhelm other people.

REVERSED

A reversed Ace implies in some way a failure of that primal experience. This can mean simply that the situation turns against us, or, especially with Wands and Swords, that we find it impossible to hang on to that force and use it beneficially. Therefore, the Ace of Wands reversed can mean chaos, things falling apart, either because it just happened that way, or because we have ruined them through too much undirected energy. This can happen on a practical level, through too much activity, too many new starts without consolidating past gains; or emotionally, through being overconfident of friendship, or simply overbearing; or finally, sexually, through refusing to contain that fiery sexual appetite.

Waite included a much lighter reading for the reversed Ace: 'Clouded joy'. Then the Ace becomes like the Four or the Sun; the wonder and happiness exists even when we cannot, or will not, see it in front of us.

CHAPTER EIGHT

CUPS

If Fire symbolizes the spirit force giving life to the universe, then Water signifies the love that allows the soul to receive that force. The sun draws the seed out of the ground, but only when water has first softened and nurtured it. Fire represents action, Water formlessness or passivity. Water does not symbolize weakness; rather it stands for the inner being, and that slow coming to life of the seed. In extreme situations water and fire are natural enemies; a flood will obliterate a fire while a flame under a container will dissolve the already shapeless water into steam. At the same time life cannot exist or grow without a blending of these two primal opposites.

This paradox has led the alchemists and others to describe trans-formation – which is not simply change, but sudden evolution from a fragmented to an integrated state – as a unifying of Fire and Water, shown in the image of the hermaphrodite (in traditional society, with its strict identification of gender and role, what more powerful symbol of opposites existed than man and woman?), and more symbolically in the six-pointed star. In that ancient image (far older than its modern use as an emblem of Jewishness) the upward pointing Fire triangle joins the downward Water triangle to form a picture of life reaching out in all directions from a unified centre.

Because the water in a river changes constantly, yet the river always retains its basic character, rivers symbolize the true self that remains constant beneath all the outer changes in a person's life.

Thus, while Fire symbolizes what we do, Water stands for what we are.

All rivers flow into the sea. However much our egos insist upon our separation from the rest of life, our instincts – the Water side of us – remind us of our harmony with the universe. Western culture has emphasized the idea of the individual as unique and separated from the world. The Tarot does not deny the individual's uniqueness – it insists on it, through the uniqueness of readings – but instead describes the individual as a combination of elements (an astrology chart, with its twelve signs and twelve houses, teaches the same lesson). And one of those elements remains a person's basic connection to the rest of life.

The suit of Cups shows an inner experience that flows rather than defines, that opens rather than restricts. Cups represent love and imagination, joy and peace, a sense of harmony and wonder. They show us love as the Way to Spirit, both the love we give to others and the love we receive from people and from life itself in its happier moments.

At times when life demands action, either physical or emotional, Cups represent the problem of passivity. All attempts to do anything, or to sort through some complicated problem, dissolve into vagueness, apathy, or empty dreams. Wands energize Cups, Swords define that emotional energy and give it direction, help it to figure things out (though an Air storm will agitate the peaceful Water), while Pentacles bring the fantasies back to the ground of real projects.

Figure 39

KING

Like the Kings of Wands, he represents his suit in terms of social responsibility, accomplishments and maturity. And like the Fire King, his position as maintainer of society does not fit him all that comfortably. Cups symbolize the creative imagination, and to achieve success he has had to discipline and even suppress his dreams. The fish, symbol of creativity, hangs around his neck, but as an artificial ornament. He has directed his creative powers into socially responsible achievements. Waite describes him as a man of 'business, law, divinity'. In a sense he has matured his suit; but Water demands to flow, not to be confined.

Behind his throne a live fish jumps through the waves, signifying that creative imagination remains alive even when pushed to the background. Similarly, his throne floats on the lively sea, yet he himself does not touch the water (compare the Queen, p. 188), indicating that his achievement derives ultimately from creativity, though he has shaped his life in such a way as to separate him from his own playful poet-like imagination.

In its extreme the imagery suggests someone who has dammed up his or her emotions and imagination. It also shows, more gently, a person who expresses these qualities, but not as central to her or his life. Responsibility comes before self-expression.

The King does not look at his cup; rather he holds it in the same way he holds his sceptre, symbol of power. Some commentators see the King as a person of troubled emotions, even anger and violence, who habitually suppresses these feelings even from himself, always maintaining a calm exterior.

In some contexts, especially the arts, the King takes on a very different meaning. Because he is the leader of his suit, he can symbolize success, achievement, mastery, and maturity in artistic work.

REVERSED

More complex, and perhaps more troubled than the King of Wands, the King of Cups reversed slides towards dishonesty. When right side up he uses his creativity for his work; reversed, he turns his talents to vice or corruption. Swindlers also use creativity to further their careers, but we would not describe them as 'responsible'.

The card upside down can mean that the violent Air emotions emerge from their calm exterior, perhaps through the pressure of outside events. Romantically, the King of Cups reversed can suggest a dishonest yet domineering lover, more often male, sometimes female.

Finally, in relation to the arts, the King reversed can suggest that an artist's achievement has proved to be insignificant, or that a person has not yet matured and cannot point to a significant body of work. In a reading, this final meaning would come out strongly if the card appeared in connection with certain Pentacles reversed, such as the Eight, or the Three.

Figure 40

QUEEN

The most successful and balanced of the Cups, in some ways of all the Minor cards, the Queen is almost a mundane version of the World Dancer. Coming between the outer responsibility of the King and the passiveness of the Knight, she shows the possibility of blending imagination and action, creativity and social usefulness. Her throne, decorated with cherubic mermaids, sits on land, indicating her vital connection to the outer world and to other people, at connection more real than the King's. At the same time the water flows over her feet and merges with her dress, signifying the unity of self with emotion and imagination. The water suggests also unconscious forces – the underlying spiritual patterns shown in the Major Arcana – nourishing conscious life. The unity of water, land, and the Queen implies that we do not feed the imagination by giving it complete freedom to wander where it will, but rather by directing it into valuable activity, an idea that most artists would endorse. This idea appears even more strongly in the Nine of Pentacles, emblem of creative discipline.

Waite describes the cup she holds as her own creation. It is the most elaborate of the Cups (whatever we may think about its style!) and symbolizes the achievement brought about through using the imagination. Notice its church-like shape. Until the modern age (and still in more archaic cultures) all art expressed and glorified spiritual experience. The Queen stares at the cup intently, showing the strong will that directs and moulds creative force without suppressing it. At the same time her look suggests that the creative person derives inspiration for future activity from her or his past achievements. Compare her fierce gaze with the dreaminess of the Knight, or the cloudy fantasies of the Seven.

Willpower alone will not unite imagination and action. Only love can give meaning to her actions, and realize her goals. These goals are not simply creative in the narrow sense of art, but in the wider sense of making something whole and alive out of the opportunities and elements given by life. They can include emotional goals, especially family, for while the King symbolizes society, the Queen symbolizes the family, for men as well as women.

What is most important is that she joins consciousness to feeling. She knows what she wants and will take the steps necessary to get it. Yet she acts always with an awareness of love.

Waite says 'loving intelligence and hence the gift of vision', terms suggesting that a vision of life as joyful can only come as a gift, but love can open us to receiving such a gift, to recognizing that it exists. With intelligence joined to love we return the gift by taking that vision and making something real and lasting from it.

REVERSED

Reversing the Queen of Cups breaks that unity of vision and action. We see someone ambitious and powerful, yet dangerous, because she cannot be trusted. The love has become lost, and with it the commitment to values greater than her own success. If she slides further from the balance, she can become dishonourable, even depraved, as her creative force lurches out of control.

(a)   (b)

Figure 41

KNIGHT

As a less developed figure than the Queen or King, he has not learned to direct his imagination into the world. Therefore dreams dominate this card, with its images of a slow horse, and a knight lost in the enticements of his cup, symbol of the imagination. At the same time the creative force is less powerful here than in any of the other Cups court cards. Only a narrow river flows through a parched land. The Knight has not learned that the true imagination feeds on action rather than fantasy. By this I mean that if we do nothing with our dreams they remain vague and unrelated to the rest of our lives.

We may make another point about the Knight's dreaminess. What feeds it – inner principles, as in myth or archetypal art; or self-indulgence, as in daydreams and escapist films or books? The English poet, Samuel Taylor Coleridge, distinguished between 'imagination' and 'fancy'. Both take the mind away from ordinary experience and perceptions. However, while the first derives from and leads to an awareness of underlying spiritual truth, the second produces only fantasies that may excite, but ultimately lack real meaning. They derive from the ego rather than the unconscious.

Nothing emerges from his cup (compare the Page; p. 192). Nor has he shaped it into something greater than it was, as has the Queen. A Knight is a figure committed to action and involvement. Water, on the other hand, symbolizes passiveness. The contrast makes it hard for the Knight to reconcile these two qualities. By denying this basic commitment to the world, he does not allow his imagination to produce anything.

Because he is a Knight the outside world of action, of sex, may pull him even while he pursues his thoughts and fantasies. His passiveness can sometimes be at pose, almost exaggerated for the purpose of denying those temptations and desires which disturb his peace. Romantically the Knight can represent a lover who does not wish to commit him or herself, who is perhaps attractive yet passive, withdrawn, or narcissistic.

These harsh images of the Knight all deal with his conflicts. At the same time his helmet and feet are winged, his horse is spirited in its slowness. And he resembles Death, symbol of transformation. If the Knight is not pulled by responsibility or desire, if he follows a genuine vision rather than escape from outside commitments, then he can go very deeply into himself, turning the Knight energy into an exploration of his own inner world.

REVERSED

In various ways we see the Knight reacting towards increased demands from the world beyond himself. It can mean simply that he rouses himself to action or else follows his more physical desires. Or it can mean that a passive person is being pushed towards action or commitment and does not like it. Without outwardly resisting he or she can resent those demands. The result can be a wall built up between the Knight and those people who are making him act out his responsibilities. This attitude can result in hypocrisy or manipulation, sometimes lies and tricks.

Figure 42

PAGE

Being younger in spirit, child-like, the Page does not suffer the same conflict with either responsibility or sensual desire. He indicates a state or a time in which contemplation and fantasy are very proper to a person. No outside demands disturb his or her gentle contemplation. As a result the fish of imagination looks at him from his cup. Amused, he looks back at it without the Knight's need to penetrate so deeply into himself. Here, the imagination is its own justification.

The fish can also symbolize psychic talents and sensitivity. And since the Pages all have a student quality, the Page of Cups can show someone developing psychic abilities, either through an actual programme of study and/or meditation, or else such talents developing by themselves, but in a peaceful way.

REVERSED

Right side up we saw a person letting his imagination bubble up before him. Because he does nothing with his fantasies they give him no trouble. If he acts upon them, however, they may lead him into mistakes. Reversed therefore means to follow our inclinations, to act without thinking, or to allow our immediate desires to seduce us, particularly if they go against our common sense. We see the reversed Page whenever we buy something we do not need and do not even really want; we see him when we make promises we cannot keep or commitments that do not really mean anything.

In other situations, if the Page refers to psychic development, or true visions, then reversed shows a person disturbed by these visions. For many people in our rationalized world the sudden emergence of psychic talent, even if deliberately sought through training, can appear very frightening. The reversed Page mirrors the fear and reminds us to calm down, to look peacefully at the fish rising from the cup of ourselves. In connection with Pentacles it calls for grounding in outer reality to avoid being washed away by fantasies or visions.

Figure 43

TEN

As the highest number, the Tens signify being filled with the quality of the suit. In Wands we saw an excess of burdens; in Cups we find joy and the wonder of life spread across the sky. The holy Grail, symbol of God's grace and love, rests at the base of this suit, showing us that love, imagination, and joy all come to us as gifts. The Bible tells us that God made the rainbow as a promise that the world will never again suffer a flood of destruction. But the rainbow carries a more positive promise as well – that life brings happiness and not just an absence of pain.

The man and woman in the picture understand these things. Arm in arm they look up and celebrate the rainbow. The children, however, dance without looking up. They symbolize innocence, which takes happiness as the natural condition of life. They expect happiness, but do not waste it. Showing a family, the card refers primarily to domestic happiness, but can indicate any situation that brings a surge of joy. It especially refers to the recognition of the valuable qualities in a situation. This meaning pertains especially in readings where the Ten of Cups appears in contrast to the Ten of Pentacles.

REVERSED

There are two basic variants here. First, all the emotion turns against itself. Some highly-charged situation, usually romantic or domestic, has gone wrong, producing violent feeling, anger, or deceit. Or, in practice, the reversed Ten can simply mean that at person does not recognize or appreciate the happiness life is offering him or her.

Figure 44

NINE

From deep joy we move to the simpler pleasures of feasting and physical contentment. As noted earlier, the Nines depict the compromises we make with life. Wands showed a strong defence; the more benign Cups demonstrate the attitude of avoiding worry and problems by concentrating on ordinary pleasures. People sometimes react antagonistically to this card, perhaps wishing to see themselves as beyond superficiality. At times, especially after troubles or a period of long, hard work, nothing can serve us better than a simple good time.

REVERSED

For once the reversed meaning gives the greater awareness – to use Waite's formula, 'truth, loyalty, liberty'. In connection with the right side up meaning, the words imply a rejection of surface values; but they also refer to very tangled or oppressive situations where, by clinging to the thread of truth, or by staying loyal to ourselves, or to others, or to a purpose, we can bring about victory and liberation.

(a)   (b)

Figure 45

EIGHT

The pleasant nature of Cups tends to lull us away from what we have to do. The Eight begins (or ends) a series of five cards dealing with the Water problem of action. In this card we see someone turning his back on a double row of standing Cups which symbolize a situation that not only has provided happiness, but actually continues to do so. In contrast to the Five, all the Cups remain upright; nothing has been knocked over. And yet the person knows that the time has come to leave. The imagery suggests one of the true uses of Water instinct – an ability to sense when something has ended before it either dries up or comes crashing down around us, to know the time to move on.

We see the figure climbing a hill, going to higher ground, with the implication of moving from a less to a more meaningful situation. Notice the resemblance of the figure to the Hermit. To reach the height of the Hermit's wisdom, we must first put the ordinary things of life behind us.

The Hermit reminds us that the image of land does not necessarily mean action or involvement in the ordinary sense, but can suggest almost the opposite: that is, withdrawing from outer activity to seek at greater self-awareness. At first the scene appears to take place at night; but when we look closer we see that actually it depicts an eclipse, with the moon moving across the sun. A moon phase, that is, at period of inner awareness, has taken over from outer-directed activity. By joining moon imagery to a scene of movement, the card teaches us that developing a deeper sense of self is also an action. Remember that the Hermit, by reversing the sexual polarity of the High Priestess above him, combines action and intuition in a definite programme of self-knowledge.

Whether we view the figure as moving away from the world, or into action, the card symbolizes leaving a stable situation. In its deepest level this card acts as at Gate, similar in certain ways to the Three of Wands. Both work through the image of a journey into the unknown, but while the Fire card is drawn to Water, the Water card is drawn to Air. The Three of Wands breaks down the ego and frees the exploring spirit, while the Eight of Cups moves from the vagueness of Water to the specific knowledge of abstract principles symbolized by the climb up the Hermit's mountain.

REVERSED

Sometimes the upside down Eight indicates the simple negation of the card's basic image – a refusal to leave some situation, a determination to hang on even when we know deep inside that we have taken all we can from it. Such a description characterizes many relationships.

Usually, however, the card reversed maintains its quality of awareness and correct response. It symbolizes that the time to leave has *not* come, that the situation will continue to give joy and meaning.

One final possibility: timidity, leaving a situation because a person lacks the courage to pursue it and take everything she or he can get from it. Many people make this a pattern in their lives; they become involved in relationships, work, projects, etc., and then run away, either when difficulties arise, or when the time comes for genuine commitment.

Figure 46

SEVEN

With the Seven, the Cups problem emerges in its most direct form. Emotion and imagination can produce wonderful visions, but without at grounding in both action and the outer realities of life these fantastic images remain daydreams, 'fancies' without real meaning or value. Notice that the visions cover the whole range of fantasies from wealth (the jewels), to a victory wreath, to fear (the dragon), to adventure (the castle), even the archetypes of mythology – a god-like face, a mysterious radiant figure, and a snake, universal symbol of psychic wisdom. It is a mistake to think that daydreams are meaningless because of their *content*; on the contrary they often spring from deep archetypal needs and images. They lack meaning because they do not connect to anything outside themselves.

REVERSED

This card reversed means a determination to make something from dreams. This does not mean rejecting fantasies, but rather doing something with them.

Figure 47

SIX

As cards of benevolent emotion and dreams the Cups signify sweet memories. Sometimes these memories truly represent the past; at other times we may idealize the past and see it through a haze of security and happiness. The emblem of this second attitude is childhood, pictured as a safe time, when parents, or older brothers and sisters, protected us and gave us everything we needed. Sometimes such an attitude can produce a warm secure feeling which will help people face their current problems. In this sense the card shows the past (the dwarf) giving a gift of memories to the future, symbolized by the child. At other times, however, a fixation on the past can prevent a person from facing current problems. The past can distract from the present just as much as fantasies of the future.

There are other meanings for the Six beside memory. The Sixes show relationships of giving and receiving. Here we see the image of a teacher or protector giving wisdom and security to someone who might be a family member, a student, or a friend.

REVERSED

Like the Seven, the Six reversed indicates a move towards action. Specifically, it shows looking towards the future, rather than the past. The two cards reversed are very similar; the difference is that the Six shows an attitude while the Seven indicates actual steps taken.

At other times, depending on the right side up meaning, the Six reversed indicates disturbed memories (compare the Three of Wands reversed), or a feeling of alienation from the past. It can also show the breakdown of a relationship based on one person protecting or teaching the other(s).

Figure 48

FIVE

The Fives concern struggle and sometimes pain. With Wands we saw the adventure of competition; Cups show the emotional reaction to loss. The picture depicts sorrow but also acceptance. Three cups lie spilled out, but two remain standing, even if at the moment the figure concentrates on the three. In readings I have often seen this card linked to either the Three of Cups as a happiness or hope that has failed, or else the Three of Swords; the two cups standing have often referred to the Two of Cups, that is, support from a lover or friend.

The woman (or man; the androgynous character of the figure indicates that sorrow unites the sexes) stands rigid, wrapped in black, the colour of grief. She needs to accept that some happiness has suddenly vanished, been knocked over. She does not yet realize that something remains, for first she must understand and accept the loss. Has she herself knocked over the cups, either through recklessness or by taking them for granted? In the sense of awareness the card relates to Justice, emblem of truth and the acceptance of responsibility. In her pose and costume she resembles the Hermit, who cloaks himself in wisdom to hold him upright in his task of looking within for a vision of his life, the vision he will accept injustice.

The river represents the flow of sorrow but the bridge symbolizes consciousness and determination. It leads from the past (loss) to the future (new beginnings). When she has accepted her loss she can then turn, pick up the two remaining cups, and cross over the bridge to the house, symbol of stability and continuity.

With its deep evocation of regret the card forms another Gate, bringing to us that sense of spiritual loss and separation which all over the world has given rise to myths of a fall or an exile from Paradise.

REVERSED

The basic meaning of the card can change in three ways when reversed. First, it can mean not accepting the loss, and as an extension of this, false projects or mistakes. Second, it can indicate support from others, friendship, new interests and occupations after some sad or disturbing event. Finally, it can emphasize an awareness of what remains important and permanent in the face of sorrow. In this sense the woman turns from the three to the two. Here the two cups symbolize the solid basis of a person's life; they remain standing because they are not so easily knocked over. And this awareness indicates that the three fallen cups symbolize something less important than might at first seem at the time of its destruction.

Figure 49

FOUR

The passiveness of Cups can sometimes lead to apathy. What we can call the 'negative imagination' makes us look at everything as worthless or boring. There seems to be nothing worth getting up for, nothing worth doing, and nothing worth examining.

The three cups symbolize the person's past experience. Bored by what life has given him he does not recognize the new opportunities being offered to him by the fourth cup. The resemblance of that cup to the Ace suggests that the new possibilities can lead to happiness and satisfaction. In the main, however, the card shows a situation when everything in life has come to appear the same. The card sometimes shows apathy resulting from a dull, unstimulating environment.

REVERSED

Again, the reversal takes us out of ourselves and awakens us to the world and its possibilities. New things are offered, new relations, new ideas. Most important, the reversed card shows enthusiasm and the seizing of opportunities.

Figure 50

THREE

The Threes show an appreciation of the meaning and value of the suit. Because of the Grail at the base of the suit, the Three of Cups indicates joy, celebration, and above all sharing the wonder of life. As if we had passed the crisis of action, the final three cards all, according to their numbers, flow with happiness. Here we see the women celebrating, as at a harvest. Either a crisis has finished, or work has produced good results.

We see the three women so intertwined we can hardly tell whose arm is whose. In bad times as well as good, the card shows a sharing of experience.

REVERSED

Again several meanings present themselves. First of all it can show the loss of some happiness. Very often it indicates that something hoped for has not come about. It can also signify the failure of friendship, and again the disillusionment of finding that friends have not supported us when we needed them, or else the break up of a group of friends.

Another meaning shows a corruption of the original. Rather than a shared celebration of life's joys we find what Waite quaintly calls 'excess in physical enjoyment and the pleasures of the senses'. Obviously Waite intended this to mean that deeper values are ignored. It is worth observing however, that most people find this phrase, especially as a prediction, not at all unpleasant.

(a)   *(b)*   *(c)*

Figure 51

TWO

In many ways this card acts as a lesser version of the Lovers. While the trump shows the great power of mature sexual relationships the Minor card emphasizes the beginning of a relationship. This is not a hard and fast rule as far as readings are concerned. The Two can often show a long-term union or friendship, perhaps on a lighter level than the Lovers. In study, and most commonly in practice, however, it indicates the pledging of friendship, the beginning of a love affair.

In the trump we see the Angel, symbol of super-consciousness. In the Two of Cups we see the winged lion over the caduceus of Hermes, symbol of healing and wisdom. In both cases, the card shows how two people by uniting their separate qualities and abilities through love, produce something in their lives beyond what either would have achieved alone. The lion symbolizes sexuality, the wings Spirit. Love gives a greater meaning to the sexual drive that leads us to it.

In Part One of this book we saw how the Lovers can serve as a diagram of the unified self. We can look at the Two of Cups in a similar way. While the man symbolizes action and movement, the woman symbolizes emotion, sensitivity, and an appreciation of experience. By uniting these two qualities we give our lives value.

Notice the resemblance of the man to the Fool. In a reading these two cards came up linked together. The woman, an artist, wanted to know what direction her work should take. She was especially concerned to investigate whether her art came from a real centre in her life or was simply an intellectual exercise. Now, other cards indicated she had reached a level of technical mastery in what she had been doing, while the Fool, as an outcome, showed her taking a leap into a new area. But the Two of Cups showed she would find success if she linked her technical ability and explorations to the spiritual grounding symbolized by the woman.

REVERSED

In different ways the reversed card shows a breakdown of the ideals symbolized right side up. It can mean a love affair or friendship which has gone sour in some way, in particular because of jealousy and a breakdown of trust. It can mean simply the end of a relationship. Depending on the cards around it, it can signify a relationship endangered by internal or external pressures. Another possibility is infatuation, when people pretend to others, to themselves, that a love affair means more than it actually does. In a similar vein the reversed card can show people going through the motions of a love affair, with one or both of them not really caring.

If we look at the card as signifying the self, then reversed indicates a split between what we do and what we feel, between action and emotion.

Figure 52

ACE

From the King's conflicting emotions, through the various balances of celebration and passivity, we arrive finally at the Ace – emblem of love underpinning life. The Ace of Cups has the immediate meaning of a time of happiness and love, a gift of joy. Just as fire makes the world, so love gives it value.

The Smith picture, with its dove and wafer, specifically shows the Holy Grail, said to contain the physical presence of the Holy Ghost at work in the world. In the more subtle versions of the King

Arthur legend, it was not really chivalry – that is, a moral structure – that held together King Arthur's glorious kingdom, but rather the secret presence of the Holy Grail hidden in the land. When the Grail left (because Arthur's knights failed to approach it in a spiritual way) the kingdom fell apart. The allegory tells us that the world does not function primarily by its laws, its moral order and its social structures, but rather by the spiritual basis which gives all these things meaning, and protects them from corruption. When we look at existence as something solely to be conquered (the way Arthur's knights went after the Grail) we bring only chaos. Cups – Water – symbolize receptivity. Love, and ultimately life, cannot be seized, but only accepted.

REVERSED

The reversed Ace always brings disruption. Here we see unhappiness, violence, destruction – the very conditions acted out in the King Arthur legend when the Grail had left the kingdom. The reversed card can indicate simply that the times have turned against us and we can only accept that life brings problems as well as joy. Or, the card upside down can imply that we ourselves bring about our unhappiness by not recognizing what life offers us, or by reacting violently when what we need is calm.

CHAPTER NINE

SWORDS

In many ways Swords are the most difficult suit. The very object, a weapon, signifies pain, anger, destruction, and it is mostly these experiences that the Swords image depict. Yet a sword can also symbolize cutting through illusions and complicated problems (remember Alexander cutting through the Gordian knot). Galahad, the knight who achieved the Holy Grail, could not begin his spiritual quest until he had received his magic sword from Merlin, the kingdom's guide. Similarly, we cannot begin our own quests for meaning and value in life until we have learned to recognize and accept the truth, whatever pain it brings.

Swords belong to the element of Air, or wind, often seen as the closest to Ether, or Spirit. The word 'spirit' relates directly to the word 'breath', and in Hebrew the word for 'spirit' and the word for 'wind' are the same. Just as air constantly moves, so the mind never rests, twisting and turning, sometimes violent, sometimes calm, but always moving. Anyone who has tried to meditate will know how persistently the mind moves.

One problem connected with Swords is that of 'ungrounded thought' or what we might call a 'Hamlet complex'. The mind sees so many sides to a situation, so many possibilities, that understanding, let alone action, becomes impossible. Because our culture has always emphasized rationality, many people today see thinking in general as the cause of all life's problems. If we just stop thinking, they tell us, then everything will work out all right. Even if such a thing were possible, the Tarot tells us it would not benefit us. We do not overcome the problem of an element by banishing it or replacing it with something, but rather by combining it with other elements. The fact is, the more confused we are the more we need our minds, because nothing else can sort out the truth. We need also, however, to combine Air with Water – that is, emotion with receptivity. We need also to combine it with Ether, Spirit, the deep values grounded in spiritual/psychological truth that we see embodied in the Major Arcana. Then the problem of Air changes to the Way, wisdom.

The more obvious problem shown in Swords is that of sorrow, pain, anger - the stormy side of Air. We cannot overcome these things by ignoring them, but we can add to Swords the optimism of Wands, and we can use Pentacles to take ourselves out of our emotions through an involvement with work, nature, the outside world.

(a)   (b)   (c)

Figure 53

KING

As a maintainer of the social structure the King represents authority, power, and judgement. He takes the mental energy of Air and uses it to uphold and rule the world with the keenness of his mind and the force of his personality. His crown is yellow, the colour of mental energy, while his mantle is purple, for wisdom. His cap, a burnouse-like head-dress, is red, the colour of action. The King's intellect does not exist for itself alone, but rather for what it can *do,* as a tool of authority. Similarly, his sword, unlike that of the Queen of Swords or of Justice, does not point straight up, for pure wisdom, but rather tilts slightly to the right, the side of action. The requirement to act upon his judgements tends to distort the power of judgement itself, a fact we can see if we compare the situation of an academic observer of politics with that of someone running a country.

Moreover, the emphasis on social-minded 'realism' may narrow his viewpoint to a very limited materialism. We can see him in the man or woman priding him or herself on tough-minded common sense, with no time for 'mystic mumbo jumbo'. Such people usually ignore how much of their thinking depends on preconception and prejudice, rather than observation of life.

Notice the resemblance to the Emperor. We can call the King the Emperor's representative in the real world. While the trump embodies the archetype of order, law, society, the King of Swords maintains these principles in practice.

Two birds, the animal emblem of the Swords court cards, fly behind the throne. The bird symbolizes the mind's ability to take us into the high air of wisdom, removed from fiery passion, watery emotion, or earthly material corruption. The number two, on the other hand, symbolizes choice, the constant tension between abstract thought and the action that must be taken in the world.

But if the birds symbolize the mind's ability to climb above the world they also symbolize the remoteness such an attitude can produce. Notice, that the King's throne is seemingly in the clouds. Like the King of Wands, the Swords King can tend towards arrogance, his powerful mind and will setting him above the more confused people around him. In social terms the imagery suggests the tendency of government and rulers to divorce their judgements from the real needs of people. In more personal terms, we see the remote King in men or women who are harsh, cold, judgemental. As a husband or lover, the King of Swords often indicates a domineering or controlling person.

In his best sense the King of Swords evokes Justice, the card directly beneath the Emperor in the Major Arcana. When he connects with this trump, the King stands for social justice, wise laws, and above all, a commitment to intellectual honesty, and the need to put knowledge into practice. Like Justice, and alone of all the court cards, he stares directly out at us, a master of wisdom compelling us to recognize and hold to the truth.

REVERSED

Right side up the King walks a narrow line between committed intellect and power for its own sake. Reversed, he tends to fall on the wrong side of that line. He is authority corrupted, strength used for its own ends of power and dominance.

In readings, we must always take such strong imagery into consideration The reversed King (or any reversed court card) may simply mean some person in difficulty. In connection with the Queen or the Knight it may mean a difficult relationship or a failure to mature (see the section on Readings for relationships between court cards of the same suit). By itself, however, it symbolizes the arrogance of a powerful mind turned in on itself, recognizing only its own desire for control.

Figure 54

QUEEN

As the yin aspect of the suit, the Queen of Swords symbolizes experiences of both sorrow and wisdom, and especially the connection between them. Having experienced pain (the card sometimes signifies widowhood), and having faced it with courage, acceptance, and honesty, she has found wisdom.

The tassel hanging from her left wrist (the side of experience) resembles a cut rope (compare the Eight of Swords, p.219). She has used the sword of her intellect to free herself from confusion, doubt, and fear; now, although she frowns at the world, she opens her hand to it. Though clouds gather around her, her head remains above them in the clear air of truth. One bird, a symbol of the purity of her wisdom, flies high above her. Her sword, like that of Justice and the Ace, stands straight up.

In the sense that powerless women will often suffer from the actions of men, the card refers specifically to women. In its character, it can represent someone of either sex, for neither sorrow nor courage are restricted by gender.

REVERSED

The reversed Queen can indicate an overemphasis on sorrow, someone who makes life seem much worse than it is by ignoring the good things around her. She can also show a strong mind turned nasty, especially as a reaction to pain or pressure from unpleasant situations or people. Sometimes she represents a person so forceful she or he expects, not just demands, that everyone around her, even life itself, will do what she wants.

When people oppose her, the Queen turns malicious, narrow minded, bigoted, and like the King, uses her attitudes to force her personality on the people around her. Whether she represents an excess of sorrow or egoism, she has lost the right side up commitment to truth.

Figure 55

KNIGHT

The young Knight, whose youth makes him both freer of social responsibility than the King, and less tempered by experience than the Queen, rides directly into the storm, waving his sword in his eagerness to overcome all difficulties. He is brave, skilful, strong; yet he tends also towards wildness, even fanatacism. He recognizes no limits.

And yet he often does not know how to sustain a long struggle. He expects his enemies and life's problems to fall under his charge and cannot so easily handle a situation that requires long, steady plodding.

His eagerness suggests a certain innocence, like a young knight who has never lost a battle. His bravery, his skill, his readiness to charge all problems, can sometimes contain a fear of losing that innocence, that strong belief in himself. For he knows inside that he has yet to face and overcome life's greater difficulties. The opposite in many ways of the Knight of Cups, he directs all his energy outwards; he is perhaps nervous of being quietly alone with himself.

REVERSED

As with the King and Queen his weaknesses take over. He is extravagant, careless, excessive. His charge becomes wild, a mistaken response to a situation that calls for a quieter more careful approach.

Figure 56

PAGE

A much lighter card than the other court Swords, the Page represents a very different approach to problems than the Knight (notice that while the King and Queen emphasize wisdom, the two 'younger' cards deal with Swords' more immediate quality of conflict). Rather than charge them he finds it sufficient to simply get above them, to find the high ground. Instead of solving conflicts or meeting opposition he detaches himself.

If the situation is one that calls for such an easygoing approach then the Page's unattached attitude is very beneficial. But if a more difficult problem is involved, then the Page's practice becomes hard to maintain. It requires 'vigilance' to use Waite's term, making sure that people or situations do not get too close. Much of the Page's energy goes to looking over his shoulder. As a somewhat aged student, Hamlet embodied the Page's attitude of observation and irony. His situation, however, called for the aggressive approach of the Knight.

Because of his detached quality the Page can sometimes indulge himself in spying on people, either literally, or figuratively, as an attitude to life. In other words, he may look on human life as a kind of curious spectacle in which he himself does not expect to take part.

REVERSED

Here we see the effect of the Page's aloof attitude in a situation that requires more force. The vigilance turns to paranoia; everyone appears to be an enemy. What began as a feeling of 'I'm above all that, I don't need to concern myself with that,' becomes an obsession with problems and a seeming inability to do anything about them. Such feelings of weakness are endemic to Swords; they require Wands for courage and optimism.

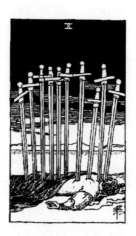

Figure 57

TEN

From the blue skies of the court cards to the black gloom of the Ten and Nine. Just as the Ten of Cups showed joy overflowing, so the

Ten of Swords fills us with pain. Despite the extreme picture the card does not represent death, or even especially violence. It signifies more of a reaction to problems than the problems themselves.

It takes only one sword to kill someone. The ten swords in the man s body, even including one in his ear, suggest hysteria, and the adolescent attitude that 'no one has ever suffered so much as me', 'my life is over', and so on. Notice that in contrast to the Nine the sky clears in the distance, the black clouds give way to sunshine, and that in contrast to the Five or the Two, the water lies placidly. The situation is not so bad as it looks.

REVERSED

Turn this card round and we can imagine the swords falling out of his back. Waite describes it as success and advantage but not permanent. These ideas suggest that when a situation changes, the problems may go away for the moment. However, the person must now take advantage of this relief by making a real change in her or his condition – either practical or mental, depending on the need – so that the situation will not revert to what it was. The card bears a relationship to the Ten of Wands reversed, where we saw the danger of picking up the sticks again once the situation has calmed down.

Figure 58

NINE

The image of deepest sorrow, of utmost mental pain. Where the Queen frees herself by turning sorrow into wisdom, and the Three suggests the calm of acceptance, the Nine shows the moment of agony, of dissolution. The Swords do not stick in her back, but hang in the black air above her. Very often the Nine refers not to something happening directly to us, but rather to someone we love.

Love, in fact, fills the card and gives it its meaning. The blanket design shows roses, symbol of passion, alternating with the signs of the zodiac. In the card's deepest sense it shows a mind that takes on itself all the sorrows of the world, the Lamed Vav, or Just Man, of Jewish legend.

Can we see a way out of such dreadful pain? Both Buddha and Christ pictured the world as a place of unending sorrow, yet both also said that tragedy remains always a half truth, that the universe seen as a whole brings joy and peace. And Nietzsche wrote of embracing existence so completely, with such total ecstatic honesty, that we would gladly repeat, endlessly, every moment of our lives, whatever the pain.

REVERSED

For the Nine reversed Waite gives one of his most suggestive formulas: 'Imprisonment, suspicion, doubt, reasonable fear, and shame'. The words delineate a state of mind or rather a progression of states that result when people retreat into themselves from some problem they do not dare to confront.

As with the card right side up, the reversed card deals with our reaction to something outside ourselves, but here it is oppression rather than tragedy. The key term is 'reasonable fear', which can refer to, say, political oppression – as of racial or sexual minorities; or social oppression – a feeling of being a scapegoat because of appearance, speech, etc.; or simply the personal oppression of a domineering family or partner. The important thing is that the problem is real, but because we cannot directly attack it, we tend to hide in ourselves, keeping in our anger and resentment.

Anger turned in on itself becomes depression and from there suspicion. The person who was laughed at as a child for her big nose thinks that everyone is looking at her. The black person believes that any complaint at work is a racial slur. And suspicion easily leads to self-doubt and shame. Often it does not even help, at least not completely, if we rationally know that we have no reason to feel ashamed, that in fact those who have ridiculed or oppressed us should feel the shame. Unless the oppressed self-doubting person takes action, expresses her or his anger, makes real changes in her or his life, the deep hidden shame will remain.

Figure 59

EIGHT

From the Nine reversed we move to an even clearer image of oppression. We see a person tied up, surrounded by swords with a castle – symbol of authority – behind her; she stands in the mud, an image of humiliation and shame. Notice, however, that the swords do not actually fence her in, and the ropes do not go around her legs, while the people who have tied her up do not appear at all in the card. In short, nothing prevents her from just leaving.

The clue to this card is the blindfold – symbolizing confusion, oppressive ideas, isolation from other people in similar situations;

what political liberationists call 'mystification' – keeping people down not by direct force, but by training them to believe in their own helplessness. In that remarkable way the Tarot has of summing up a complex situation the card can almost stand as a diagram of the oppressed condition.

On a very different level the Eight of Swords acts as a Gate to a special awareness. By identifying with it we gain a sense of our own ignorant condition, something which many people will intellectually recognise (paradox of paradoxes) but not really accept. Because we live such lives, bounded by our physical needs, the limitations of our senses, and the conditioning of language and culture, we can know reality only through filters. Without enlightenment, or what some Sufis and others call 'conscious evolution', we can never really know ourselves or the world, can never say 'This is the truth; this is the way things really are'. Recognition of ignorance is the first (and often the hardest) step to true knowledge.

REVERSED

Freedom begins when we throw off our blindfolds, when we see clearly how we have arrived in whatever situation we are in, what we have done, what others have done (particularly those who have bound us, but also others in similar situations), and what we can do about it now. The reversed Eight means, in general, liberation from some oppressive situation; primarily it refers to the first step of such liberation, that is seeing things as clearly as possible.

Figure 60

SEVEN

The theme of struggle continues. Here we see an image of taking action against problems. Sometimes the card means simply a daring act, even a coup that takes the sting out of opposition. More often, it stands for an impulsive act when a careful plan is required.

The picture shows us someone grinning as he makes off with his enemy's weapons. He has not attacked the camp, he cannot even carry all the swords. The card implies schemes and actions that do not solve anything. Not as obvious, but sometimes more important, is the sense of isolation involved. He is acting alone, unable or unwilling to get anyone's help.

Going a step further, this card can indicate craftiness, but with the flaw of habitually hiding, often for no real reason, one's true plans or intentions.

REVERSED

The isolation turns around to become communication, in particular seeking advice on what to do about one's problems. Valuable as the specific instructions can be, just as important is the person's readiness to listen and to seek help. The card can sometimes refer to the *act* of finding help, such as consulting a reader or a therapist or simply friends.

Like all else the value of the image depends on context. Where self-reliance is required the Seven of Swords reversed can imply an overdependence on others telling us what to do. When the card reversed appears in opposition to the Fool or the Hanged Man, we must look to the other cards to determine which course – independence or seeking advice – will produce the best results.

Figure 61

SIX

A strange and powerful image, this card more than any other illustrates how Pamela Smith's images reach beyond Arthur Waite's formulas. *The Pictorial Key* says 'journey by water, route, way, expedient'. But the picture of a ferryboat at twilight, carrying shrouded figures to a wooded isle, suggests a more spiritual journey – in myth, Charon carrying the dead across the River Styx. A great silence fills this card, like the silence of Salvador Dali's paintings.

Usually this card does not signify death, though it can indicate mourning; nor does it show transformation, in the sense of Death in the Major Arcana. Rather it depicts a quiet passage through a difficult time. Waite says, 'The freight is light'; and Eden Gray writes, 'The swords do not weigh down the boat'. Though we carry our troubles with us we have adapted to them; they will not sink us or bear us down. On a simple level it means functioning in some difficult situation without attacking the problems. It can refer to an immediate problem or a situation that has gone on for years. Looking deeper we see the image of a long sorrow – mourning is an example, but not the only one – which a person has felt for so long that it no longer gives pain, but has become part of life.

There is another, less disturbing meaning - that of a quiet passage, physically (certainly the literal meaning of a journey must not be forgotten) or spiritually, a time of easy transition. Notice the ferryman's black pole. Black indicates potentiality; where nothing final has happened, all things remain possible. By staying calm we waste neither energy nor opportunity.

The Six of Swords is a Gate. Looking at it with sensitivity and then entering the picture will produce first a quieting effect on the mind and then later, slowly, a sense of movement within the self.

REVERSED

Seen in one way the balance and peace become disturbed; the passage is no longer serene for the water, symbol of emotion, becomes stirred up. So the reversed card can suggest a stormy journey, physically or spiritually. It can refer also to the idea that when we try to attack some longstanding problem, especially one accepted by everyone else, we agitate the situation. As one example, an unsatisfying or oppressive relationship can go quietly along for years until one of the members decides to do something about it. To try to remove the swords from the boat can sink it, for the swords, after all, are plugging up the holes.

In another way, the Six reversed can show communication, reminding us that right side up the people maintain their composure by not speaking or looking at each other. If the swords symbolize unhappy memories and the silence is a defence then communication can be painful. It can also begin healing.

Figure 62

FIVE

One of the most difficult cards, and one of the reasons why some people find the Rider pack too negative. And yet it mirrors a real situation that most people will experience at some time in their lives.

All the Fives show conflict or loss. Swords carry this idea to the extreme of defeat. Sometimes the meaning of the card will focus on the large figure in the foreground – the victor. More commonly we identify with the two figures turned away. They have lost some battle, and now the whole world bears down on them – the water choppy, the sky jagged. A sense of humiliation as well as weakness goes with their defeat.

The image of an enemy can refer to a real person, to an overall situation or to an inner feeling of inadequacy. Once I did a reading for two people who had suffered at the hands of a disturbed and vengeful boss, and who now wanted to know if they should bring him to court. They decided against it when the Five of Swords indicated they would lose. Later two other people did sue the man for the same kind of misconduct. They lost the case.

REVERSED

The painful quality remains, though the emphasis may shift. Where right side up indicates the moment of defeat, reversed extends this to the despair felt afterwards. It is a difficult state to overcome, though other influences, particularly those symbolized by Wands, may help.

Swords are more pessimistic than any cards in the Major Arcana. Taken alone, no Minor suit can show the true balance of life. They break experience into parts and therefore distort and exaggerate. An excess of Swords cards needs more than any other suit to be balanced with experiences and attitudes from the other suits elements.

Figure 63

FOUR

Fours relate to stabilization; for the unhappy Swords this translates as rest or even just retreat. The image shows not death but withdrawal. People sometimes respond to difficulties by isolating themselves, literally hiding in their houses, or simply flattening their emotional reactions to hide inside themselves. This card once appeared in a reading for a man accustomed to dealing forcefully with everyone around him. The card showed him that when his aggressiveness failed, or when his confident mask grew too heavy for him, he hid from the world rather than show his other side or try to work with other people.

Withdrawal, however, can also lead to healing, if the purpose is not to hide but to recoup strength. The card can mean holding back from a fight until there is a better chance of winning. Similarly, by withdrawing for a time after some deep hurt a person gives him or herself a chance to recover.

Notice that the knight lies in a church, and that the window shows Christ giving a healing blessing to a supplicant. The imagery suggests the Fisher King of the Grail legend, whose physical wound mirrored the spiritual sickness of the kingdom. The picture also recalls Sleeping Beauty. Both these figures needed outsiders to awaken them. The King lay ill until Galahad brought the Grail's blessing; and the princess, symbol of a neurotic fear of life, remained asleep until the prince, refusing to be stopped by the fence of thorns (the neurotic will use the force of her or his personality to set up barriers against other people), roused her through sexual life-energy (in the Disney version he kisses her; in folk tales he has intercourse with her). Withdrawal, even for the purpose of recovery, can shut a person off from the world, creating a kind of spell only outside energy can break.

REVERSED

Reversed this card shows a return to the world. Whether this comes about quietly or dramatically depends on the situation. Sometimes the card refers to caution, as if the knight emerges carefully from his sanctuary. At other times the Four reversed can represent other people perceiving and breaking through the fence – the prince coming after Sleeping Beauty.

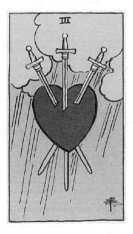

Figure 64

THREE

The Golden Dawn title for this card is 'Sorrow'. Of all the Swords, the Three most simply represents pain and heartbreak. Yet, for all its gloom, the picture brings a certain calm in the symmetry of its swords. To true sorrow we can make only one response – take the pain into our hearts, accept it and go beyond it. The Nine raised the question of how to continue after a great anguish. The Three tells us that we must not push the pain away from us, but somehow take it deep inside until it becomes transformed by courage and love.

Once, in a reading for myself, after a death in my family, the Three of Swords came up crossed by the Three of Cups. At first I thought this meant setting joy and friendship against sorrow. Two cards of the same number, however, often mean a transformation. And the crossing card often emerges from the first in some way. Looking deeper into the reading, I saw the two as connected, not opposed. Acceptance and love can turn pain into joyful memory, an embracing of life.

REVERSED

The healing process becomes blocked when we fight acceptance. If something in life appears too painful we may push it away, try not to think about it, and avoid any reminders. Such an attitude keeps the pain forever with us, and in fact increases its hold. Waite writes: 'mental alienation ... disorder, confusion'. A reading once for a woman showed great potential for development in many areas, yet the outcome appeared very mediocre, weak. In the position of background lay the Three of Swords reversed. Earlier the woman had spoken of the ways in which she had never got over the death of her father.

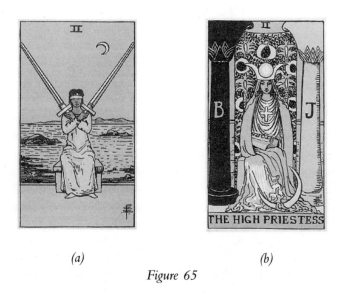

(a)   (b)

Figure 65

TWO

One method of handling problems or opposition is to push every-thing away beyond an emotional fence. If we let nothing approach us, then nothing can hurt us. In contrast to the Eight, the blindfold here shows not confusion, but a deliberate closing of the eyes. The figure has tied it on herself so that she will not have to choose between friend and enemy, for such choice becomes the first step in once again involving herself with other people. The swords remain ready to strike anyone who tries to come close. They represent anger and fear creating a precarious balance; the one wants to strike out, the other wants to hide, and so the person remains tensed between them.

Notice, however, the effect this posture has on the woman First of all, the crossed arms close off her heart. The imagery of blocked emotions continues in the way the grey dress seems to merge into the stone seat. At the same time the heavy swords raise the centre of gravity from the solar plexus to the chest. When a person holds in emotions the breathing becomes shallower, the body becomes rigid. Paradoxically, the attempt to stop emotion makes a person more emotional, as she or he thinks and acts not from the centre but from the constricted chest, seeing not the world, but her own image behind the blindfold.

Compare the Two of Swords to the High Priestess, number 2, in the Major Arcana. They sit in similar postures, but where the Priestess appears relaxed, tension coats the Two of Swords. A veil separates the Priestess from the waters of the unconscious hidden behind her; no veil protects the blindfolded woman from her disturbed pool of emotions. And yet that shallow pool is not the same water as that behind the Priestess.

The weight of the swords makes it easy for the woman to be tipped over into the choppy waters. Because it makes us concentrate on the emotions, a defensive attitude makes us more prone to outbursts, to anger and hysteria. We also might compare the Two of Swords to Justice, whose number, 11, reduces to 2. Justice carries one Sword, for a sharp mind, but she wears no blindfold, preferring absolute honesty.

REVERSED

The balance is lost – or given up. Either the person becomes knocked over by people or problems charging her defences, or else the blindfold is given up for the purpose of either seeing truth or communicating. The latter experience can prove very emotional, even shattering if the person does not receive help from outside.

Figure 66

ACE

The final (first) Sword card returns us to the true essence of the suit – intellect. Pointing straight up for true perception, the sword pierces the crown of the material world. Wisdom leads us beyond illusions and limitations to the spiritual truth contained within life. Many of the Swords cards suffer from the illusion that life contains only sorrow and pain. The mountains symbolize 'abstract truth', objective facts of existence, independent of personal viewpoint and experience. The Major Arcana depicts this truth for us; more than any other Minor card the Ace of Swords reaches through to the fifth element. However, intellect alone, divorced from intuition, will only lead to more illusion. We need the Ace of Cups, that is, love, to find the truth; yet only intellect can take us beyond immediate experience.

Many people maintain that only our emotions express the real us, that emotional reactions alone will lead us to the truth. Often, however, emotions are exaggerated, egotistic, or self-indulgent. But neither will intellect alone bring real awareness. Both truth and awareness must come from a deeper level of spiritual values and experience. And so the hands come from clouds, leading us back to Spirit.

The symbolism of truth holds for mundane experiences as well. In confusing, emotional, or oppressive situations, the mind can pierce the fog and knots to give a clear understanding of the real facts. Truth expresses the Ace in its most valuable form. On another level the card signifies simply emotional force, both love and hate, in extreme forms. Notice the tight grip. The emotions, too, are a gift, enabling us to experience life intensely, but they always remain hard to hold and harder still to direct. For people who have suffered abuse of some kind, focusing on the Ace of Swords can act as a way of bringing to the surface repressed anger.

REVERSED

The grip fails, bringing illusion, confused ideas and feelings, overpowering emotions. The more violent feelings overcome the benevolent ones. Without a clear sense of reality, the mind can fall prey to mistakes created by emotion. Problems become exaggerated; everything, including attractions, appears to be more important than it actually is. In such situations, the Ace of Swords reversed tells us to take hold of ourselves and try to find a balanced sense of reality.

CHAPTER TEN

PENTACLES

Our culture has a long history of despising the physical world. We see Adam's creation out of clay as a humiliation – 'ashes to ashes, dust to dust'. We insult people by 'treating them like dirt'. Emotions and abstract thoughts are seen as 'higher' than anything which actually exists. And yet, just as a painting is the end result of an artist's conception, so we can see the mortal world as the product of God's creative force. For us, creation means the world of our senses. However far we may travel in spiritual meditations we must begin and return *here* – or lose ourselves in the process.

A famous Kabbalistic tale illustrates this need for 'grounding'. Through study and meditation four rabbis entered Paradise. Rabbi Ben Azai experienced such ecstasy that he fell dead on the spot. Rabbi Ben Zoma, overwhelmed by the flood of experience, went mad. Rabbi Ben Abuysh saw what looked like two Gods, a contradiction of the basic tenet or monotheism, and thereby became an apostate. Only Rabbi Akiba entered and left in peace. We can explain this story in terms of Tarot symbolism. Rabbi Ben Azai went too far in the direction of Fire and so burned himself out. Rabbi Ben Zoma allowed his emotions (Water) to overcome his reason. Rabbi Ben Abuysh, overbalanced with Swords energy, took both what he saw and what he read in the Scriptures too literally. Rabbi Akiba, able to balance the other elements in Earth, understood his experience in the true way.

In its earlier form of Coins, Pentacles stood primarily for materialism in the narrow sense of money and work. We still see these important qualities in the Rider pack, and indeed Pentacles carry the problem of becoming so involved with these things that we forget anything else exists – the reverse, in a way, of Rabbi Akiba. The Rider pack, however, adds the greater dimension of nature to the fourth suit. We ground ourselves not just in our work but in a love for the world around us.

As a magical sign, Pentacles symbolize the 'magic' of ordinary creation. Taken simply this means the beauty of nature, the joy of satisfying work. The symbolism, however, carries a deeper meaning, hinted at in the story of Rabbi Akiba. The mystic or magician does not simply ground the self in a negative way, using the world as the opposite of spiritual experience. Rather, the natural world, because it carries a firmer reality than the other elements, because it does not lead so easily to confusion or misconception or ill use, opens the way to more mystic experience.

The very mundaneness of day-to-day life ensures, by a kind of law of reciprocity, that such things possess a greater 'magic' than the more immediate attractions of the other elements. We cannot understand this paradox immediately. We need to ponder and experience it. Two facts about Pentacles/Earth will hint at its true value. First, in a study of religious leaders ancient and modern, the astrologer Ronnie Dreyer has found that Earth signs predominate throughout their charts. Second, Pentacles contains more Gate cards than any other suit.

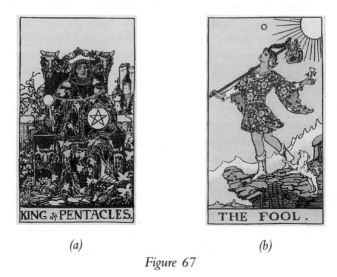

(a)   (b)

Figure 67

KING

The mundaneness of Pentacles goes very well with the social responsibility of the King, who presents to us the very image of the successful business or professional man. The casual way he sits on his throne, the fond way he looks at his pentacle – here the symbol of his capabilities and his achievements – show him satisfied with life. He is generous, even courageous, though not especially given to adventure. The role of King does not frustrate him as it does the Kings of Wands and Cups. Perhaps at an earlier stage of his life and career he might have suffered from impatience or doubt. Now his success has justified his life, allowing him to relax and enjoy it.

Enjoying life means a closeness to nature as well. Though his castle – symbol of his dominant place in society – rises in the background, he sits in his garden, with flowers on his crown, and with grapes – symbol of life's sweetness – decorating his robe. The very leaves and flowers seem to merge with his robe, just as the water flowed into the Queen of Cups' dress. Life is good to him and he means to enjoy it.

A Tarot reading once produced the Fool crossed by the King of Pentacles (the two cards greatly resemble each other in their colour schemes). The conjunction forms a fine example of what I call vertical and horizontal time, that is, the inner and outer worlds. The King symbolizes ordinary activity, accomplishments, social position, success, while the Fool stands for the inner spiritual freedom that allows a person to enjoy these things and build upon them without getting trapped in a narrow materialist view. Consider two people with the same outer worlds – both successful, respected, wealthy; yet inwardly one may be tense, or frustrated, or afraid, while the other remains joyful and at peace.

If we see the Fool as the beginning of the Major Arcana, the King of Pentacles as the final card of the Minor, then the two stand at opposite ends of the Tarot. But this polarity holds true only if we see the cards in a line. If we envision them in a circle, then the Fool and the King of Pentacles become joined together.

REVERSED

The King is meant for success. Reversing him suggests failure or simply mediocrity. The lack of fulfilment brings dissatisfaction, feelings of weakness, and doubt. Taken another way we can see the upside down King as symbolizing the idea of success corrupted, the image of a man or a woman who will use any means to achieve his or her goals.

If we describe the King of Pentacles as someone who needs a vital connection with nature (and not everyone does, despite contemporary assumptions), the King reversed stands for the state of being cut off from that rejuvenating flow. Here too the break results in dissatisfaction, weakness, even psychic danger.

(a) *(b)*

Figure 68

QUEEN

Where the King sits before a castle the Queen's throne stands entirely in a field, framed by roses. Where the King simply glances at his Pentacle, the Queen holds hers in both hands, intensely aware of the magic in nature and the strength she derives from it. More than any other Minor card she represents a love for and unity with the world. The rabbit in the lower right-hand corner stands not only for sexual fertility, but also for the spiritual fruitfulness of a life that has found its own rhythm in the world around it.

Her qualities, as well as the sexual symbolism, relate her to the patron of Pentacles, the Empress. At the same time, as a Minor figure she carries a quality lacking in the archetypal trump of passion: self-awareness. She knows and believes in herself, and in the magic of her life. In readings, this quality of self-trust will often prove the most important.

If the King stands beside the Fool then the Queen belongs with the Magician. Like him she wears a red robe over a white shirt; leaves and flowers frame both of them; a yellow sky shines behind each. Where the Magician manipulates the forces hidden in the world, the Queen of Pentacles joins herself to those forces, allowing them to flow through her into her daily life.

REVERSED

In readings, the Queen reversed can mean not trusting oneself in some specific situation. More generally it refers to psychic weakness. For cutting off the Queen from her vital connection to the earth results, even more so than with the King, in nervousness and confusion. She becomes afraid, even phobic, mistrustful of others and especially of herself, doubting her abilities and her value as a person. This separation means more than being isolated from plants and animals. Rather it means a loss of daily rhythm in life, a dissatisfaction with the whole environment, and an inability to appreciate what the environment has to offer.

In a reading the Queen reversed not only points out these qualities in the subject, but suggests a dual remedy. First, a build up in confidence; besides emphasizing his or her accomplishments and good qualities a person can do this through meditation with the Queen right side up. Second, a grounding of the emotions in natural things, ordinary pleasures, satisfying work.

Figure 69

KNIGHT

The Knight's responsibility for action brings out the suit's practical qualities. At the same time, denying the Knight's natural penchant for adventure tends to distort and narrow his attitude to life. He is responsible, hardworking, uncomplaining. In his best sense he is deeply rooted to the outer world and to simplicity, a quality suggested by the way his horse stands firmly on the ground, with its rider sitting upright.

Though he also holds a pentacle he does not look at it, but instead stares over it. The symbolism suggests that he has lost sight of the source and meaning of his strength in life. In dedicating himself to purely practical matters, he has cut himself off from the deeper things in Earth.

REVERSED

Sometimes the Knight reversed can mean an awakening of those other awarenesses. More often it shows a failure – or exaggeration – of the Knight's more obvious virtues. His steadiness slows down to the point of inertia, his plodding responsibility gives way to idleness. A mild personality, taken just a little too far, becomes weak and depressed, especially if his placidity has covered a repressed desire for either adventure or greater advancement.

The Knight of Pentacles reversed can sometimes indicate a crisis. If a person has dedicated her or his life to a job or some similar outer responsibility, and that meaning is taken away – say through dismissal or retirement – then discouragement and depression can overcome him or her. Another example would be a woman who has dedicated her life to her children and now finds that they have grown up and away from her.

Though such extreme meanings of course occur rarely in actual readings, they remain implied in the Knight's basic paradox: deeply grounded in, yet unaware of, the magic beneath him, he identifies himself with his functions. He needs to discover the real source of his strength, within himself and in life.

Figure 70

PAGE

In direct contrast to the Knight the Page looks at nothing but his pentacle, holding it lightly in the air. Where the Knight is the prototypical worker the Page represents the student, lost in his studies, fascinated, feeling little concern for anything outside them. Nevertheless he partakes of the suit's practical nature by symbolizing the actual work of the student, the study and scholarship, as compared to the inspiration symbolized by the Page of Cups.

The student here acts as a symbol; the Page need not refer to someone actually in school, but simply anyone approaching any activity with those qualities of fascination, of involvement, of caring less for rewards or social position than for the work itself.

REVERSED

Again the Page appears as the converse of the Knight. In reality the two of them split the Pentacles double qualities – practicality and magic. Where the Knight, without his job, becomes discouraged and inert, the Page, without his sense of hard work, gives way to wildness and dissipation, what Waite calls 'prodigality'. Sometimes, however, the card can mean simply relaxation after a difficult task, like a student unwinding after examinations.

Figure 71

TEN

One of the most symbolic and deeply-layered Minor cards, the Ten shows us the very image of the Gate opening to hidden experience in ordinary things. Like the Ten of Cups it deals with domestic life, but where the men and women in Cups celebrate the gift, the family here does not notice the magic all around them. On the surface the card represents the established home, the good life, a secure and comfortable position in the world. The people concerned, however, appear to take the comfort for granted; they find the security boring or stifling. In contrast to the Ten of Cups (the two cards will often appear together in readings) the family here does not seem to communicate with each other. The man and woman face opposite ways, though the woman glances anxiously over her shoulder at the man. The child hangs on nervously to its mother, but looks away. And none of them notices the old man outside the arch.

Though the card expresses mundaneness, magic signs cover it. The ten pentacles form the Kabbalistic Tree of Life, something which appears nowhere else in the deck. Notice also the magic wand resting against the arch; no other Minor card contains one. The arch itself bears a relief of balanced scales (just above the old man's head). Now, scales stand for Justice, and further, for subtle forces which keep the everyday world from breaking into chaos. By 'subtle forces' I do not mean only so-called 'occult' laws, such as polarity, or the law of correspondences (as above, so below). The term applies also to nature's generally more accepted workings, such as gravity, or electro-magnetism Because we learn about these in school we should not consider such phenomena as any the less marvellous. The fact is, we all take the universe for granted simply because it works so well.

Even more than the other images, the old man evokes magic. He resembles the image, from every culture, of the god or angel who comes disguised as a beggar or traveller to visit some family, test their virtues of hospitality and generosity, and then leave them a magical gift. In the case of Abraham and Sarah the angels gave them a son, Isaac. In many such stories only the dogs recognize the visitor (just as in other tales the dogs alone run from the Devil when he comes in disguise). Because they have not buried their instincts in blasé human rationalism, the dogs can sense the wonderful when it comes to call.

Now, most of these tales emphasize the moral 'Be nice to everyone. You never know whom you might turn away'. But we can give the story a more subtle interpretation. By acting a certain way, people create in *themselves* the ability to recognize and receive the blessings in the world around them.

All these hidden signs and wonders point up the basic theme of Pentacles: the everyday world contains a magic greater than any of us can usually see. The magic is all around us, in nature, in the very fact that life exists and that this vast universe does not fly apart.

Inside the arch we see a bright ordinary day; outside darker tones prevail, even in the old man's coat of many colours, with its signs of astrology and ritual magic. The family stand under the arch posed as in a play. For all its firm reality, the everyday world, the comfortable lives we take for granted, and even the troubles and miseries that often occupy our minds, are only a play, in which we all follow the parts set out for us by our upbringing and by society (the recognition that we are a product of our conditioning is the first step to freeing ourselves from it).

The true reality remains ancient, dark, and mysterious. Though we look through the arch the perspective of the card places us outside it, with the mysterious visitor. By merging with this card we can find ourselves beyond the Gate, looking in at the little dramas of our own daily lives. By going further with it we can experience that wild vibrant universe existing in the very centre of the ordinary.

When the hero Odysseus arrived home from his wanderings in the wild, monster-ridden world outside civilized Greece, he came disguised as a beggar. Only his dog recognized him Though he wore rags, they were glorious rags (much like the visitor's patchwork coat) for the goddess Athena had given them to him. Odysseus returned to the domestic world from the wild; he destroyed the evil in his house and re-established the moral order. Yet first he had to experience what lay beyond. The Ten of Pentacles takes us there as well.

REVERSED

If the sense of boredom with life increases it can lead to taking risks, especially financial or emotional ones. Sometimes, depending on the contexts or the projected results, the risks are justified; for instance, the Fool beside the Ten of Pentacles would urge the gamble. At other times the risks come less from need than from impatience with what we already have. This situation becomes more pointed when the Ten of Pentacles appears with the Ten of Cups.

The parallel with Odysseus stands out when the card becomes reversed. Most of that hero's troubles arose because of a streak of recklessness that made him do wild things at just the wrong moment. The urge to gamble stood in opposition to his basic qualities of caution, skill, and foresight. And yet the wildness maintained the balance. Without it Odysseus would not have seen the world beyond the home and family to which he finally returned.

(a)   (b)

Figure 72

NINE

As material cards Pentacles deal with success and what it means in a person's life. Unlike the figure in Ten the woman here is sharply aware of the good things in her life. Her hand rests on the Pentacles, her thumb hooks on a grapevine. Awareness is one of the card's basic meanings, especially self-awareness and the ability to distinguish what matters in life, what goals truly demand our best efforts. The card signifies success – but not simply the material benefits; it means as well the sense of certainty that comes with knowing one has made the right choices and followed them with the necessary actions. The pentacles growing on the bushes symbolize a life that is productive and alive.

'Success' here means not so much worldly achievement as success in 'creating' ourselves out of the material given us by the circumstances and conditions of our life. And 'certainty', in its strongest sense, means more than looking back and seeing that we have done the right thing. It also means the ability to *know* where others can only guess. The Nine of Pentacles stands as the emblem of this quality, the true mark of the evolved person (for a further discussion see the end of the section on Readings);

study and meditation with this card will therefore help achieve such certainty.

We have seen that the Nines show compromises and choices. This theme emerges in Pentacles as well. The woman stands alone in her garden. To achieve what she has, she has had to give up normal companionship. In readings, this symbolism does not mean that the card inevitably advises giving up a relationship; but it does call for self-reliance and a certain loneliness in pursuit of goals.

The image in Fig. 72(b), slightly different from the official Rider version (Fig. 72(a)), comes from an American edition of several years ago. In this Nine of Pentacles a shadow darkens the woman's face, as well as the grapes on the card's right-hand side. Clearly she is turning away from the sun. The symbolism suggests a sacrifice. To make of her life what she wants she has had to give up not only companionship, but also such things as spontaneity, wandering, and recklessness. If the sacrifice seems too great, it perhaps means that we do not value enough the rewards of self-development.

The image of the bird carries these ideas further. A soaring hunter, the falcon symbolizes the intellect, the imagination, the spirit. The hood, however, subdues it to its mistress, that is, the conscious will. Therefore, while at first glance the card means success, a more intimate knowledge of it shifts the primary meaning to that of discipline. And an entry through the Gate of this card will help bring one to the joy of true discipline, which does not cripple, but soars.

REVERSED

The qualities of the card become denied or turned around: lack of discipline and the failure that comes from it; projects taken up and then abandoned; an inability to channel energy into useful purposes. It can mean not knowing what we want, or what really matters to us. The lack of self-awareness brings irresponsibility and faithlessness, to others as well as ourselves.

Figure 73

EIGHT

The way to Spirit for Pentacles lies not so much in success, or even awareness of value in ordinary things, as in the work that allows us to appreciate those things. The Nine shows discipline; the Eight shows the training that brings both discipline and skill.

Work, whether physical, artistic, or spiritual (the Sufi Idries Shah speaks of 'work' as the most basic of Sufi doctrines), cannot succeed if the person thinks only of the end result. Many artists and writers have testified to this fact, warning hopefuls that if they just want to become famous or rich they will never succeed. We have to care about the work itself.

Therefore we see the apprentice lost in his task. And yet work also needs to be related to the outside world. However much we follow our standards and instincts or seek our own development the work we do lacks meaning if it does not serve the community. Therefore, behind his shop – though far away – stands a city, with a yellow road (yellow for mental action) leading to and from the workshop.

REVERSED

When reversed the card suggests primarily impatience and the situations resulting from it: frustration, unfulfilled ambition, envy or jealousy. These things may result from the attitude of looking only to success, and not to the work that brings it. They may also arise from unsatisfying work, that is, a job or career which calls for no skill, no personal involvement, no pride.

Figure 74

SEVEN

From the image of work we move to its reward. Like the Nine the Seven shows the pentacles as a living development from the person's labour. Meaningful work gives more than material benefit; the person too grows. The Seven shows that moment of being able to look back with satisfaction on something accomplished. The 'something' may be as broad as a career or as simple as an immediate project. The card implies that whatever has been built up (including relationships between people) has reached a point where it can grow by itself, and the person can step back from it without it collapsing.

REVERSED

For many people, meaningful work is simply not available. In general the Seven reversed shows the pervasive dissatisfaction, the trapped feeling, that comes from unsatisfying jobs or commitments. Again, the Seven reversed can mean any specific dissatisfaction or anxiety, in particular one arising from some project that is not going well.

Figure 75

SIX

The next two cards, related by their symbolism, stand among the most complex cards of the Minor Arcana, indeed of the whole deck. At the same time they demonstrate the difference between layers of interpretation and that extra dimension I call the Gate; for while the Five allows quite a few meanings the Six shows us the Gate mechanism itself.

On the surface the Six of Pentacles illustrates the idea of sharing, generosity, charity. Notice, however, that the people form a hierarchy, one above two others. The card therefore signifies a relationship in which one person dominates others. He or she gives, but always from a basis of superiority. The scales are balanced;

such relationships are often very stable, precisely because the people are well matched. Just as one wishes to dominate, the other(s) wishes to be dominated. The lower position does not really imply weakness; the dominated person often instigates the relationship, and in fact will subtly insist on maintaining it when the one who plays the dominant role might wish to change.

Sometimes the hierarchy does not indicate a person but rather a situation – emotional, economic, or other – which dominates a person or a group of people. It may give them very little, but just enough to keep them from looking for something else. This can happen in a job which gives material benefit but little satisfaction or chance for improvement; or a relationship in which the people are unhappy but comfortable; or a political situation where people recognize they are oppressed, but do not wish to endanger what little security they have.

The card bears a (distorted) relationship to all those Major cards (the Hierophant, the Lovers, the Devil, and others) in which some force holds together or reconciles the opposites of life. Here nothing becomes truly reconciled, but the situation maintains the balance and keeps it going.

So far the meanings emphasize the two beggars. But what of the giver? He shows generosity, yet the balanced scales indicate he does not give spontaneously, but rather measures out what he thinks he can afford. In other words he gives what he will not miss. Emotionally this symbolizes a person who relates really easily to others yet always holds back his or her deepest feelings.

As we said above, the relationship comes from both sides. Many people will only accept limited 'gifts' from others. A display of strong emotions, for instance, may embarrass or scare them. The same may hold true for people who resent 'charity' and put any offer of help in that category. Therefore the Six of Pentacles may indicate *giving people what they are able to receive.*

I have emphasized these words because they imply something beyond their literal meaning. Most people will unconsciously measure out their giving according to what other people expect from them; they avoid making themselves or other people uncomfortable. On the other hand, in order *consciously* to give people what they need and can use (rather than what they may think they want) one must have achieved a great degree of self-knowledge as well as awareness of human psychology in general. Few people really reach this level of giving; many people who think they perceive what someone else needs are actually projecting their own requirements and fears onto that person. As a more objective source of information the Tarot can help us understand our own or someone else's needs. Because of these meanings, the Six of Pentacles relates to the Nine in the context of that card as an emblem of certitude.

The idea of giving what people are able to receive carries a religious meaning as well. Mystics and esotericists often say that the truth hidden within a specific religion may run almost opposite to what that religion appears to say on the surface. For instance, while doctrine may teach us to control our desires through pious thoughts, the occultist may attempt to bring forth and work with her or his most hidden urges. This split exists because most people are not only incapable of but even unwilling to deal with religious/psychological teachings in their undisguised form. Even many who try may find the truth impossible to assimilate. Consider Rabbi Ben Abuysh, who lost his faith when he thought he saw two Gods.

Idries Shah tells the fable of two men who come upon a tribe which harbours a great fear of water-melons, believing them to be demons. The first traveller tries to tell them the truth and is stoned as a heretic. The second accepts their orthodoxy, gains their confidence, and slowly works to educate them. Like this tale, the Six of Pentacles indicates the manner in which religion, and also esoteric teachings, give what we are capable of receiving. Waite, in describing this card, says 'a person in the guise of a merchant' – not a merchant, but a person 'in the guise' of one. And Nietzsche, in *Thus Spake Zarathustra,* has a hermit tell Zarathustra, 'If you want to go to them, give no more than an alm, and let them beg for that.' Give more and no one will listen.

Yet who is this person in his merchant 'guise'? Is he simply a teacher, or a religious or psychological doctrine? The scales suggest something more – Justice, which stands for truth, not just as 'correct information' but as a living force holding together and balancing the universe. In the Ten of Pentacles we saw this force as the old man at the gate; here we see it as the merchant. *Life* gives us what we need, what we can use. Especially when we put our-selves in a position to receive.

People who work with meditation or the Tarot or similar disci-plines (as well as people doing artistic work) often notice a curious phenomenon. Life appears to conspire to give them what they need to help them on their way. Not a great burst, but just enough to give them a little push when they can most use it. Here is an exam-ple. At the time when I was working with these meanings for the Six of Pentacles I did a Tarot reading for myself in which the Six came up crossing the Knight of Cups. I took this to mean that by keeping a meditative frame of mind I would receive benefit. Now, this occurred some months after my mother's death, and while vis-iting my father I found and began to wear a *mezuzah* (a kind of Jewish amulet) of my mother's. The *mezuzah* was inscribed with the name 'Shaddai'. I recognized this word as a name of God, but did not know what it meant. Two or three days after the reading I went with my father to a synagogue for the Saturday prayers (some-thing I would not have done on my own). On the way in I saw the name Shaddai on some jewellery on display, and mentioned my curiosity about its meaning.

When I looked at the Bible reading for that day I discovered a note explaining the meaning of Shaddai. Translated as 'Almighty' it comes from a Hebrew root meaning 'to overpower'. But it relates also to an Arabic word meaning 'benevolence, giving of gifts'. Not only did the book answer my immediate question, but it gave me a greater understanding of the Six of Pentacles. The 'merchant' symbolizes the force of life, which not only gives us what we need and can receive, but can also overpower us (yet ordi-narily does not if we do not wish it) with spiritual wonder. And I had gained these insights (which, because I experienced them, meant more to me than they would have as intellectual ideas) by literally putting myself in a position to receive, that is, by going with my father to the synagogue.

From the Six of Pentacles we learn that the value of studying the Tarot or other disciplines lies not simply in the specific knowledge gained but also in the frame of mind created by the *act* of doing it. The work itself changes us. We can develop these changes con-sciously and deliberately through the mechanism of the Gate cards.

By contemplating and joining their pictures we allow ourselves to receive their gifts.

The possible meanings relate to the meanings right side up. A lack of generosity, selfishness when sharing is expected. Sometimes this refers to a situation where the person is in a superior position. Then the giver is challenged to give more freely, not to measure out what he or she can afford, but really to share. At other times the card will point up the resentment of those people receiving charity, or its emotional counterpart, pity.

Often the Six reversed indicates that some stable, but basically unequal or unsatisfying, situation has been disrupted. Whether or not this disruption results in a freer or more equal situation will depend on various factors, not least of which is the desire and courage of the people involved to continue a process which they, or some outside agency, have started.

Finally, of course, it means not putting ourselves in a position to receive; either cutting ourselves off spiritually, or missing some practical opportunity, perhaps through arrogance or suspicion of other people's motives.

(a)

(b)

Figure 76

FIVE

The various meanings for this card illustrate again that problem of certitude discussed in the section on Readings. How can we know for sure which meaning will apply in a real situation? At the same time the meanings show the way in which a situation can turn in very different directions.

The Fives illustrate conflict and loss of some kind; in terms of Pentacles this means first of all material troubles, such as poverty or illness. Sometimes it implies a longstanding hardship. Observe that the people, though bent and crippled, are surviving. This card may indicate love, especially that of two people holding together in a bad situation. It may turn out that hardship has become one of the major factors keeping them together, so that relief from their material troubles may strain their unity – or they may think this will happen and therefore fear change.

Notice that they are passing a church. Now, as a place of sanctuary, the church represents rest and relief from the storm. The people, however, do not see it. Human beings can get used to anything, and when they do they will often not see opportunities for change; they will even resist an end to their problems. If we compare these people with the kneeling beggars of Six we see that Five represents pride and independence, sometimes to a foolish degree when help is genuinely offered.

As we examine the card more closely we can discover alternative, even opposed, meanings. The card shows no door to the church. As with many real churches today, which lock their doors like businesses at 5 pm, this church has perhaps shut the people out. The sanctuary has failed. We see first of all a comment on modern religion, which many feel has failed in the task of giving comfort and healing to people's troubled souls. On a simpler level, in many countries the churches have grown rich at the people's expense. Again, compare the Five with the Six. The merchant there may symbolize the modern secular church, giving what material assistance it can (or will), while the people's spiritual needs go unattended.

We can call the previous paragraph the 'sociological' interpretation of the doorless church. If we shift the emphasis to the people we can see a psychological view. Sometimes we may find ourselves in a situation where outside forces – social institutions, family, friends, etc. – cannot help us and we must struggle against the problems on our own.

We can extend this idea of a 'magic' or occult interpretation. In Part One of this book I discussed how the magician, by setting out on a course of personal development, pits him or herself against the established Church, which traditionally acts as an intermediary between human beings and God. The choice may bring practical as well as political consequences. If the magician encounters danger-ous psychic forces, then traditional religion cannot (let alone will not) help him or her overcome them. Compare the Five of Penta-cles with the Hierophant, number 5 in the Major Arcana. There two supplicants submit to a doctrine that guides them in all situa-tions. Here the people have rejected such doctrines, or have simply found them irrelevant.

REVERSED

Waite gives the meaning 'chaos, disorder, ruin, confusion'. This suggests that the situation right side up has collapsed. The people are no longer surviving. While the immediate situation may seem much worse it can sometimes lead to improvement. When people accustom themselves to suffering, a collapse may release them. Whether they now can build something more positive depends partly on themselves and partly on the influence and opportunities around them.

Figure 77

FOUR

We see first of all the image of a miser, and by extension, dependence on material comforts and security for the stability symbolized by the number Four. As if in response to the troubles shown on the previous card the man has given himself a protective layer against any economic (or other) problems that might arise in the future. However, while the Five showed two people, here we see one person, excluding others through his need for personal security.

As magic signs the pentacles symbolize basic emotional/psychic energy. The man here uses his pentacles to close himself off from the outside world. He has covered his most vital points: the crown of the head (literally a crown here), the heart and throat, and the soles of the feet. People working with chakra meditation will recognize the first two as vital point connection to Spirit, and to other people. Covering the feet symbolizes blocking ourselves off from the world around us The man cannot, however, seal his back. We always remain vulnerable to life, no matter how self-centred we try to make ourselves.

In certain situations, the Four, usually viewed as 'problem' card, becomes very appropriate. When life has broken down into chaos,

then the Four indicates creating a structure, either through material things, or by turning emotional and mental energy inwards. The
card remains an image of selfishness but sometimes selfishness may
be precisely what is needed. People who meditate through their
auras will usually, at the end of each meditation, follow a ritual of
'sealing' the aura at the chakra points. This practice prevents both a
leaking of their own energy and a flooding of the self by outside
influences.

Finally, on a very deep level, the Four of Pentacles symbolizes
the way in which the human mind gives structure and meaning to
the chaos of the material universe. This idea does not contradict the
concept of forces balancing nature, as described in Ten and Six.
Rather it adds to that idea, by showing that the mind not only per-
ceives, but actually helps those forces to function. The fact that
human beings exist in the universe as creators rather than as passive
observers forms one of the meeting points between mystical/eso-
teric teachings and contemporary physics.

REVERSED

Here the energy becomes released. The act can signify generosity
and freedom – if right side up indicates greed or confinement within ourselves – but it can also represent the inability to hold our life
together, to give it structure. Once again, in an actual situation the
meaning depends on other influences.

Figure 78

THREE

We return here to the theme of work, seen both in its literal sense and as a symbol of spiritual development. The man on the left is a sculptor, a master of his art. The card sometimes appears in connection with the Eight of Pentacles, signifying that the hard work and dedication have resulted or will result in mastery.

To the right stand a monk and an architect holding the plans of the church. Together the three figures signify that the best work combines both technical skill (Air) and spiritual understanding (Water) with energy and desire (Fire). Observe how the pentacles form an upward pointing Fire triangle, showing that work can raise us to higher levels, while below them a flower sits within a downward pointing Water triangle, symbolizing the need to root such work in the reality of the world and the needs of the community. Reflecting this duality the card, like the Nine, refers to actual work yet may also stand as a symbol of the developed self. These two meanings do not cancel each other out. As observed earlier, practical work, done consciously and with commitment, may serve as the vehicle for self-development.

Part of this card's meaning lies in the fact that such symbolism of psychic development should occur in mundane Pentacles, rather than the often more exotic images of the other suits.

REVERSED

Mediocrity: the work, physical or spiritual, goes badly, often from laziness or weakness. Sometimes the meaning extends to a general situation in which little happens; things continue either getting worse or improving, at a slow steady rate.

Figure 79

TWO

Like the Two of Swords the Two of Pentacles strikes a precarious balance, though in general a happier one. We see, in fact, the very concept of balance in the image of the juggler. At times the card means juggling life itself, keeping everything in the air at once. More simply, it carries the idea of enjoying life, having a good time – similar to the Nine of Cups, but lighter, a dance more than a feast.

Like so many Pentacles, the card implies a hidden magic in its ordinary pleasures. The juggler holds his magic emblem within a loop or ribbon shaped like an infinity sign, the same sign which appears above the head of the Magician, and the woman in Strength. Some people believe that spiritual development occurs only in serious moments. Pleasure and amusement can also teach us a great deal, as long as we pay attention.

REVERSED

Here the game become forced: Waite says 'simulated enjoyment'. Faced either with some problem we do not wish to face, or else with social pressure not to make a fuss, we may pretend to ourselves as well as to others, to take everything lightly. The juggling act is likely to fail.

Figure 80

ACE

The gift of the Earth: nature, wealth, security, a joyful life. On this Ace alone we see no Yods falling from heaven. The Earth, in its completeness and solid reality, bears its own magic.

We have seen with the other cards (primarily the Ten) how the magic will often remain hidden from us simply because we see its products as so ordinary. Here the hand gives its gifts in a garden, a place sheltered from the wilderness seen beyond it. Civilization, when it works well, gives us this basic protection. Through the work of civilization humanity shapes the raw material of nature into a safe and comfortable environment.

Spiritual work leads us to recognize the magic in normal things, in both nature and civilization, and then to go beyond them to the greater knowledge symbolized by the mountains. The exit from the garden forms an arch very similar to the wreath of victory surrounding the World Dancer. As the Minor Arcana comes to an end the Ace of Pentacles shows us once more how, when we are ready, the Gate always opens to the truth.

REVERSED

Because material gifts exist in a way that the gifts of the other Aces do not, they are more open to abuse. The Ace of Pentacles reversed can signify all the ways in which wealth corrupts people – selfishness, extreme competition, mistrust, overdependence on security and comfort.

Taken another way the garden can sometimes stand for protection, either by events or other people, from the problems of life. Reversed then indicates that this protection has ended, and that the person must deal with her or his problems; or that the person wishes to hang on to this shelter after the time has come to leave it. Like the Hermit reversed, it can symbolize a refusal to grow up – specifically, to become independent of our parents.

At other times, however, the Ace reversed can mean recognizing (as with the Eight of Cups) that the time has come to leave the familiar behind and travel through the Gate to the mountains of wisdom.

PART THREE

READINGS

INTRODUCTION

The use of Tarot cards for doing readings – 'divination', to give the practice its proper name - has been controversial for at least as long as the occult, 'serious' study of the cards began in the eighteenth century. Paradoxically, while many occultists will sneer at divination, most people know of no other purpose for Tarot.

Many people today still believe the Romany (the 'Gypsies') invented Tarot, despite clear evidence to the contrary. The connection between the two remains so strong that many women wishing to read professionally will dress in bright scarves and flouncing skirts and gold earrings (balloon pants and brocaded vests and *one* earring for men) and take names like 'Madam Sosostris ' in order to satisfy the public.

The long association of Tarot reading with cheap theatricals probably explains, at least in part, the contempt or lack of interest many Tarot students have shown towards divination. Seeing the Tarot as both a diagram and a tool of conscious evolution, occultists and esotericists will automatically dismiss the use of the cards to usher in 'tall dark strangers' or mysterious inheritances. And yet, by seeing only the abuse and not the deeper possibilities in readings, these occultists have themselves limited the Tarot's true value.

Here is Arthur Edward Waite commenting on divination in his book *The Pictorial Key to the Tarot:* 'The allocation of a fortune-telling aspect to these cards is the story of a prolonged impertinence.' This brings us to an interesting paradox. Because they looked down on fortune-telling, Waite and others have extended the misuse of readings. The derogatory way in which they wrote about it has fixed in many people's minds the image of trivial attempts to predict the future. As to why they wrote of it at all, we can only guess that they or their publishers assumed the public demanded such an approach. After all, even today most people who pick up a book on Tarot care more about mysterious messages than they do about achieving psychic transformation. Certainly the best-selling Tarot books give the simplest formulas for the cards meanings — and at the same time promise all knowledge.

More important than why they bothered to write about it is the simple fact that few esotericists have done much to dispel the image of divination as trivial. This disregard has even extended to the entire Minor Arcana. Because the Minor cards are associated with readings many serious books on Tarot treat them very lightly, if at all (Waite's remark applied only to the Major cards). Paul Foster Case's book *The Tarot*, gives only the barest formulas in a kind of appendix at the back. Many others treat only the Major cards. Almost alone of modern esoteric studies Crowley's *The Book Of Thoth* goes deeply into the Minor cards, linking them to a complex astrological system.

As for methods of doing readings, the most important esoteric studies have given only the barest information, a few 'spreads' or designs for laying out the cards, with formula explanations for the different positions. Again, Crowley is the exception, presenting a characteristically complicated system of readings via an astrological 'clock'.

The impact of depth psychology and humanistic astrology has led many contemporary writers to seek a more serious use of divination. Unfortunately, by treating readings in such an offhand manner, the earlier writers have created a tradition of formulas which modern writers have found hard to shake off. Thus we still find the same sorts of explanations for the Minor cards, such as 'All is not yet lost; good fortune is still possible' (Douglas); and the same brief descriptions of spreads, with explanations such as 'best possible outcome' for the positions. Following Crowley and others, several contemporary books have attempted to widen the meaning of the cards by linking them not only to astrology and the Kabbalah but to the I Ching, Jungian philosophy, Tantra, even Central American mythology. Such linking aids understanding, particularly for those people with a previous knowledge of the other system (it would be interesting to see a book about, say, gestalt psychology which explains its subject in terms of Tarot correspondence rather than the other way round). Still, the emphasis for any careful study of Tarot must remain with the cards themselves, and with their use in meditation and in readings. This section of the book hopes to give at least a sense of just how complex and deeply instructive a tool Tarot divination can be.

COMMON SENSE

Many people say that Tarot readings 'scare' them. What they mean by this is first a discomfort that anything should expose their experiences, as well as their inner fears and their hopes; and second, that a pack of cards should do so. They may approach the Tarot first as a game, especially if a friend or relative lays the cards so that they do not have to pay for the reading. They mix the cards, grinning a little, for they feel foolish; the reader lays them out, perhaps looking up the meanings in a book, and amazingly, out comes the new job, or the unfaithful lover or, if the reader approaches it a little more subtly, perhaps the fear of illness or a painful rebellion against a parent. 'You're making that up from what you know about me', they say, or 'You could tell all that from looking at me, couldn't you? You didn't really get that from the cards.' And then the next time someone suggests laying out the cards they laugh and say, 'No thanks, that stuff scares me.'

The fact is, the future does scare most people. They do not expect anything good to happen. They will settle for things staying the same – a balance of pain and happiness with a large measure of boredom, frustration, and low-level misery; but even such stability appears unlikely. In most people's eyes things can only get worse, and probably will.

Tarot readings teach us many things beyond the particular information we get from them. One of these is the predominance of pessimism. If a person's cards all come out positive, glowing with promised happiness, the person will probably say, 'Oh yes? I'll believe it when I see it.' But if just one card hints at trouble or illness the response changes to 'I knew it, I knew it. What am I going to do?' With such an attitude, imagine how the fear, and perhaps resentment, rises when the dread information comes to them from a pack of cards.

There is another side to this question of accepting the cards. People who go to Tarot readers often do so with a 'show-me' attitude. Since they look at divination as something 'magical' (though not really knowing what that means) they want the reader to demonstrate magical powers. The value of the reading for them lies in how accurately it matches what they know to be true about their lives, plus, of course, a bit of fresh information. To make sure the reader is 'honest', they conceal as much of their lives as possible. I remember one woman who came for advice about her work. Throughout the reading she stared blankly at me or the cards, giving me no indications at all if what I said meant anything to her. Afterwards, however, she went over every card, explaining how it related directly to her current experience.

Another time I had promised to do a Tree of Life reading (see below) for a friend as a present for her twenty-first birthday. When she told someone at work she was going to have her cards read the woman said, alarmed, 'Oh, you mustn't do that. You don't know what these people do. They go down to the city hall and look up everything about you, where you were born, where you live …' My friend didn't tell the woman I already knew all these things.

It does not seem to occur to such people that they have wasted their time and money if they only learn things they already know, along with a smattering of new facts. They seem to forget that they have not come to test the reader but to get advice. How much more the woman could have learned about her career if she had given me the opportunity to go deeper into the relationships between the cards instead of just seeing how close I came to the facts.

Behind the fear and the scepticism lies the same problem: Tarot cards offend 'common sense', that is, the image of the world we hold in common, which is usually the image taught to us by society. We can call this image 'scientific', though only in the strict historical sense of that word as meaning the view propagated by officially recognized scientists (excluding, for instance, astrologers and yogis) since the seventeenth century. Ironically, the natural sciences themselves, particularly physics, are moving away from a strict mechanistic universe. However, culture lag ensures that most people still think of science in nineteenth-century terms.

Thus, the 'common sense' view of the world that arose in one culture – Europe – has held sway for no more than two or three hundred years, and has already started to fade. We cannot deny the achievements of this view, whatever its shortcomings. Most people who denounce science cannot offer any replacement other than nostalgia for a romanticized past that never existed. The danger which humanity now presents to nature ironically testifies to the extent to which humanity has overcome the great threats – starvation, wild beasts, disease, etc. – that nature once presented to humanity. But accepting science's achievements does not require us to banish all other contributions to human knowledge.

Modern Western science began as a consciously ideological movement, deliberately opposing the religious world-view of its time. Its early practitioners and theoreticians, such as Francis Bacon, saw themselves as revolutionaries, proposing a whole new relation to nature, one that would do more than increase knowledge. Science, they preached, would create a new world. Even today, the institution of science retains a dogmatic evangelist character. The fame and popularity of Immanuel Velikovsky derived, at least in part, from the hysterical attacks on him by scientists (in Holland, land of tolerance, scientists attempted to get the government to ban Velikovsky's books). And witness the organization recently formed by Carl Sagan, Isaac Asimov, and others for the purpose of attacking the popularity of astrology.

Interestingly, while traditional science's reputation has fallen on hard times its view of the world remains mostly unchallenged. With some justification and some confusion people blame scientists for the various threats facing life on earth. And yet 'common sense' still means the world as created by eighteenth- and nineteenth-century science. Such is the power of conditioning.

How then do we characterize this 'common' (shared, ordinary) sense? Primarily it insists that only one kind of relationship can exist between events, objects, or patterns. This is the relationship of direct physical cause. If I push something it falls over. That makes sense. Does it make sense if I think about something and it falls over? Or if I push a toy model of it and it falls over?

The common-sense person says no, if events turn out that way it is coincidence, a word meaning that two or more things have a relationship in time; they *have coincided,* but have no other relationship. Causality remains restricted to observable physical action.

But science, even in its most mechanistic period during the last two centuries, had to extend this concept to dubious limits in order to explain the observable world. The earth and the other planets move around the sun. This is a demonstrable fact. We can calculate the mathematical relationships of these moving bodies to such a degree that we can discover new bodies by an irregular movement in those already known (Neptune and Pluto were discovered this way). But the facts do not explain how this happens. No giant hands push or pull the earth around the sun. Yet the regularity of the movement prevents us calling it coincidence. Therefore, scientists invented such concepts as 'natural laws' and 'force fields'. The same person who will say that it 'makes no sense' for someone to knock over a chair by thinking about it will find it perfectly sensible that 'gravity' makes the earth go round the sun (in the twentieth century Einstein's 'general relativity' produce a more complex explanation for the movements of large bodies such as planets, but most people still will invoke the 'natural law' of gravity).

What then of the earlier view – that of 'correspondence', where the relationship between objects and events is that of similarity? Here it does 'make sense' that someone can knock over a chair by knocking over a toy model of it. And it makes sense that the position of the planets at the time of birth should influence personality.

Actually, both these views exist side by side today, though the correspondence view remains less respectable. Certain plants resemble human organs. Various people (particularly 'new age' or alternative healers) will claim that it makes sense that these plants should help keep those organs healthy. Other people will say it makes sense that the two things have nothing to do with each other. The 'sense' of the two groups is not common at all.

Despite this uncommonness, the two views will sometimes overlap. People who wish to justify astrology to the majority often invoke the 'law' of gravity to explain the astrological influences, despite the fact that the kind of influence that each planet is said to exert depends largely on the mythological associations assigned to that planet by ancient civilisations.

Suppose we accept the earlier common sense; does that help us accept the observable fact that Tarot readings accurately reflect a person's life? We do interpret them according to correspondences – the pattern of the shuffled cards reflects the pattern of events. Nevertheless, for many firm believers in the sense of astrology the Tarot still offends. The planets form a fixed and specific pattern at the moment of birth, one determined all the way back to creation when gravity slotted them into their predictable orbits. But shuffled cards carry no such determination. Besides, the planets are mighty beings, ponderously moving through the sky. Cards can appear so trivial. How can we accept them?

For many people, the authority of astrology derives from the vastness of the cosmos and ultimately from God. It makes 'sense' that something so small as a human being should receive its personality from the vast movements of the planets. And even if it might embarrass people to say so, we know *who* set those planets and stars in motion in the first place. But only people shuffle cards. And if they shuffle them again, why, they get a new pattern. So how could the first possess any serious meaning?

Behind this last question lies a very important assumption: that only fixed patterns are real. The fact is, the correspondence worldview can tend to mechanistic attitudes as much as the natural law view does. Both beg the question of God, or first causes. Just as neither explains how the mechanism came into being, the natural laws or the patterns of the zodiac, so neither really requires us to worry about it. God may have set it all in motion, but now it works by itself. Though a good astrologer uses intuition to interpret a horoscope, the chart itself can be constructed by anyone with a little training.

The Tarot, however, is dynamic rather than determinist. No fixed rule governs how a person will shuffle the cards. And they can always be shuffled again. (I have done as many as six readings on a question and had basically the same answer every time, though with important variations, with many of the same cards appearing in every reading. The observation that something works, however, does not explain *how* it works.)

In the 1930s Carl Jung and Wolfgang Pauli decided to study 'meaningful coincidence'. Jung became interested in the subject through astrology and experiments with the I Ching – which frightened him in much the same way the Tarot frightens most people. Pauli took up the subject from a more personal involvement; coincidences seemed to follow him like a faithful, and often clumsy, dog.

Their investigations did not really go much beyond the stage of proclaiming that such coincidences exist and some sort of principle must lie behind them. They did, however, add a new word to the world's languages: synchronicity. Events are synchronous when no observable cause connects them and yet a meaning exists between them. For instance, if we need to consult a certain rare book, and without any knowledge of this need someone comes to our house carrying a copy of this book, we call this conjunction synchronous.

People often use the word 'synchronicity' as a charm against the philosophic difficulties of events which have no apparent cause. When something seemingly impossible happens we say, 'It's synchronicity' and escape the assault on common sense. Jung and Pauli, of course, saw the term as something more than that. They were trying to suggest that an 'acausal principle' could connect events as surely as the causal ones of natural laws. In other words, if we bring bits of information together in a random way, free from the causal connections of conscious direction, then the acausal synchronicity will bring them together in a meaningful way. This is, of course, what happens in divination. The important thing to notice here is that the synchronous principle can only take over if we first remove the causal one. In other words – any method of producing random patterns – shuffling cards, throwing coins – is necessary to give the principle a chance to work.

In a way, divination really derives from a world-view older even than that of correspondences. We can call this view 'archaic' and describe it as one in which God or the gods are present at all times, taking an active part in destiny and the running of the universe. In such a world nothing happens because of any laws, but rather because God chooses to make it happen. Thus, not gravity but the

Great Mother causes spring to follow winter. And she may just as well choose not to make it happen.

For people who held this view, communication with the gods was not only possible but necessary. Not only did they want to keep the gods happy, or at least not angry, but it helped if they had some idea of what the gods intended. People who could not depend on the predictability of natural laws, or the measured movements of the planets, had to ask.

They could communicate with the gods in two ways. First, it was (and is) possible to go into a trance and visit the gods in their celestial retreats, as the great shamans have always done. More easily, and less dangerously, they could let the gods speak through code, that is, divination, using dice, entrails, bird patterns, yarrow sticks, cards.

But why should these random patterns constitute God's speech? As with synchronicity the answer is because they *are* random, because they *do* offend rational common sense; they bypass the ordinary moment-by-moment way in which people experience life. Like dreams they step outside the normal logic-bound language of conscious humanity. And by stepping outside it, they transcend it.

In this archaic view God is present in all things, all events. God speaks to us all the time. Our limited perception, however, prevents us from sensing this communication. It is just as well this limitation exists. As the three rabbis who entered Paradise with Rabbi Akiba learned, God's speech overwhelms, blinds. In fact, as we say in Part One of this book, the veil of ego exists not only as a cumbersome limitation but as a saving mercy from the true power of the universe. The purpose of esoteric training is not simply to remove the veil, but rather to train the self to make proper use of the lightning flash of God's speech. Nevertheless, if as ordinary people we want some information from God – that is, from beyond our own limited perceptions – we need a way to see round the blinkers which cut us off from the world of Truth. We need to produce synchronicity.

Any device which produces a 'random' pattern will serve this function. It is possible that all the gimmicks people use for gambling originally served for divination, and for the same reason. Dice and mixed cards and spinning wheels all cut through the conscious mind's control of the outcome.

Identifying some of the Tarot's ancient roots (I am not suggesting that the Tarot itself goes back to ancient times, only that the concepts behind its working do) does not explain it to modern minds. However, certain aspects of the archaic world-view have begun to return, suitably clothed in the modern terminology of physics and depth psychology rather than the mythological language of gods and goddesses. 'Synchronicity' is one such term.

Modern quantum theory suggests that on the most basic level existence does not follow any rules or determined laws. Particles interact at random, and what we observe as natural laws are actually aggregates of probability giving the appearance of determinism, something like the way a coin flipped enough times will come out to an equal number of heads and tails, so that someone might think a 'law' of balance required even distribution. (Indeed, many people believe the 'law of averages' can order the outcome of some particular' event – 'You've failed every other time, the law of averages says you've got to make it this time' – when the whole point of probability is just the opposite, that it cannot predict specific events.)

At the same time that physics is eating away at the universe of fixed laws, so modern psychology (or at least some branches of it) has begun to look at non-rational theories of knowledge. Where archaic people spoke of the 'other worlds' or the 'land of the gods', today we speak of the 'unconscious'. The terms change but the underlying experience remains: a realm of being in which time does not exist and knowledge is not limited to the images received from our senses. And the methods used to 'contact the unconscious' have not changed from those employed to listen to the gods thousands of years ago – dreams, trances (of which Freudian free association is a kind of lesser version), tossed coins.

We come to the notion that the Tarot works precisely because it makes no sense. The information exists. Our unconscious selves already know it. What we need is a device to act as a bridge to conscious perception.

As pointed out earlier, reaching this level of connection, this synchronicity of uncommon sense, does not depend on what system we use. The Tarot, the I Ching, dice, tea leaves, all really serve the same function. They produce random information. Perhaps in the future more 'modern' ways of producing random patterns will emerge. Most 'pure' might be a system of divination based on the movements and energy jumps of sub-atomic particles. For it is at this most basic level that we can see the most important implication of synchronicity, that existence does *not* follow rigid determinist laws in which all events arise from fixed causes. And yet at the same time, events have meaning. Or rather, meaning emerges from events. From all the random darting and spinning of particles emerges solid matter. From the separate actions and experiences of a person's life emerges a personality. From the mixing of Tarot cards emerges awareness.

If any device will provide meaning, why Tarot ? The answer is, any system will tell us something, but the quality of that something depends on the values contained in the system. The Tarot contains a philosophy, an outline of how human consciousness evolves, and a vast compendium of human experience. Shuffling the cards brings all these values into play with each other.

We might argue that assigning a philosophy to the cards destroys their objectivity in terms of predicting events. Human values and interpretations have intruded in an otherwise pure system. Such an idea, I think, would come from a misunderstanding of 'objectivity'. The Tarot is objective because it bypasses conscious decision, but it is not impartial. On the contrary, it attempts to push us in certain directions: optimism, spirituality, a belief in the necessity and value of change.

The meanings for the cards given in this book leave a good deal of room for interpretation by the reader. In fact, they require it. This is because the practised reader brings far more to her or his work than a detailed knowledge of the cards and their traditional meanings. Just as important is sensitivity – both to the pictures and to the person sitting there nervously and excitedly staring at the cards. A good reader does not simply repeat traditional fixed meanings. Rather, he or she will find new meanings and interpretations, will extend the patterns.

While some people desire objective readings and dislike interpretation, others argue that a reader should not use any definite meanings at all, but always work from 'feeling' the pictures at the moment. Yet to do so will limit the reader to the narrow range of his or her own perceptions. And those perceptions will always come at least partly from his or her own experiences and cultural conditioning. Very few people have reached a level of awareness where they can escape the bias of their own history. For most of us, our emotions cloud our intuition. The subconscious gets in the way of the unconscious. (See the footnote on page 298 for the difference between 'unconscious' and 'subconscious'.)

A reader who trusts feelings can be led away from the truth as well as towards it. But there is another reason why we should work with the traditional meanings belonging to the images. If we do not use the wisdom others have put into the cards, then we deprive ourselves of their knowledge and experience. Therefore, part of a reader's training lies in simply studying the cards, while another part lies in gaining personal sense of them through practice, meditation, and creative work.

Tarot readings teach us many things. One of the most valuable is this necessary balance of objective and subjective, action and intuition. Recently experimental science has 'discovered' that the two halves of the brain do not perform the same functions; the left hemisphere (governing the right side of the body) deals with rational and linear activities, while the right hemisphere (governing the left side of the body) deals with intuitive, creative, and holistic activities. This 'discovery' is reminiscent of the argument about whether Columbus, Leif Ericson, or St Brendan discovered America.' Just as the Native Americans had lived there for thousands of years, so esotericists had known about the split brain for centuries.

When a person has mixed the Tarot cards the reader, if right-handed, picks them up in the left hand, then lays them down with the right. We do this to give just a little more emphasis on that necessary combination of intuition and conscious knowledge. The left hand helps channel sensitivity but we turn the cards with the right because we want the rational brain to explain the pattern intuitively.

In Part One of this book I wrote that readings partake of both the Magician and the High Priestess principles, consciousness and intuition. We can go further and say that doing Tarot readings helps achieve a balance and unity of these principles in their practical states, that of will and openness. Each time we do a reading we assert our will to impose a meaning on the patterns thrown out by chaos. The act suggests not only the Magician (number 1) but the Wheel of Fortune (number 10). The latter card carries a vision of the world in time (remember the Wirth version of the Wheel as resting in a boat – consciousness – floating on the sea of existence) However, meaning imposed by consciousness carries true value only if we open ourselves to the pictures and the impact they make on us. Therefore, Tarot readings Suggest the High Priestess (number 2), but also the Hanged Man (number 12), the image of such a close connection to life that we no longer see ourselves as separate or opposed to it. And the card that connects trumps 10 and 12 can also stand for the emblem of Tarot readings themselves: Justice, her scales forever balanced not by a careful weighing of opposites – so much intuition for so much objective knowledge – but by a living commitment to the truth.

CHAPTER ELEVEN

TYPES OF READINGS

BEGINNING STEPS

The true psychic readers, who are rarer than many people think, can simply take a few cards from anywhere in the deck, lay them out in no particular pattern, and use them as the trigger for going into a trance or simply for releasing the information from unconscious sources.

For most people, however, a spread helps them find the meaning in a divination. As the cards are taken off the top of the pile the reader places them in specific positions, each of which carries its own meanings, such as 'past influence', hopes and fears. The meaning of that card then becomes a combination of the picture and the position. From the symbolic meanings of all the cards a whole pattern will (we hope) emerge.

Whatever spread the reader uses, first comes the mixing of the cards and before that the choice of one card to represent the subject or 'querent' as many writers call the person mixing them. We often call this card the 'Significator' (not everyone follows this practice; some follow it only for specific spreads, in particular the Celtic Cross). We choose the querent card and set it aside for two reasons. First, so that the person shuffling can focus on the picture to keep the attention from wandering. Second, so the deck will then reduce to seventy-seven which is seven, the number of will, times eleven, the number of balance.

Some writers suggest using the Fool to represent the querent in all readings. Often, readers will choose some other major card, depending on their favourites. I usually discourage this practice on the ground that the Major cards symbolize archetypal forces, whereas the subject is a whole person, existing in a specific time and place. Besides, removing a trump from the deck removes the chance of having that card come up somewhere in the reading.

Most readers prefer to use one of the court cards to signify the querent. Traditionally, the Pages have stood for children (some people see the cutoff between childhood and adulthood as the loss of virginity), the Knights for young men, the Queens for women, and the Kings for older, more mature men.

People who have read Waite's *Pictorial Key* will remember his confusing assignation of Knights to men above forty, and Kings to younger men. This system comes from the Golden Dawn Kabbalistic Tarot. In that deck the Knights represent Fire, and Fire, as we might expect from an order of magicians, stands at the head of the suits. Therefore, the Golden Dawn Knights represent mature men. But the Golden Dawn deck (and Crowley's Thoth Tarot) does not contain Kings, or for that matter, Pages, at all; it uses Knight, Queen, Prince, and Princess. It makes sense for a Prince to represent a male younger than a Knight. It does not make sense for a King to do so, and most readers do not follow Waite's instructions on this point, even when using his deck.

The traditional system contains a symbol for a young man, but none for a young woman. Since women jump from childhood to full maturity no more abruptly than men do, I have found it valuable to make the Knights serve either gender, as the Pages do. In fact, since the Kings and Queens symbolize different values and approaches to life, they too may signify either a male or female questioner. A former student of mine, a psychotherapist who uses Tarot as an approach to her clients' problems, follows this practice.

Unless I see a clear indication otherwise I generally choose a Queen for a woman, a King for a man. I remember one man, however, who struck me forcibly as the Queen of Swords, with her great sense of sorrow. When I showed him the card and described it he agreed completely.

Once the reader and client have decided on the figure, they must choose the suit. Usually the reader does this, following one of two methods. The first is colouring. Wands, or whatever suit stands for Fire, represent people with blonde or red hair, Cups light-brown hair and light-brown or hazel eyes, Swords dark-brown hair and eyes, Pentacles black hair and eyes. It does not take much thought to see the drawbacks of this system. Besides its general arbitrariness it makes most Chinese people Pentacles, most Swedes Wands, and so on.

A more objective system uses astrological signs. As described earlier, the four elements signify signs of the zodiac as well as the suits of Tarot. Most people know their own sun signs and if not the reader can readily determine it from the birthday. Of course, most astrologers say that the sun sign constitutes only one twelfth of the person's chart and another element may dominate.

In my work I find it worthwhile to increase the subject's involvement by letting him or her choose the suit. After I have decided the level (Queen, King, Knight or Page) I remove the four appropriate cards from the deck and place them before the person. If the person knows some Tarot symbolism I ask her or him to disregard formal attributes and choose simply by reaction to the pictures.

Usually we do not interpret this 'Significator' card. It stands for the whole person rather than whatever aspects belong to that card. In some situations, however, the choice becomes important. Suppose a married woman chooses the Queen of Cups to represent herself; if the King of Cups comes up in the reading it may represent her husband, or more precisely, since the reading looks at the situation from the querent's point of view, her husband's influence on her. If the husband tends towards immaturity and/or dependence on the woman, then the Knight may appear instead of the King.

Other cards of the same suit may also stand for the subject rather than someone else. If the subject chooses the King of Wands to represent himself, then the appearance of the Queen may indicate the emergence of a more 'female' side appreciation and receptivity. If the querent is a Knight, then the appearance of the King or Queen may represent immaturity, or regression, or a more youthful attitude.

We can call these changes 'vertical' – moving up and down in the same suit. 'Horizontal' changes are the appearance of one or more cards at the same level but from different suits. If the person chooses the Queen of Swords, then the Queen of Cups appearing in the reading may indicate a change in the person. These 'transmutations' as I call them often carry great meaning.

The question of how to interpret court cards – as someone else or as an aspect of the subject – remains for most people one of the most difficult elements of Tarot reading. Usually it takes experience and a strong feeling for the cards to help indicate the correct interpretation. Even very practised readers will often find the alternatives confusing.

After the choice of Significator comes the mixing. If the person is not asking a particular question I instruct him or her to empty the mind and concentrate on the hands, or simply on the Significator. If the reading does concern a specific question I ask the person to focus on that and even say the question out loud to fix it more firmly in the mind.

The method of shuffling does not matter, except that it must be thorough and some of the cards must become turned around to allow reversed meanings to emerge. One method I sometimes recommend is to lay the cards on the table or floor (many readers always do their readings on the silk scarf they use to wrap the deck), then with both hands scatter them all around, like a child playing in the mud. Then I tell the person to bring the cards back together. Besides its thoroughness this method carries a nice symbolism. Any Tarot reading represents a personal pattern emerging from the chaos of possible combinations. Even if we only read ten cards the whole deck bears the imprint of the person who last mixed them. By scattering the deck we return it to chaos; when we bring it back together, it carries the new pattern.

With the cards mixed the subject must separate them into three piles in the following way. Using the left hand he or she must remove a pile from the top and place it to the left, then from that pile again remove a pile from the top and lay it down on the left.

Now the reader takes over, and here again people disagree about how to put the deck back together. Some simply pick up the pile on the right with the left hand, place it over the middle pile and then put these two piles over the pile on the left. Others hold their left hand a few inches over each pile until a warmth seems to rise from one of them. They then place this pile over the other two.

Either way, when the deck has re-formed, the reader, using the right hand, begins to turn over the cards in whatever pattern he or she has decided to follow. Hundreds of patterns exist. Of the three presented here, one I made up, while the other two are variations on traditional themes. Almost any book on Tarot will give further patterns.

THE CELTIC CROSS

Over the years this pattern has proved the most popular. The Cross derives its name from its shape, a cross of equal arms (one card on each side of the centre), with four cards lined up as a 'Staff' beside it (see Fig. 83, p. 288).

As we might expect, commentators disagree on the meaning of particular positions and how to describe them. Some, such as Waite and Eden Gray, provide a sort of ritual for the reader to pronounce while laying out the cards: 'This covers him' or 'This lies beneath him'. Others prefer more convention phraseology. It does not matter which system we use as long as we remain constant. The meanings described below are the ones I use. They follow the traditional system, with certain changes.

THE SMALL CROSS

In every way of laying out the Celtic Cross the first two cards form a small cross of their own with the first one, the 'cover' card, lying directly on top of the Significator and the second lying horizontally across it.

Now, the cover card usually stands for some basic influence on the subject, a general situation or starting point for the reading. The second card, which we always read right side up, despite how it comes off the deck, represents in traditional systems an 'opposing influence', something counter to the first. In practice, this 'opposition' may actually form a second influence supporting the first.

For example, suppose the cover card was the Fool, indicating a sense of following instincts despite what may seem the more

sensible practice. If Temperance crossed it, we could call it an opposition, since Temperance usually refers to caution. But if the Knight
of Wands crossed the Fool, the two cards would tend to support
each other, and in fact the other cards might suggest a need for a
more temperate influence to balance all that eagerness.

In my work I have developed a slightly different way of looking
at the first two cards, referring to them not as cover and 'opposition' but as 'Centre' and 'crossing'. For their meanings I term
them the 'inner' and 'outer' aspects, or some times 'vertical' and
'horizontal' time, or simply 'being' and 'doing'. The Centre card
shows some basic quality of the person or the person's situation.
The crossing card then shows how that quality affects the person,
or how it translates into action. Put another way, the first shows
what the person is, the second how he or she acts.

Consider the example in Fig. 81. The Fool would indicate a
person with an inner tendency to take chances, to follow instinct.
Temperance crossing it would mean that when it comes to action
the person tends towards a more careful approach, blending instinctive energy with more practical considerations.

Figure 81

Another example will help illustrate this most valuable part of a
Celtic Cross reading. The Ace of Cups in the Centre would indicate a time of happiness in a person's life, or more precisely a

chance of happiness, since the Aces represent opportunities. If the Ten of Cups crossed the Ace the two would imply that the person recognizes the opportunities and will use them. But if the Four of Cups should cross the Ace a different meaning will emerge, showing an apathetic attitude that prevents the person appreciating what life offers him or her. The apathy, however, would not cancel out the opportunity.

I have stressed the small cross because of its importance. In some readings the first two cards can tell the whole story, with the others filling in details. As described in Part One the terms 'vertical and horizontal time' derive from symbolic interpretations of the crucifixion, where Eternity, embodied in Christ as the Son of God, intersected the 'horizontal' movement history, that is, the death of one human being. For Christian mystics the fact of the crucifixion allows them – through meditation on the cross and other methods of identification with Christ – to bring a sense of 'vertical' time into the horizontal facts of their own physical existences. In many other cultures the image of a cross symbolizes the four horizontal directions along the surface of the earth, while the crossing point, the meeting place of the four, suggests the essentially vertical direction of the centre. The cross, therefore, also symbolizes the Tarot itself, the four arms being the four suits and the centre the Major Arcana.

In terms of readings, the cross symbolism can show the way in which a person's substance, or inner being, can mix with the way that person acts in the world. It is worth repeating here the original example which suggested the symbolism of crossed time. The reading was done for a man unsure of the direction of his life. A long love affair was ending, his chosen career as a professional singer had not materialized. The reading began with the High Priestess crossed by the Hierophant. Now these cards, sometimes called the Papess and the Pope, at first glance represent contradictory values. The High Priestess stands for instinct, mystery, stillness, while the Hierophant, as the preacher of a doctrine by which people may guide their lives, stands for orthodoxy, planned behaviour, clarity. Therefore, it appeared that the two symbolized conflicting approaches to life. The more I looked at them, however, with their religious imagery, the more I thought of conjunctions, rather than opposites. The two seemed to prescribe almost a way of dealing with life. The High Priestess indicated that within himself this man carried qualities of instinct and understanding that might never fully emerge but could give his life substance. The Hierophant, on the other hand, showed that in his daily life he needed a more rational plan of action; he needed to organize and make definite decisions to achieve what he wanted. But these plans and practical steps would work best if backed by his own instincts and inner awareness rather than by socially-acceptable ideas of proper goals and behaviour. Just as I was trying to explain how these qualities could complement each other the man broke in to say how he saw them as constantly in opposition, how he swung back and forth, giving in first to his desires or simply to passivity, and then moving the other way to very directed orthodox action, such as getting a responsible middle-class job rather than pursue his singing. Part of my job in the reading became to show him how these qualities could work together.

'BASIS'

After the small cross the reader places the next card directly below the Centre. This position represents the 'Basis' of the reading – a situation or event, usually, though not always, in the past, which has helped create the current situation. Because of the way our past shapes us this card can sometimes explain and tie together all the others. In one remarkable reading about a woman's difficulties relating to her husband the Emperor in the Basis position indicated that her relationship to her father still dominated her unconscious sexuality and was preventing her from working out her current problems.

Usually the Basis does not show such a broad theme, but often it does indicate a previous situation, especially if a connection exists with the number or suit of one of the first two cards. Consider these three cards: the Magician crossed by the Five of Cups, with the Five of Swords beneath them (see Fig. 82). The Magician, as the person's being, shows a strong, highly-creative and dynamic personality. The Five of Cups, however, indicates that the person is currently preoccupied with some loss so that the powerful personality has become subdued. In terms of the pictures, the Magician

Figure 82

has covered his dazzling white and red robe in a black cloak. The Five of Swords, however, shows that the loss began as a painful and humiliating defeat. It is this defeat which has dimmed the Magician's fire. But the move from Swords to Cups shows that already a process of renewal has begun. The person can begin to see the situation as one of regret rather than shame. What makes this movement possible is the Magician qualities, currently concealed yet still active in the person's life.

'RECENT PAST'

The next card lies to the left of the small cross and bears the title 'Recent Past'. The term is really a misnomer, for the difference between this position and the Basis lies not so much in the timescale as in their impact on the person. The Recent Past refers to events or situations that affect the subject, yet have passed or are passing out of importance. Usually it does refer to recent events; sometimes, however, it can show something reaching far back or of great importance. In the example above, of the woman whose father affected her so strongly, if the Emperor had appeared in the Recent Past instead of the Basis, it would have indicated that the block was receding from her life, and would not affect her so much in the future.

'POSSIBLE OUTCOME'

The next card goes directly above the small cross. Some people term this position the 'Best Possible Outcome'. However, a little practice will demonstrate the narrowness of this optimistic title. If, say, the Nine of Swords shows up here it can hardly be called the 'best' result. Therefore, like many others, I refer to this position as simply 'Possible Outcome'. Now, since we call the final card 'Outcome' people may find the two terms confusing. By 'possible' we mean first of all a more general trend that may result from the influences shown in the reading. At the moment, it remains vague and may never actually come about. It simply means the person is heading in this direction.

Sometimes the relationship between the Possible Outcome and the Outcome includes cause and effect. The Possible may result from the Outcome. As a simple example, suppose the Outcome shows the Eight of Pentacles and the Possible Outcome shows the Three. The Eight indicates that the person will go through a period of hard work and learning. The Three indicates that this effort is likely to produce the desired result of great skill and success.

Sometimes the Possible Outcome indicates a more tentative result than the Outcome. Here is an example from a reading done several years ago for a woman who had applied for a job and wanted to know her chances of getting it. The Outcome card indicated delays and suspense but the Possible Outcome showed success. When the woman went to find out, the hiring agent told her that they had hired someone else but had put her on an alternate list. Several days later he called to tell her that the someone else had changed her mind and he wanted to hire the woman. The possible had become real.

There is another way of comparing the Possible Outcome and the Outcome, especially if the two contradict each other (rather than complement, as in the examples above), or if they show a direct relationship, such as the same suit or number. In these situations I read the Possible Outcome as something that might have happened but will not. The task then is to look at the other cards for the reason why the outcome should happen instead.

Suppose the Star lies in the person's Possible Outcome, indicating that the person might emerge feeling very free, full of hope, open to life. Suppose then that the Devil comes up as the actual Outcome, indicating bondage to an oppressive situation. What has gone wrong? If, say, the Nine of Swords reversed lies in the position of Basis, this would give us a clue, for it would say that the person holds inside her or him a sense of shame and humiliation coming from past weaknesses and fears, and that the 'imprisonment' symbolized in the Nine prevents the person from realizing the potential of the Star.

These examples will help us to see that the true meaning of a Tarot reading does not come from specific cards but rather from the configurations they form together.

'NEAR FUTURE'

The final arm of the Cross comes to the right of the central pattern. Lying opposite the Recent Past it bears the title 'Near Future'. It shows some situation that the person will soon have to face. It does not carry the same totality as the Outcome; rather it forms yet another influence, in this case the influence of events. If a situation begins in a certain way but ends very differently, then the reason might lie in the Near Future bringing in some new situation or person to change the direction. On the other hand, if the Outcome is very different in character from the Near Future this might indicate that the coming situation will have no lasting effect. For example, if the Five of Wands lies in the Near Future, and the Three of Cups in the Outcome, it can indicate that the person will go through a period of conflict with friends, but that this conflict will not last long, giving way to closer ties, and co-operation. Often such information can greatly help a person come through a difficult time by reassuring him or her that it will not last. And if the opposite should appear (that is, a happy situation will give way to a bad one) the reader can simply hope that the person can use this information well. Bad news is always less pleasant to give than good.

After laying out the Cross the reader turns up the final four cards, one above the other, to the right of the Cross. The final pattern looks like this:

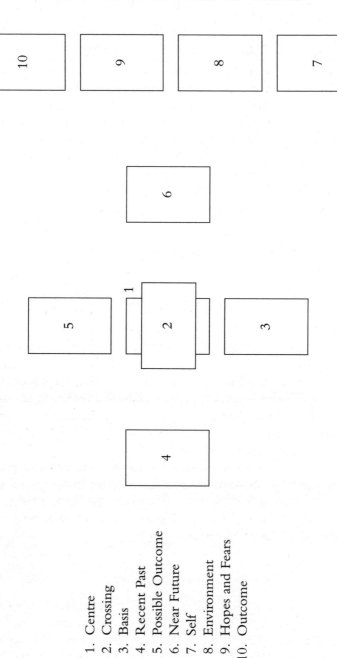

Figure 83 The Celtic Cross Pattern

1. Centre
2. Crossing
3. Basis
4. Recent Past
5. Possible Outcome
6. Near Future
7. Self
8. Environment
9. Hopes and Fears
10. Outcome

'SELF'

The card on the bottom of the Staff is called 'Self', and refers not to the whole person, but to some way in which the person her or himself is contributing to the situation. What attitudes does the subject show? What is she or he doing that will affect the situation described in the other cards? Suppose, in reading that began with the Two of Cups, the Self position shows the Two of Swords. This would indicate that the subject finds it difficult to open up to the new relationship indicated by the first card. The subject's tense, even hostile behaviour greatly affects the overall situation. The outcome would indicate the result of the conflict.

'ENVIRONMENT'

Just as the subject affects the reading so also do the people and general situations around him or her. We call the eighth card the 'Environment' or the influence of 'Others'. If a court card appears in this position it will usually mean a person influencing the subject. Otherwise the card can show either the effect of one important person or of a more general situation. Often it will indicate whether the environment is helping or hindering the direction in which the subject is heading. For instance, in a reading done about work, the Five of Wands reversed in the Environment would suggest that an atmosphere of hostility, trickery, and backstabbing competition is making work unpleasant.

Sometimes the Environment indicates the querent rather than other people. It shows how the subject reacts to her or his surroundings. In a reading done some time ago the Four of Swords in the Environment showed the person's habit of retreating from conflicts with the people around him.

'HOPES AND FEARS'

Above the Environment comes a position similar to Self but one with a sharper focus. We call this position 'Hopes and Fears' for it shows how the person's attitudes to the future affect the working out of events. Often this card will almost dominate the reading,

especially if the Outcome is very different from the Possible Outcome, indicating that what seems likely will not happen after all.
The influence shown by this card can work either for or against the
person. Suppose the reading concerns a love affair, and most of the
cards tend to success, with the Two of Cups as the Possible Outcome. Yet the Outcome shows the Lovers reversed, a clear sign that
the relationship goes badly. If the Hopes and Fears card was the
Three of Swords it would show that the person's fear of heartbreak
has prevented the necessary emotional commitment. At other
times, a very positive card in this position, such as the Star or the
Six of Wands (both cards that mean hope), would indicate that the
person's attitude can create success.

Sometimes this position and that of Basis or Self will work very
closely together, with the Basis explaining the origins of the subject's attitudes to the future. For instance, if the Two of Cups
reversed came up as the Hopes and Fears, and Eight of Wands
reversed was the Basis, it would indicate that a background of
jealousy was leading to a very negative attitude towards the continuance of the love affair.

Notice in this last example that the Two of Cups reversed might
be a fear, but it might also be a hope. We call the position
Hopes *and* Fears rather than the more usual Hopes *or* Fears. The
terminology reflects the fact that the two often go together (something originally pointed out to me by my therapist student). In
work, often people hope for and fear success at the same time,
while in relationships many people will fear the love they seek, or
will half consciously hope for rejection. The duality of Hopes and
Fears shows up most strongly in cards dealing with change, or the
emergence from confined situations to open ones.

Death, the Eight of Cups, the Two of Wands reversed, and the
Four of Wands all deal with these themes of freedom and change.
Some others are the Devil reversed, the Eight of Swords reversed,
and the Star. Very often if the subject and the reader together
examine the subject's attitude to one of these images in the Hopes
and Fears position, an ambivalence will emerge. Confinement is
more secure than freedom. Because the unpleasant component –
the fear of love (or success), or the hope of rejection (or failure) –
often remains hidden from the conscious desires, the discovery of

this ambivalence can help the subject work on creating what he or she really wants.

Seeing this duality at work in one reading after another teaches the reader some basic facts about conditioning. The subconscious (the repressed material we might call the lower layer of the ego – again, see footnote on page 298) is basically conservative, even reactionary. It not only resists any change, whether desirable or distasteful, it also prefers to deal with all situations in the same way it dealt with similar situations in the past. For many people each new friend or lover becomes the stage for repeating the story of Mummy and Daddy. We face each new problem or task the way we we learned to deal with problems as children. No matter if we dealt with them successfully; that counts for less than the safety of having a fixed pattern to follow. The subconscious looks first to security and then to other considerations. And security comes through repetition.

Now, this hidden mechanism of repeating past patterns has built-in survival value. When new problems arise we can handle them because the subconscious automatically compares them to previous problems and then clicks into the ready-made response. Unless a person wishes to embark on a deliberate programme of self-creation (such as the Major Arcana outlines) this system will work fairly well and probably should not be tampered with. However, if a person finds one love affair after another collapsing into jealousy and bitterness, or one job after another failing, then she or he might do well to examine the way the subconscious insists on arranging new situations to repeat the past. One way of at least beginning such an examination can be Tarot readings, with their emphasis on past experience, and what we really hope for and fear.

'OUTCOME'

Finally, the Outcome. This card brings together all the others. More, it balances them out and shows which influences are strongest, and how they work together to produce the result. Sometimes the Outcome will be an event. Then the important question becomes how it came about, not just what it is. If the subject finds it an unpleasant event, then she or he can look at the other cards to see what influences are pushing in that direction, with the hope of changing the situation. If the Outcome appears desirable then a similar study can help increase those influences, already strong, which are tending towards that result.

The Celtic Cross, like any spread, consists of a fixed number of cards. If the reader and subject find the mixture ambivalent, they can either turn over some more cards without a fixed pattern, or else do further reading. In turning over extra cards I usually stick to no more than five (Sometimes asking the subject to choose a number), though at times the initial reading has served as the basis for turning over most of the deck. Usually, beginning readers find it more difficult to interpret cards at random and therefore avoid using them.

Sometimes we may do further readings to get information about a specific card in the first reading. We might have a question about a person referred to in the Near Future position. In this situation some readers will use the card in question as the Significator for the new reading. Just as the original Significator helped the person to concentrate on him or herself, so the new card helps the person focus on the particular question.

A SAMPLE READING

Before leaving the Celtic Cross I would like to present a sample reading done by me some months before writing this book. (I should state that the subject gave her consent for it to be included.)

The reading was done for a woman who had just passed her bar exam, who had recently begun a new love affair, and in general appeared happy and excited about her life. Yet when I turned over the cards I received an immediate sense of sadness. Trusting the cards rather than my conscious impressions I asked the woman if she had been feeling sad recently. To my surprise she immediately said yes.

The cards came out as follows. For the Significator the woman chose the Queen of Pentacles. The first two cards were the Three of Wands crossed by the Knight of Cups. The Basis was Death, the Recent Past the Nine of Swords, the Possible Outcome the Five of

Swords reversed, and Near Future the World reversed. The Self was the Six of Cups reversed, the Environment the Three of Cups, the Hopes and Fears the Tower, the Hermit the Outcome. (See Fig 84).

I began by giving the woman a general interpretation. She was going through a time of transition when many old patterns were dying out. The effect of this was frightening as well as exhilarating. The sadness came from realizing what she had lost, and also from the fact that she had grown up and cut her ties to her childhood. The situation would not resolve itself very quickly – there was even a chance it would develop badly, especially if she let the Near Future, showing stagnation, frighten her into a very negative attitude. The people around her, however, gave her a lot of support, even if ultimately she needed to work it out herself.

All this, of course, was very general. We then went over the cards one by one. The cover card, the Three of Wands, indicated first of all her immediate achievements, not just graduating from law school, but even going in the first place. For as we discussed what she had done she told me how before she had gone to law school she had never taken her life or her abilities very seriously. Now she had reached a point where she not only knew her own strength and intelligence, but the accomplishment of passing the bar exam on the first attempt had given her a solid base from which to look for future work. Even before we discussed these facts the meaning of them came through the image of the man standing on the cliff while sending his boats out to explore new lands.

But the Three of Wands carries another meaning, one very suited to this reading. It implies a contemplative attitude as a person looks over her memories. Actually, this looking over her life came out of the sense of accomplishment. The things she had done made her aware of how her old life had ended. At the same time the boats going out to unknown waters symbolized her situation of not really knowing what she would do next, or even what shape her life would take in the future.

The image of accomplishment and exploration bore reference to other things in the woman's life besides her career. She had recently begun psychotherapy; she had also joined a support group called 'the healing circle'. Both of these activities increased the sense of newness and the unknown, for while they gave her confidence and

Figure 84 A sample Celtic Cross Reading

belief in herself they also made it much more difficult to hold on to past patterns.

Now, the Knight of Cups lay across the Three of Wands and here the second card appears very much as an outcome of the first. For the Knight of Cups signifies an involvement with oneself, with looking inward. The two cards together said that in the centre of her life the woman at that moment was contemplating the past, thinking about what her life had been, and looking to the future. But the Knight of Cups is the least connected to action of any of the Knights. When it came to practical steps she found herself very hesitant.

Below the small cross came Death, the first Major card. Death emphasized the experience of seeing the past die away. All her life the woman had maintained certain patterns: certain ways of dealing with the world, with other people, with herself. Now, because of her achievements these old ways no longer applied. Almost without warning she found herself cut off from the safe patterns without much idea of how to face the future. More about these patterns became clear as we considered cards of Self and Outcome, but here it was simply important to see that the old, whatever shape it had taken, had died.

Notice the resemblance of the Knight of Cups to Death. Since the trump lies in the Basis – the past – and the Minor card in the present, we can call the Knight a practical development from the archetype of Death. That is, underneath she is experiencing the loss of her old life, but on the surface she finds a lack of confidence, emotional as well as practical, about what to do next.

The Recent Past came directly from the Basis. It shows how the two positions can exist almost in the same time frame. In other words, the Basis did not come first and then give way to the Recent Past, but, like the small cross, the Recent Past came out of the general pattern shown by the Basis. Now, the Nine of Swords indicates sorrow, grief. It can at times symbolize mourning. In this case we can think of 'mourning' as a metaphor. The person she grieves for is herself, for we have seen in the Basis that something has 'died'. That something was not harmful, it had simply lost meaning. However, the fact that her life had gone beyond it did not stop her from missing the safe and comfortable ways of dealing with the world. Nor does the card really suggest that she misses her old self because she fears life. The sadness here is more genuine and, in fact, coexisted with the equally real joy and excitement I had seen before the reading.

The first four cards have stressed her inner life; the next two showed the Tarot's ability to indicate trends and events, and in particular to give a warning. First the Possible Outcome. The Five of Swords reversed indicates defeat, producing shame and humiliation. Its presence here showed that despite all that the woman had accomplished her efforts might still come to nothing. Now, sometimes the Outcome card will clearly contradict the Possible Outcome, showing that for some reason the possibility will not become reality. Here the relationship is more subtle. The Hermit is a good indicator that she will not lose what she has gained, but it does not guarantee anything. It shows her headed in a good direction, but not yet arriving, at least not in the practical sense. Therefore the Five of Swords remained a possibility, and the Tarot was warning her to do what she could – use the support of her friends, not give in to her fears, especially during periods of stagnation – to avoid this result.

The World reversed stands for non-movement, a lack of success, the inability to put things together. As the Near Future it indicated that her life would remain unsettled for some time, without much advancement in her career and in other ways. We see therefore that the defeat of her new self shown as possible might come when that self fails to achieve practical results. The fact that the Tarot has warned her of this stagnant period could help her get through it, as could knowing that it is only the Near Future and not the Outcome.

After the Cross comes the Staff. The first of the four cards, the Six of Cups reversed, lay in the position of Self. And here we found a clearer indication of what had died. The card, when right side up, shows a child in a garden with a larger figure giving her a gift. It implies protection, security, the child whose parents take care of all its needs. Here, however, we see the card reversed. Together with the other cards, especially Death and the Hermit, the image implied that she had overthrown this enclosed, protected way of life. In discussing this card it became clear that in fact the woman had spent most of her life with her parents treating her as their 'little girl'. She had let them do this because of the security it gave her. Even now, as she explained to me, her parents, especially her father, could not accept that she had grown up and must make her own decisions, take her own chances. And of course she herself had found the change hard to accept. Going to law school had been the first step. Before that she had never taken herself seriously enough to do something important. At the same time the school had remained another 'garden' – a situation where she did not have to make any choices, but just follow the strict pattern laid out for her. When the time came for her to take her exam, she had become frightened, and in fact had gone to the therapist to help her pass. The therapy had done this, but it did other things as well. It made her see that she was no longer a child who could let other people make her decisions. The sadness came from this loss.

The next card was in some ways the most important, as well as the simplest in the whole reading. The Three of Cups in the Environment indicated great support from friends. In particular it represented the 'healing circle' and the therapist. Its importance lay in the fact that it showed how much uncritical support she could draw from these people, especially important with the possibility of defeat from a period of stagnancy. The Three of Cups does not show support in any sense of charity or self-sacrifice. The three women dance together. The people around her give her strength simply from being with her, from sharing her experiences and letting *her* support *them*. Notice also the contrast between the Three and the Six. Here the women are all equal; the card carries no sense of sheltering or coddling.

The Three of Cups bears a 'horizontal' connection (two cards of the same number) to the Three of Wands as the Centre. Some of the grounding influences in that image – the figure firmly planted on the hilltop – derive from the support given in the environment. Even though looking back on her life, and exploring new areas, remained essentially lonely activities, she could draw courage from the people around her.

In the position of Hopes and Fears lay one of the more fearful images in the Tarot, the Tower. It signifies destruction, collapse, painful experience. Clearly it represents the woman's fears that all she has accomplished will somehow fly apart. This fear could easily make itself a self-fulfilling prophecy, leading to the Five of Swords reversed, especially without immediate success to reassure and encourage her.

The exaggerated fear goes back to the Six of Cups, and its overthrow. She may have given up a sheltered childlike attitude, she may have been looking on her life with excited expectation, yet a part of her still thought, 'How can I do this? I'm all alone now. I'm not protected any more. I've got to make my own decisions.' And from there it crosses to 'I can't do this. I'm not strong enough, it's all going to fall apart.'

When opposition or delay arose, the fear would take over, making it seem like the expected collapse. And the half-conscious thought then becomes 'See? I knew I couldn't do it. Why did I ever cut myself off?' In the reading we discussed the possibility that the Tower also represented a subconscious hope. The subconscious, a very stupid as well as very conservative organ,★ will often refuse to accept the loss of a situation it considered safe or secure. No matter that the self knows, even consciously, that it can never return to parental protection. The subconscious does not accept reality. It can easily convince itself that defeat of the current plans will bring a return to safety.

To become aware of such hidden attitudes goes a long way towards overcoming them, for the subconscious depends a great deal on concealment. We can see this by thinking of the times we have harboured some secret anxiety, only to find when we say it out loud that the sheer silliness of the idea dispels it from our mind. A Tarot reading can act in this fashion by identifying the hidden

★Do not confuse the 'subconscious' with the 'unconscious', whose attributes include courage as well as true knowledge. A great deal of confusion has resulted from the use of these two terms as synonymous. I am using the term 'subconscious' here to stand for material – desires, anxieties, fears, hopes – repressed by the conscious mind as it deals with the outer realities of life. 'Unconscious' means the basic energy of life, that area of being beyond the personal ego. The subconscious, despite its hidden qualities, is really an extension of the ego. In a sense, it embodies the ego's absolute domain, that realm where it makes no compromises with reality. Because it does not concern itself with consequences the subconscious will walk you in front of a truck to avoid an unpleasant conversation. The unconscious, on the other hand, balances and supports us by joining us to the great surge of life beyond our individual selves. The Hanged Man in the Major Arcana gives us a powerful image of this vital connection.

material and showing its probable consequences – in this case, the Five of Swords.

In the position of Outcome lay the Hermit. The first thing to observe about this card is that it does not show success or failure. In contrast with the Three of Wands and the Five of Swords it does not indicate likely practical developments. Instead it points to qualities in the woman herself that in turn will show the way she faces her new situation.

The most obvious meaning of the Hermit derives from its name and basic image. It shows her facing life alone. Now, this does not mean that she loses or denies the support from her environment. If anything, it indicates the need to draw on that support as much as possible. For the Hermit signifies the fact that as much as others can help her she alone must make the decisions. Like the figure in the Three of Wands the Hermit stands alone on his mountain.

The Hermit's aloneness, however, does not exist for its own sake. In the Major Arcana it symbolizes the act of withdrawing consciousness from the outer world and events to consider meaning. And of course the idea of meaning fits quite well in this particular reading. To have the Hermit as the Outcome means that the fears, the delays, and the possible defeats not really matter so much – once the woman accepts her situation. Indeed, the Hermit directly symbolizes psychotherapy.

At the same time the Hermit also hints towards the success of her coming to terms with life. For in its most archetypal aspect it signifies wisdom, true knowledge of the soul gained through removal and introspection. The Hermit's mountain, like the Hanged Man's tree, stands for the conscious mind's connection to the wisdom and life energy of the unconscious.

As the Outcome, therefore, the Hermit indicated that she would understand and accept the changes she had made, half unconsciously, in her life. The mountain symbolism connects the last card to the first, the Three of Wands. The connection, in turn, hints at practical as well as emotional success.

Finally, the Hermit signifies maturity. Through its awareness it carries on the process begun in the Six of Cups reversed, the overthrowing of childlike dependency. It shows her that the situation will resolve itself as the woman overcomes her hesitancy and fears.

In the long run the Hermit's mountain stands not for isolation at all, but simply for a quality the woman was only then beginning to experience – self-reliance, confidence in her own ability and judgements.

Because the Outcome showed a working out rather than a result, I decided to turn over another card to get an indication of how events might eventually turn out. The card was another three, the Three of Pentacles. As a card of accomplishment and mastery, it showed the long-term success that was delayed in the Near Future.

THE WORK CYCLE

Despite its power, the Celtic Cross stills works mostly as a descriptive tool, showing us the different influences surrounding some situation. Though it often implies a course of action ('Take a careful approach, work at setting everything up before you do anything' or 'Things won't work out with this person. You'll find your own self again if you let him go.') People sometimes find themselves left with the question 'What should I do?' While the Tarot does not often give suggestions as concrete as 'Study pottery', or 'Visit your grandmother' it may indicate the sort of action or approach a person needs, leaving the specific details to the individual. As a simple example, the Eight of Pentacles can advise a person 'Keep working at what you are doing. It will take time, but it eventually will bring good results.'

There are other, more subtle, questions that people sometimes ask themselves after a Celtic Cross reading: What if I followed a different set of influences? What if I didn't take this particular attitude to the future, or looked to something different in my past? How would that change the outcome? In other words, what are the possible changes I can make?

To emphasize the possibilities of advice I have devised a new layout for the cards. Based partly on the Celtic Cross and partly on my own arrangement of the Major Arcana, it carries three innovations. First, its whole outlook leans towards advice rather than description. Second, it is open ended; after the reader has reached the last position she or he can lay out more cards, up to ten times the original amount. Of course the reader can do this in any reading, but not in definite positions. The structure of the Work

Cycle, as I call this spread, allows the reader to repeat, and keep repeating, the original positions. The effect is to let the reader look at the situation from different sides.

The third innovation involves reading cards in combinations. In many readings (though certainly not all; see the Tree of Life method below) the cards are read individually, even though we attempt to combine the meanings, as in the Cross. In the Work Cycle, however, the positions include the idea of combinations. Readers will remember that my interpretation of the Major Arcana divides the trumps into the Fool plus three lines of seven cards each, with each line showing a different stage of development. They may also remember that each line breaks down further into three parts. The first two cards signify the starting point for the line – the archetypes or basic qualities the person must use in going through the experiences shown in that line. The middle three stand for the basic work of the line – what the person must assimilate or over-come. The final two cards show the result. Thus, in the first line the Magician and the Priestess indicate the basic archetypes of life. The Empress, the Emperor, and the Hierophant show the different aspects of the outer world facing us as we grow up. The Lovers and the Chariot symbolize the development of the successful individ-ual. The Work Cycle borrows and adapts this tripartite structure.

THE LAYOUT — POSITIONS AND MEANINGS

The reading begins with choosing the Significator and mixing the cards in the same manner as with the Celtic Cross. Similarly, the first two cards from a small cross, interpreted much the same way as in the older method of reading, with perhaps more emphasis on the crossing card being an outcome or development of the Centre card.

After the small cross the reader turns over seven cards in a row below the Significator rather than around it, with the Significator and Cross standing above the middle card. (See Fig. 85).

This line forms the basic cycle, and the reading may stop with these nine cards. However, if after interpreting this line, the reader and subject desire more information or simply another approach, the reader turns over a second line of seven directly below the first, and so on, until the meaning becomes clear.

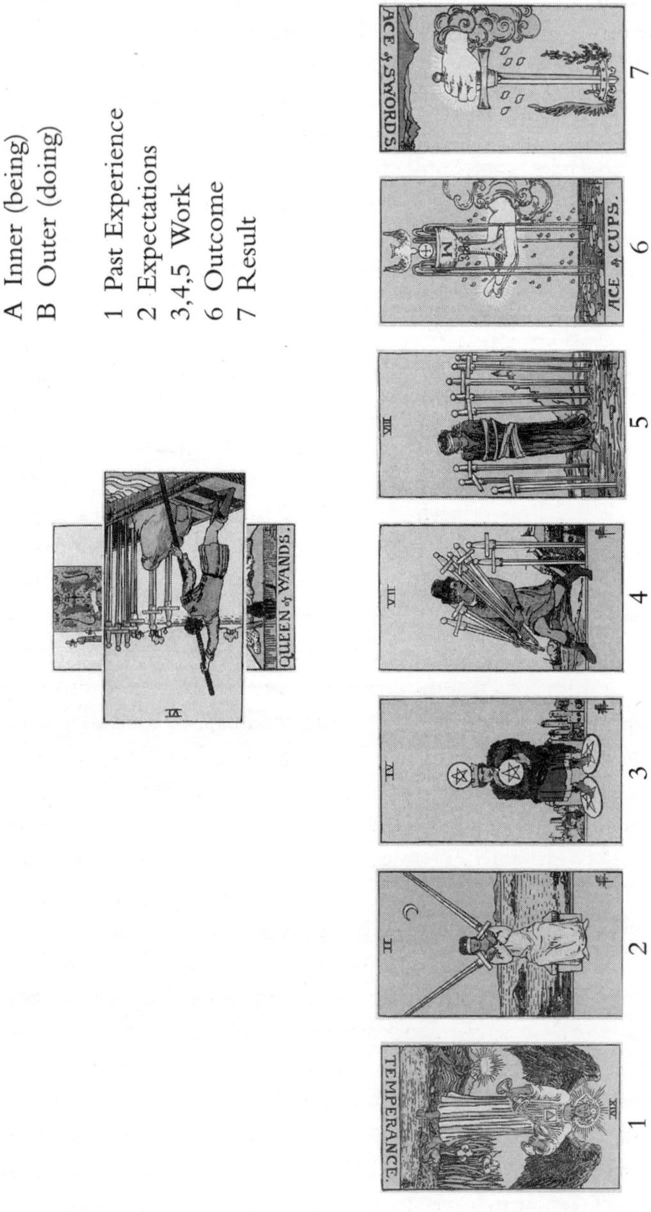
A Inner (being)
B Outer (doing)
1 Past Experience
2 Expectations
3,4,5 Work
6 Outcome
7 Result
QUEEN of WANDS.
TEMPERANCE.
ACE of CUPS.
ACE of SWORDS.
1
2
3
4
5
6
7

Figure 85 A sample work cycle pattern

In each line the first two cards form the starting point. Their specific meanings derive from the Celtic Cross, the first being Past Experience, interpreted similarly to the Basis card in the older form. The second is Expectations, the person's attitude to the future. In practice, we interpret this card in much the same way as the Hopes and Fears position of the Celtic Cross. Together, the two cards show what has happened and what the person hopes, fears, or simply believes will happen.

The next three cards depart more strongly from the older system. They show what I call the Work – situations, influences, or attitudes the person can use or must overcome. In the Cross the positions represent fairly fixed patterns. This is the way it is. The Work cards indicate possibilities, even opportunities. It emphasizes how the person creates the situation – and can change it.

When I began this form of reading I assigned a meaning to each position. The card in the centre indicated Self, the one in the left Others, and the one on the right Events. I soon found it better to give no specific quality to any of them, but rather to interpret them together as simply what the person has to work with in the situation, a combination of possibilities. At same time the three designations are worth remembering, for one or more of them may help to pinpoint the meaning in specific readings.

Let me give an example of the three as a combination. Suppose a reading deals with that old favourite, a new romance. A woman has met someone she likes but does not know how he feels about her, or whether she should do anything about her feelings. The Work section of the reading shows the Five of Wands, the Hermit reversed, and the Two of Cups (see Fig. 86).

Now, the Two of Cups obviously indicates that the man feels about her in a similar way, just as it would in the Celtic Cross. But here the card further advises the woman to tell the man about her feelings. It also suggests she has much to gain from being with the person, and that the love affair, whether long or short, will affect her life quite strongly.

The Hermit reinforces these ideas. Here its reversed position does not mean immaturity, but rather the idea that now is not the time for aloneness. Instead, the woman will gain most from being involved in the relationship. The Five of Wands, however, suggests

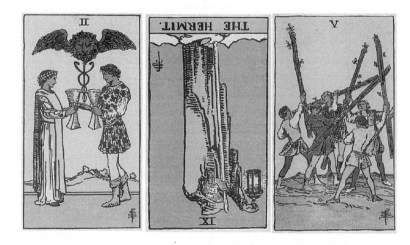

Figure 86

that the situation includes conflict. Because it appears right side up, it does not indicate bitterness or even a serious disturbance that the woman should try to avoid. Instead it shows a quickening quality to their fighting, one that exhilarates rather than drains them. And because it occurs in the Work section, it implies she should *use* the energy released through conflict rather than try to avoid it.

The Hermit coming between the two cards indicates perhaps that the woman has spent some time cut off from other people and now wishes (or needs) to return to the world. On the one hand she can use her new relationship to bring her out of herself. On the other hand, she will find involvement with other people brings quarrels and competition, and she must learn to accept and use these things.

Notice that the three cards do not simply show what is, but rather directions and potentials – things to work with. Now let us consider two possible starting points for this imaginary reading and the different ways in which they modify the Work cards. First of all, let us consider the meaning if the first two cards are the Five of Cups and the Three of Cups, connected by the image of the three cups. The first, as Past Experience, indicates the loss of something – most likely the end of a love affair – and would give the background to the Hermit. Therefore, Past Experience tells us that the

Hermit stage came as a reaction to an event, but a reaction the woman can now put behind her. The Three reinforces these ideas of new involvement. It shows a very optimistic attitude that will likely carry her over the conflicts that arise.

Suppose, however, that we switch the starting point to Swords, specifically the Eight followed by the Four. The Eight would indicate a history of repression, isolation, confusion, while the Four would suggest that this past situation has left the woman scarred, for as the Expectation it shows a desire to hide from the world, to avoid involvement with others. At the same time the Four would represent a fear – or belief – that she will spend her life alone, with no one breaking into the closed church to awaken her and return her to the world.

With such a starting point the Work cards would indicate an important opportunity for the person. They would tell her that this relationship can bring her out of her lonely Hermit state. The time has come to emerge, and if this emergence brings conflicts and arguments she must accept these too, even use them to involve herself more strongly in life.

The last two positions in the line again feature the idea of combination. As the Outcome and the Result, they go beyond the Celtic Cross's single use of Outcome to sum up the reading. The Outcome indicates the likely way things will develop. The Result, on the other hand, indicates the person's reaction to this development, or the effect it will have on the person's life. This effect can be either experience or attitude. For instance, it can indicate an event or further development that comes about because of the Outcome. The Five of Cups followed by the Eight of Cups would say that the person loses something, or something ends badly, and as a result of this, the person decides to leave, go somewhere new, or start a new phase in life.

Or, the Result card can show the Outcome's effect psychologically. A classic example is the Tower followed by the Star, indicating that an explosion in the person's life would lead to a release of hope and energy. This example also illustrates the potential great importance of seeing not just the Outcome, but what comes afterwards. If a reading showed only the Tower, and not the Star as a result of it, it would leave the subject with a sense of devastation.

Very often the first line will give such a strong picture that the person will need no further information. At other times, however, the line may leave the person slightly confused, or simply wishing to see the situation from a different point of view. In this case, the reader may simply turn over another line directly under the first. The positions remain the same, and the seven cards still relate to the original small cross that set out the basic situation. And yet, because we begin with a different starting point, the line enables us to see the situation in a different way.

Besides the new information gained, this method helps answer a question many people ask about Tarot readings: 'If I did it again, different cards would appear, so how can these cards really mean anything? The answer is that the new cards will look at the same situation from a new point of view.

Very often, if a reader sets out a Celtic Cross, then mixes the cards and does it over again, many of the same or similar cards will appear in the second reading. In one pair of readings I did for a married couple (with someone else's reading in between) six out of the ten cards were the same, and the Environment card in the woman's reading was the one used as the Significator for the man. The Work Cycle, because it actually prevents the same cards from appearing, tends more to show different sides to the question.

Sometimes the second line will almost mirror the first, indicating that the situation is heading so strongly in this direction that the person will not easily change it. At other times, however, the Outcome-Result will show a definite alternative to the first line, and then the reader must look to the starting points and to the Work cards.

A SAMPLE READING

Once I did a reading for a woman with a jealous lover. Theoretically the two did not expect each other to be monogamous but the woman knew that if she went with someone else – and someone else had come along – her lover would be upset. She wanted advice on what to do and we did a Work Cycle (see Fig. 87 a, b).

Before the reading I remarked to the woman that the Three of Cups often appears in such situations, right side up if it is going well, reversed if it is not. The reading began with the Three of Cups reversed crossed by the Ace of Cups. The combination showed that despite the jealousies and arguments the situation was giving her a lot of happiness, if only she could work it out. The first line then began very positively with the Ace of Pentacles as the Past, and the Sun as a highly optimistic Expectation for the future. Now, the Ace of Pentacles, besides showing happiness and pleasure, also carries a sense of security, of protected and enclosed situations. For some time the woman and her lover had not related much to other people, building up a tight emotional 'garden' around themselves as the Ace symbolism shows (they were, in fact, living in a remote house in the Welsh countryside).

The Sun shows the child riding out of a garden. The woman hoped now to break loose into wider experiences. And, since the Ace of Pentacles had changed in the present to the Ace of Cups, at least as a possibility, the cards showed that she had begun to let loose, to pour out her emotions regardless of security.

The Work seemed even more to suggest freedom. The Star, the Tower, and the World, all trumps from the last line, showed first of all the power of the situation. In the centre the Tower symbolized the stormy battles and overpowering emotions involved. It also suggested the danger of her secure relationship being broken down by the lightning bolts of jealousy and resentment. Now, the Star here did not particularly indicate a release coming after the Tower, as it would at the end of the line. Rather, it told her that in this difficult situation she needed optimism and extreme openness about her own desires and emotions. The World also indicated Optimism, implying the possibility of combining the opposing goals of a firm relationship and freedom.

And yet, despite all these positive influences, the end cards looked very unpromising. The Eight of Swords reversed followed by the Devil implied that she would make an attempt to break loose from the confining qualities of her situation. The Result, however, showed she would probably fail to get free. The happy and comfortable security of the Ace of Pentacles had become changed to Devil-like repression, with her and her original lover chained to a situation that neither of them really wanted.

Figure 87 (a) A sample work cycle reading

To try for another viewpoint – and also to understand what went wrong in the first line – we laid down a second row (see Fig. 87(b))

This line began more soberly. The Past Experience showed the Seven of Swords, indicating half-hearted attempts to break out of the confinement in her life. It implied that previously she had never seriously pushed the question or faced the real problems involved. This card alone hinted at the reasons for the Devil asserting itself – the woman had never tried to work out what had to be done, had never confronted her lover or the problems between them.

The second card carried this idea further. Justice showed not just a hope for everyone to be 'fair' rather than repressive or selfish, but even more, a desire to see everything clearly and face the truth about herself – what *she* had done with her life, as well as dealing with the reactions of the others. A harsher, much tougher attitude than the Sun, Justice symbolized a commitment to reality, to creating a real future for herself. Notice that the Sun shows a free child, without responsibilities – the opposite of Justice.

The Work in this line – the Nine of Cups, the Four of Pentacles, the Wheel reversed – continued the theme of realism. The Nine of Cups showed a need to balance the emotional pressure with light enjoyment. On the other side the Wheel reversed indicated being able to sort through all the illusions involved. It showed as well the need to gain control of the situation, to refuse to allow the Wheel of events to simply spin her along whichever way it turned. Justice became then not just a hope but the primary method of moving away from passiveness and subjectivity.

Of the three cards in the middle, the Four of Pentacles proved the most interesting, especially compared with the Tower above it. Where the trump had shown her flying apart under the impact of everyone's charged emotions the Four of Pentacles showed her protecting herself. It showed her holding on to her own needs, her own understanding of the situation, despite the pressure on her from her two lovers. The two cards around it indicated ways to do this; first by enjoying herself and using that pleasure to hold herself together; and second by understanding what had happened and why it had happened. The Wheel reversed on the right indicated the need – and the opportunity – actually to apply her hope for Justice, that is, to work hard at understanding the true meaning of all the changes going on in her life.

Figure 87 (b) A sample work cycle reading continued

In discussing these two lines the woman said that the first looked to her like what she *should* want, and the second what she really wanted. People around her talked so much of 'freedom' and open relationships without painful consequences that she felt pressured to want this 'Sun' kind of behaviour. In reality she cared much more for Justice, the truth. The result of the second line's harsher, more realistic starting point showed the sense of what she said. The Outcome card was the Queen of Wands, with the Six of Wands as the Result. The Queen indicated that by looking first to Justice rather than an overly optimistic Sun, the woman would find a sense of her own strength and joy. She would become more dependent on herself rather than the outside situation. From this would come the confidence and belief of the Six, an optimism which would carry the other people along with her.

THE TREE OF LIFE

Any Tarot reading originates in a particular moment; by describing the influences and trends it reaches to past and future. The shorter forms tend only to reach far enough to illuminate some particular situation. When we begin to know the cards better, we may look for some method to give a wider picture of a person's place in the world. The Tree of Life reading, which uses the whole deck and is similar in scope to a natal astrology chart (though perhaps more narrowly focussed on the spiritual/psychological), provides this fuller understanding.

The image of the Tree comes from the Kabbalah. We can see it in the Rider pack on the Ten of Pentacles, drawn in the following way:

Figure 88

In meditation with the Major Arcana, we use primarily the twenty-two positions or links between the different Sephiroth (the ten positions). In divination we use the Sephiroth themselves, adapting their classical names and connotations to enable them to serve as positions in a spread, similar to the Basis, Self, etc. of a Celtic Cross, but much wider in scope. The Kabbalist titles and descriptions are necessarily abstract; they contain a mystic description of the universe's creation and structure, as well as a way towards a greater knowledge of God. Therefore those Tarot readers like myself, who have wished to use this powerful image for divination have chosen more mundane meanings to correspond to the positions.

THE STRUCTURE OF THE TREE

Before going through these meanings, we should look briefly at the Tree's structure. There are two basic patterns within the Tree, shown as follows:

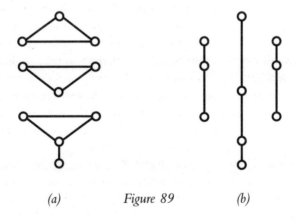

(a)   *Figure 89*   (b)

Figure 89 (a) emphasizes levels of awareness. The top triangle remains closest to God, from whom the original point of light emanated to create the first Sephirah. As the light of creation travelled through the different triangles it became more and more diluted, or even for some people corrupted, until in the last, single, Sephirah it became contained within the physical world of flesh and rock and water. (Such a brief description of course greatly distorts Kabbalist philosophy. I give it here only to show something of the background for the Tree of Life reading.)

The concept of a downward descent of the light is used in divination in the following way. Since we wish to describe a person's life we look at each triangle as an aspect of that person, using a tripartite system similar to the three lines of the Major Arcana. The top triangle signifies a person's spiritual existence, pointing upwards to the subject's highest potential. The middle triangle pointing downwards to manifestation, represents the ways in which the person deals with the outer world, the practical matters of life. The bottom triangle again points downwards but this time into the hidden areas of the self. It stands for unconscious drives and imaginative energy. We can also refer to the triangles as super-conscious, conscious- and unconscious.

The bottom position, standing apart, represents not a personal quality as do the others, but the outer world in which the person lives. We can think of it as similar to Environment in the Celtic Cross, but on a much wider level.

Figure 89 (b) derives from the idea of polarity or opposing forces. In Kabbalah the right and left sides of the Tree signify the way in which God directs existence. The right pillar, that of Grace, tends towards expansion. Its qualities enlarge and open out. The left pillar, called Severity, contracts, emphasizing qualities that restrict. The one gives, the other takes away, thereby maintaining the conservation of energy. But if only those two forces existed the universe would swing wildly back and forth, constantly expanding and contracting. Therefore the middle pillar stands for Reconciliation, a blending and harmonizing of the two principles. Notice that the last Sephirah, symbolizing physical existence, falls in the middle pillar. In the material world the archetypal elements merge into a stable form.

The image of the three columns appears in less abstract form in the Rider pack version (as well as a number of others) of the High Priestess. The dark pillar stands for Severity, the light pillar for Grace. The High Priestess herself fulfils the function of Reconciliation, balancing the yin and yang opposites within perfect stillness.

Just as we need a 'practical' version of the triangles, so our purpose requires a more direct interpretation of the three pillars. We therefore use a recurring pattern for each triangle. The position on the left tends towards the problems arising from that level, the one on the right depicts the benefits of positive direction. The position in the middle describes the quality itself, where the oppositions are blended together. These distinctions will become clearer when we look at the individual Sephiroth.

One further point about the structure. Kabbalists picture the path made by the light of creation as a zigzag, sometimes referred to as the lightning bolt of God. Beginning beyond the first Sephirah (for God's true essence remains unknowable and transcendent) it runs like this:

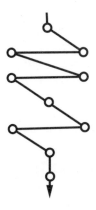

Figure 90

In meditation we use this image primarily to help us advance through the Sephiroth towards union with that aspect of God we experience in mystic ecstasy. In other words, through meditative discipline we travel backwards along the lightning bolt, as if we were unravelling the universe to get to its source. The lightning striking the Tower in the Major Arcana symbolizes this light of illumination.

Another form of meditation, mixed with ceremonial magic, attempts to follow the lightning downwards, or rather to call it down upon the person. Called 'Practical Kabbalah', this use of Kabbalistic principles for magic bases much of its work on the idea that proper ritual and meditation can bring a lightning flash, not just of understanding, but of great power onto the magician. The person following these occult practices is warned not to seek this power for personal gain but only for projects serving the community. (The warnings against misuse given in magical grimoires sometimes strike one as similar to the warnings on pornographic books: 'This material is for medical use only'.)

THE LAYOUT

In divination we follow the lightning pattern in a much more mundane way, as the method of laying out the cards. To do a Tree of Life reading the reader first removes the Significator as in the other methods, and places it high on the reading surface (obviously a lot of room is needed to lay out seventy-eight cards). When the subject has shuffled and cut the deck, the reader takes the cards and begins laying them face down according to the pattern:

1

3   2

5   4

6

8   7

9

10

Figure 91

The Significator remains exposed above the reading. When the first ten cards are placed the reader lays down another ten on top of them, and so on, until each place contains a pack of seven cards. Now, removing the Significator from the deck leaves seventy-seven cards, or eleven times seven. Therefore the reader will end up with seven extra cards. Many Kabbalists speak of an 'invisible' eleventh

Sephirah, known as Daath, or Knowledge. Usually Kabbalists will place this extra Sephirah in the middle pillar, between the first and sixth Sephiroth, that is, between the top and middle triangles. In Tarot readings we place it to the side or on the bottom, and read it after all the others. The fact that we do not place it down in order with the other cards but simply use the 'left over' seven cards emphasizes its uniqueness. The Daath pack does not belong in any of the general areas of influence. Some readers see it as signifying the immediate future.

When I first began doing the Tree of Life readings I used the Daath pack as a general commentary, an extra bit of information applying to the reading as a whole. I have since found a more specific meaning for it, that of Transformation.

In Part One I described the idea, derived both from Kabbalah and modern quantum mechanics, that any change comes not as gradual alteration, but as a jump from one state to another. We may lead up to changes with years of gradual preparation but the actual change occurs as a leap across an abyss. We cease being one thing and become another. In these moments of transformation we can sometimes sense the essential Nothing underlying all fixed existence. Some people describe Daath as the aspect which senses this truth of the abyss. Others point out that Daath links Wisdom (Sephirah 2) and Understanding (Sephirah 3) through its qualities of awareness and reflection.

With these meanings in mind I found it worthwhile to use the Daath pack as a description of the means by which a person changes. Related to the whole reading it emphasizes the connections a person makes between the different levels. The different Sephiroth/positions tend to show distinct levels and conditions of being. The Daath pack helps us see how we move between them. Therefore, the name I have given it is Transformation.

THE POSITIONS AND MEANINGS

What then are the specific Sephiroth positions? The following list is my own, based partly on suggestions from various commentaries. I offer it as a possible system and a guide. Readers who want to work extensively with Tree of Life divination will want to formulate their own positions.

Using the number pattern shown on p. 315, the positions are:

1 KETHER OR CROWN — HIGHEST SPIRITUAL DEVELOPMENT

By this we mean the truest and best qualities of the person and the ways in which she or he reaches these levels. The Crown will not always show very positive or joyous qualities. Some people reach their best development through struggle or sadness. I remember one reading where the Tower occupied the centre of the Kether line, with the Star two cards away from it. The person found it very difficult to develop in any stable way. He tended always to go through cycles of tension, explosion, and release, a theme echoed all the way at the bottom of the reading, when the Devil appeared in the centre of his Daath line.

2 HOKMAH OR WISDOM

The second Sephirah, Hokmah or Wisdom, stands for Creative Intelligence, the ways in which the person moves towards the goal of Highest Development. Usually related to the Crown line it emphasizes the process of development rather than the result. For example, if the Sun appears in the Crown line we would interpret it as joy and freedom, appreciated for themselves. If it appeared in Creative Intelligence we would think of those qualities as the means towards whatever we had seen in the Crown. Like the first line, Creative Intelligence may include unpleasant or difficult cards, if these are what the person uses to grow.

When such cards do appear it is important to consider them not only in relation to their function – to see how the person can use them creatively – but also in relation to the other cards in the line. For example, suppose the Nine of Wands appeared in Hokmah. The reader would first emphasize the strength and determination rather than the rigidity inherent in the card. But suppose the Four of Wands appeared in the line as well. Then the Nine has to be seen as part of a cycle of defence and openness, each of them helping and feeding on each other.

And because they appear in the second line of the Spirit triangle, we would think of them not simply as a cycle repeating the same experience over and over, but as a spiral, leading to whatever images appeared in Kether.

It should become obvious that the Tree of Life reading requires a good deal of experience with the cards and with divination to work properly. Not only must the reader interpret seven cards for every position, but each position must relate to the others.

3 BINAH OR UNDERSTANDING

Completing the triangle is Binah, Understanding. In Kabbalah the difference between Wisdom and Understanding refers primarily to the manner in which the soul contemplates God and itself. In the more mundane experience of a reading we can think of Understanding as those experiences which hold us back from development, or Sorrows and Burdens. Here the cards show the person's restrictions and this time the more positive images need to be adapted to the terms of the line. At the same time the original title, Understanding, leads us to consider how these restrictions can be overcome.

The middle triangle stands for the more ordinary aspects life, and here we begin with the two sides and end in the middle.

4 HESED OR MERCY

The fourth Sephirah stands for Worldly Gains, which means what the person will achieve in life in terms of work, home, money, friends, etc. Usually the line will emphasize areas of success rather than failure. It may also indicate the ways in which worldly gains affect the person's character. The three triangles form one pattern, a fact that usually becomes more and more apparent as the reading develops and connections appear more strongly. Therefore, the mundane concerns of Worldly Gains will often reflect the spiritual awareness of Creative Force above it. And understanding the lower positions on the Tree will often prove the key to going back and interpreting the higher ones.

5 GEVURAH OR JUDGEMENT

Opposite Worldly Gains we find Gevurah, or Judgement, standing for Difficulties. These may include anything from money troubles to loneliness. In one reading the Queen of Swords in this line indicated to me that the woman was a widow.

6 TIFERETH OR BEAUTY

The point of the triangle stands for Tifereth, Beauty. In readings I use this position to indicate Health. Using the Tarot to diagnose specific physical problems can be a very tricky operation, though suggestions for doing this exist, usually linking the cards to astro-logical aspects or other systems. I have found it better to get a more general picture from the line, looking not just at physical condition but also emotional, spiritual health.

One recommendation – observe which elements dominate. Strong Wands suggest good general health through the person's life, though of course such Wands as the Ten or the Nine, as well as reversed Wands, might indicate the opposite. Cups and Swords tend to show the emotional and spiritual condition of the person, while Pentacles often show weaker health or the need to take care of the body. The Five, for instance, would be a definite warning. A predominance of Major cards in the line is more difficult to inter-pret, depending for meaning on which cards appear. Strength, of course, would indicate good general health, Temperance would indicate illness averted by caution, while the Devil might show sickness, or hypochondria. Sometimes a single Major card can symbolize some special situation that has appeared or will appear in the person's life. Time sequences in this line, and in the whole tree, remain a difficult problem, especially for the beginning reader.

The third triangle deals with the Unconscious, particularly the imaginative and sexual drives. In Part One we looked at the idea that super-consciousness, or spiritual energy and awareness, consists of the unconscious transformed and made conscious. Thus, the Tree will often show very strong connections between the top and bottom triangles, with the middle level – the person's conscious experiences – forming a link between the two.

Earlier I described the subconscious as the repressed side of the ego, distinct from the unconscious, or life energy of the person. None of these triangles deals specifically with this sense of the subconscious. Rather, this hidden material can appear throughout the reading, showing problems, aggression, or unfulfilled desires. Unfortunately the vastness of the subject prevents me giving detailed examples. (I apologize for indulging in something resembling the dark hints one often finds in occult books: 'Here I may say no more about this.') I will only point out that we can see the subconscious at work in the seeming contradictions of, say, the Two of Swords appearing as a block in the line of Creative Force.

7 NETZACH OR ETERNITY

The seventh Sephirah, Netzach, means Eternity. Another name for it is Victory. I have used it in this system to stand for Discipline, the ways in which the person can put her or his imagination to work. By 'discipline' I do not mean the strict sort of rules that the word normally conjures up. Instead I mean the deliberate training and direction symbolized in the hooded hawk of the Nine of Pentacles. Creative power under such discipline becomes enhanced and freed rather than weakened or closed in. For it is a quality of the unconscious that its benefit in our lives increases the more we direct it. This is something known by most artists, as well as by people who have worked seriously in the occult.

Most people who do not deliberately work with the unconscious energy simply find that it stays dormant. Their lives may seem flat, or they may think of themselves as lacking any creativity. For some, however, the unconscious is so strong it can break through on its own, bringing chaos or even madness. I remember one reading (not a Tree of Life) done for a man who had experienced a serious nervous breakdown after a series of strong psychic experiences. In the reading the Nine of Pentacles appeared, but also the Hermit, telling him that a proper teacher would train this energy that had erupted so painfully into his life. Discipline, in its best sense, stands for the process of raising the unconscious and transforming it into creative energy.

Because most people do not find themselves drawn, or pushed, to psychic or occult work, we usually find more ordinary concerns reflected in Discipline. It may refer to artistic work, but not necessarily. For some people, the unconscious expresses itself in a career or in creating a loving home for her or his family. The important thing about the line is that it shows the training or work necessary for the person to do something with creative potential. Such blocked cards as the Eight of Swords appearing in this line may hold great meaning for the entire reading, for so much of our lives depends on the release of unconscious energy.

8 HOD OR REVERBERATION

On the other side of the triangle we find Hod, or Reverberation. Other names include Triumph, or Splendour. The divination title for this line – Love and Lust – will usually make the subject sit up and listen very closely. This line shows the person's sexual drive and the way these urges work in practice – in short, what the person wants and what he or she gets. Depending on the person this line too may provide the key to all the others, though maybe not as often as we might expect.

Notice that Love and Lust comes on the restrictive side of the Tree, while Discipline appears on the side of expansion. This construction reflects the fact that our sexual drives often dominate us, making us do things we would otherwise avoid, or preventing us from releasing potentials in other areas. Discipline, on the other hand, makes use of the imaginative energy, leading it in the direction of transformation to the spiritual. Sexual cards may appear not in Love and Lust but in Discipline, suggesting that the person develops through love, in the manner symbolized by the angel rising between the man and woman in the Lovers. For such people love is as much a discipline as a temptation or an indulgence.

I should add that Love and Lust appearing on the side of Restriction does not require us to interpret it as a problem. If the cards show satisfaction and freedom, then certainly we should interpret them that way.

9 YESOD OR FOUNDATION

The ninth Sephirah, Yesod or Foundation, stands for Imagination, in many ways the true foundation of the self. For the majority of people, who do not go through programmes of self-creation the unconscious never does become conscious. It remains both the source and the driving force of the personality. We glimpse this energy in such activities as dreams, fantasies, desires – in other words, what we commonly call the imagination. By calling the Foundation line Imagination we actually mean more than such manifestations. The term here stands for the energy itself, coiled beneath the conscious personality and giving off flashes to the outer world. The cards in this line show the shape and mood of the person's unconscious. Often they will relate very directly to the line of Highest Development way above it.

10 MALKUTH OR KINGDOM

Below Imagination comes Malkuth, or Kingdom, meaning the World around the person. Here we see the external influences, other people, situations both personal and social/political. Usually, of course, indications of these outside forces will appear throughout the reading. In one reading the Emperor, as the woman's domineering husband, appeared in the centre of her Health line, that is, in the exact centre of the Tree. However, the last line emphasizes outer influences, showing also the effect upon the subject. We can look at it as similar to the Environment of the Cross, but greatly expanded.

DAATH

Finally we come to Daath. Though we set it aside from the Tree when dealing out the cards, many readers will want to lay it out below Malkuth, thereby producing a symmetrical tree as well as graphically showing how connections underlie all positions.

Sometimes these cards will clearly refer to one particular situation shown above in one of the three triangles. Usually, we do not give the Daath cards a specific function as we do with the other lines. Like the Fool in the Major Arcana, it moves between all of them, joining things together, helping the general pattern become clearer in the reader's and subject's minds.

The image of the entire Tree, seventy-eight brightly coloured cards, can be an astounding sight. I have sometimes taken photographs of it for myself and for the subject. I would recommend readers to make a chart of the Tree, marking the positions and the individual cards. Most people also find it valuable to make a cassette recording which they can play back later to help assimilate the tremendous amount of information.

If the reader and the subject have begun a regular programme of readings, then a Tree of Life, written and recorded, can help make the readings more effective. Often it works best not to do the Tree immediately, but rather to do one or two small readings first to get an idea of the issues in the person's life. A Tree of Life will then provide a comprehensive view of the subject, which both people can use as a reference in later readings.

To do such a reading requires a great knowledge of the cards and of the ways in which they mesh together. Remember that the astrologer doing a natal chart is usually able to construct the chart ahead of time and consider its various qualities before having to explain it to the subject. But a Tree of Life reading, like any Tarot reading, works best when we interpret the cards as we lay them out.

Remember also that each line contains seven cards. Each line is itself a reading. Sometimes the seven cards appear as a group of individual experiences. More often, a pattern will form within the line. Our understanding of it may move from, say, left to right almost like a story; or we might focus on the centre card as a dominant theme, with the surrounding cards interpreted partly according to their positions. I have often found symmetry an important clue – cards one and seven relating to each other, two and six, etc. Or, the three cards on the right may show one characteristic, while the ones on the left some other, possibly contradictory one. Each line carries its own movement, its own perfection.

CHAPTER TWELVE

HOW TO USE TAROT READINGS

The value of a Tarot reading, at least for the subject, depends on what he or she does with it afterwards. For those people who come to a reader out of curiosity or as a game the reading will probably pass by their lives, like a show they watch from the audience. But this show concerns them, and if the reading means anything real, they will want to put it to some practical use.

First of all, the reader and the subject cannot use the reading at all until they understand it. Therefore the reader must develop skills of interpretation, and the best way to do this is to practise. When you begin do not assume a great depth of knowledge; just keep at it. Do not worry if you cannot see how things fit together, or become confused by all the possible interpretations of some single card. After a while you will find that you notice things that would have slid past you when you first began.

Study. Learn the meanings described in whatever books strike you as valuable. Then begin the process of making your own book. Get a good notebook and record your descriptions, feelings, and experiences for each card. You can do this in words, pictures, diagrams, whatever method means something to you. In the same or another book record the readings you do and what you have learned from them. If some reading teaches you a new point about some single card or combination or the whole deck, record this as well.

Do not take for granted that you know what you have already learned. We all carry certain biases and as time goes by we tend to remember some meanings and forget others Often a card will make no sense because we insist on interpreting it in a certain way strictly from habit, when another, forgotten meaning will clear it immediately. Therefore, from time to time, even after you think you know all the cards by heart, look back on your notes and your books. You will be surprised at how much you relearn.

Keeping a notebook serves another purpose. As described above Tarot readings help teach us a balance between intuition and action, the High Priestess and the Magician. A notebook is one practical way to develop this balance, for it combines your own impressions with the ideas you have learned from published texts. Making your own book is especially important if you are the sort of person who believes what you learn from a published book or a teacher. You are the reader, and in any situation the cards lie before you and no one else. Without the ability to respond instinctively to the pictures you will never be able to choose between the possible interpretations, let alone find a new meaning just right for that reading.

We all possess the ability to respond intuitively, but like any other faculty, this kind of perception requires training and development. A notebook will help here too. Besides giving you something permanent to look at later, the very act of writing them down will give your ideas more substance. You will also find the original ideas will be greatly extended as new points occur to you while you write them down.

You can also train the intuition by spending time with the pictures, looking at them, mixing them, telling stories with them, above all, forgetting what they are *supposed* to mean. Forget the symbolism as you pay attention to the colours, the shapes, the very feel and weight of the cards.

As the reader becomes more competent the readings will become more valuable. The primary thing we get from any reading is information, but the information can be of different kinds. For people with an awareness of the spiritual undercurrents shaping all our lives the Tarot can show what particular shape these currents are taking at that moment. For others, readings may show the likely developments from some particular situation or decision. Look for a new job, start a love affair, continue writing a novel – these are all mundane issues, seemingly far from the mystic concerns of the Major Arcana. Nevertheless, these are the things most people look at in Tarot readings; and in fact they are also the ways in which we truly develop, because they are the ways we involve ourselves in life. They form the reality rising out of the spiritual undercurrents. A Tarot reading can help us examine the consequences of such actions and decisions.

Tarot readings, then, can give us information. But to act on that information, especially if it goes against our desires, remains very difficult.

We can think up endless dodges to deny the validity of Tarot readings. On one level we tell ourselves, 'It's only a pack of cards.' But even those who do not dismiss the Tarot's predictions so easily may think, 'Now that I know what it says I can make sure it won't work out that way.' Around the time I first began to use Tarot cards I consulted them on something I wanted to do but recognized was dangerous. The cards indicated disaster and spelled out quite clear the shape that disaster would take. I then said to myself, 'Well, now that I've seen the dangers I can make sure I avoid them.' I went ahead with what I wanted to do, and the situation worked out, in detail, the way the cards had predicted. Not having learned my lesson I read the cards again, hoping not for the truth, but for some reassuring message. I was using a book of meanings at that time, and when I looked up the Basis card the book gave as an interpretation, 'Failure to follow good advice'.

The problem with making a decision based on a Tarot reading is that we never know how it would have turned out otherwise. Suppose a student considers leaving college and the cards advise strongly against it. If she follows the reading she will never know what might have happened if she had followed her desire instead. Of course the whole point of the reading is that it does tell her what would have happened. But, she will always wonder, suppose it was not true? A prediction, especially from a pack of cards, can never carry the same impact as actual experience. Curiosity alone can make us do disastrous things.

It takes courage to overcome curiosity and desire. Some years ago I read that the poet Allen Ginsberg and a woman lover of his were thinking of having a baby together. They did a reading, with the Tarot or the I Ching, I forget which, and got a negative prediction. They gave up the idea. I do not know how much they really wanted a child, but I remember admiring their strength in resisting the desire. I once did not go to a potentially valuable conference because the cards showed me unpleasant consequences. I was able to recognize the truth of what the cards indicated, at least in regard to what I would have contributed to the situation. Even so, I found it difficult not to ignore the information and go ahead.

We can think up some truly marvellous excuses for avoiding the obvious truth of a reading. If we respect the cards too much to simply declare them nonsense, we will often look for certain 'false' images to discredit the whole reading. Does the Outcome card not seem to fit the situation? Rather than interpret it in the light of the others, we will write off the whole reading.

Some books advise readers never to read for themselves because of the lack of objectivity. For a long time I went to a friend for readings and she to me, because neither of us trusted ourselves to interpret our own cards honestly. When I started doing my own readings I still found it hard to overcome various mental tricks to avoid unpleasant images. My favourite worked as follows: I could not ignore the cards I did not like or simply declare them untrue or exaggerated. That would have seemed too obvious. Therefore I looked in the reading for some very positive image, such as the Ace of Cups, and said to myself, 'Well, that can't be true, nothing so good could come out of this mess.' And then I would dismiss the whole reading on the grounds that if this one card made no sense none of the others did. Another trick I discovered myself doing was to lay out the cards very casually, so if something bad came up I could think, 'Well, I didn't really mean it, I didn't do it seriously.' I could only read for myself when I began treating the readings in the same way I would anyone else's, mixing the cards carefully, working at the images, trying to get some direction for action (or inaction).

A reading will not always give a clear yes or no answer to a question. It may show simply a complex of trends and influences. Sometimes the reading does not involve a choice because of an ongoing situation which cannot easily be avoided. Then specific images and meanings become very important. The Tarot can help us pinpoint the important elements in the situation, the ones that need the most work to change, or bring about, the predicted outcome.

People may use the idea, 'Now that I know what it says, I can do something about it' as an excuse to follow their desires. Nevertheless, the statement remains true. Maybe we have a very pessimistic attitude or an exaggerated fear, or an unreasonable hope. To recognize such things helps us gain a clearer perspective. Maybe our past experience governs our behaviour or confuses what we expect from the future. Knowing this consciously can put us on the way to overcoming it. Or maybe the cards will show us someone else's jealousy or vindictiveness; we can then take steps to free ourselves from that person's influence. Or, if the cards show love, and support from someone, we know we can trust that person.

All these things require some sort of response to make them real. We cannot expect to make use of a person's friendship if we do not make ourselves open to it. Wherever possible the reader should try to point out to the subject definite steps which can be taken to make best use of the information. If the reader cannot recommend a concrete course of action then he or she should point out what area the subject needs to work on.

Above all, the reader must learn to form a coherent pattern from the reading. Often, beginning readers will learn the cards and advance to the point where they can skilfully interpret each image in its specific position. At the end the subject finds him or herself with a jumble of different points and no clear idea of how it all fits together. A good reader can sum up what the reading says in a few sentences. Usually I will try to do this at both the beginning and end of the reading, impressing on the subject's mind the most important points . Does the Environment support or hinder? Do the person's Expectations help or hurt ? Will the Outcome bring a valuable Result? The subject needs these questions answered, not just in all their complexity, but also in as simple a way as possible. And how does one thing come out of another? How does the past help form the future? What does the person contribute to the overall situation?

Along with coherency comes the need for a positive approach. It is not enough to depict things as they are. The person wants to know what to do, what not to do. If the cards show something good, the subject still needs to know how to help this along. And if they show disaster the reader must say so, but can also say what, if anything, the person can do. What brings about this unpleasant Outcome? Can these influences be altered or avoided? How can the person counteract, or at least cushion it ? What elements show other possibilities? Can we look for anything good to come out of it?

If the Outcome arises from some particular course of action, should the person abandon it? When we do a Tarot reading for someone we take on the responsibility of trying to send that person in a positive direction.

Beyond specific suggestions of do this rather than that, lies a wider area of possible action derived from the ways the suits balance each other. In the introduction to each suit we considered its problems and the way we could 'add' other suits/elements. In practice, this adding is often difficult to achieve, because it means breaking the pattern shown in the reading itself. For this very reason, however, it is worth trying in situations where the reading shows a dead end if the person stays with the elements given.

The most direct way to bring in an outside influence involves simple suggestions. If the reading indicates a need for the grounding influence of Pentacles, the subject can try doing more physical things, such as sports or gardening, or paying more attention to more mundane activities, such as work or study or keeping busy around the house. If the reading shows a need for the watery qualities of Cups, then the reader may emphasize the person's dreams and fantasies, and may suggest activities such as meditation or drawing. A person can fill a need for Wands by becoming more active physically, competing with other people, or starting new projects. And a need for Swords would call for a sober, carefully thought out approach to the person's situation. The important thing about these recommendations is that they reach beyond the reading. They deal with the cards that do not appear as well as the ones that do. Therefore, beginning readers should use this method carefully, lest they assume too much knowledge and control on their part.

MEDITATION

So far, we have considered practical responses to the information gained from a reading. But a Tarot reading is not the words describing it; it is rather a series of pictures. And the most direct response to a reading depends on working with the pictures themselves. For people who know the cards well, or for people with some experience in meditation, it becomes possible to work directly with the images to help bring about the effects associated with that card. There is nothing vague or mysterious about this process. It requires concentration as well as instinctive feeling, and it does not replace practical steps. On the contrary, it helps to make those steps more accessible. For if the card Strength appears in a reading as something we need in our life, why not let the card itself help give it to us?

Besides actual meditation I often recommend to people that they carry a certain card around with them, and try to remain conscious of it being there, taking it out from time to time looking at it, thinking about what it means. The constant awareness helps keep the entire reading in focus as well.

Meditation can also help to bring in new influences from outside the reading. Suppose the Star does not appear in the reading, but as the reader we think it *should*. In other words, the archetype of the Star seems to us to symbolize exactly those qualities the person needs. Now, we can show the person the card and discuss the ideas associated with it. It is more valuable, however, to give the person an actual experience of the card.

Briefly, the method works as follows. We begin by leading the person into a meditative state; help him or her to relax, to breathe deeply, to release all the thoughts and tensions cluttering up consciousness. When the subject has reached this level (and with a little experience we can sense this), we then begin to give suggestions leading into the card. The suggestions may be a description of the card to set the scene (with the Empress, for example, 'You are in a garden full of flowers, with a river running alongside it. There is a woman lying on a couch …') or more simply, basic images such as sun, water, wind, that belong to the card's archetypal qualities.

Usually it is best to keep these opening suggestions as simple as possible. If we describe the card we should not try to include all the details. Let the subject create the actual impressions. We function only as a guide to urge the person along. Some people follow an alternative approach, often called path-working because they use it for moving along the paths on the Tree of Life. In this method, the guide talks more or less the whole time, making sure the person experiences a particular set of images.

We can keep the experience on this basic level or we can develop it further. We can give more complex suggestions, and start asking questions – 'What do you see?' 'What is the person doing?' 'Can you hear anything? ' – so that the subject begins to extend the fantasy beyond our directions. Sometimes the meditation will allow the person to experience the archetypal elements in a new way. At other times it may go even further; the images will transform themselves, releasing some intense awareness from inside the person. A number of times I have led a group meditation with a class, and afterwards have had someone tell me that the meditation has allowed him or her to resolve some longstanding problem or emotional block. Such breakthroughs, of course, came from the people themselves. They were ready to go beyond their current state to a new level, had been ready for some time, but could not bring themselves to cross over. The meditation allowed them to do this without realizing it until it had happened.

Meditation can also help a person develop a deeper and more personal sense of some particular card. Once, I did a meditation with someone who found the Emperor a hard remote image, almost frightening, and certainly unattractive. I began by setting the scene for her – a stony desert by a narrow image. This then opened out to a vast plain filled with the Emperor's subjects. When I pushed her to describe these people she saw them all hooded – that is, faceless – and bent over, working on robot-like tasks. The Emperor's fierce expression kept the people from daring to look at him. The people symbolized the woman, and her unwillingness to go more deeply into the card.

I then told the woman to do just that – not just look at the Emperor but go right up to him. When her fantasy-self did this a strange thing happened. The Emperor changed from a despot to a kind of harmless puppet, while from behind him rose a vast ghost or spirit figure, beautiful and benevolent. The woman's fear and reaction against the social structure of the Emperor had given way to a sense of the spiritual structure underlying the universe.

This experience not only gave the *woman* a much greater sense of the Emperor's deeper significance; it had the same effect on me. With her I went beyond the image of the Emperor as society to the more occult meaning of the card as symbolizing the cosmos itself. Whenever we give someone a meditation we take part in it ourselves.

At the same time, we can only lead such an exercise with another person after we have gained some experience ourselves. If you are a beginner in meditation you should realize above all that meditation tends to work better the more you do it. If you have never tried it before, it may have a powerful effect the first time you try. More likely, however, you will find it difficult to concentrate, or will simply become physically uncomfortable trying to sit without moving. Keep at it, and if possible go to a teacher for lessons in such basics as breathing and posture.

I am not going to recommend any specific techniques for putting yourself into a meditative state. There are a great many books and classes on this subject, and many people will find they need to try a few before they find the best method that works best for them. Though most of these technique will adapt themselves to work with Tarot, those which involve visualization (as compared to those emphasizing chanting or total emptiness of mind) will transfer most easily.

Different people use different methods to bring the card into their meditations. Some start with the eyes closed and do not look at the card until they have reached a certain state; others do the opposite. They begin by staring at the card until they reach a certain unity with it, then close their eyes and let the images continue from there. Others hold the card at arm's length, then draw it slowly towards the solar plexus, 'bringing it into the aura'.

However you begin I recommend working with the images and the feelings arising from the card instead of the symbolism you have learned to associate with it. Let the picture affect you, allow your reactions to it to surface and then slide away from you before they block any further experience. I have sometimes found it useful to stare without focussing at the card, so that the symbols and forms dissolve into colour and shape.

At other times, particularly when giving a meditation to someone else, I will ignore the actual picture and suggest some scene associated with it. For instance, for the Fool, instead of that particular person in his multi-coloured suit, I will use a simpler image of a mountain top and clear sunlight. It is more important to set the person, or yourself, in the scene than to follow the card exactly.

Movement or posture can also help to evoke some cards. For the Magician you might stand or sit with one arm raised 'towards heaven' and the other pointing at the earth.

Sometimes the meditation will go no further than an awareness of the card, or a discovery of new ideas about it, and about your self. At other times you will find yourself 'entering' the card, that is, finding yourself within the image acting out some situation with the figures in the picture. This may happen overwhelmingly, so that you find your whole being *there* instead of *here*. More likely you will experience it as a fantasy unrolling before you, with an awareness at the same time of yourself sitting on the floor or lying on the bed. Either way, it is difficult to describe in words these intense experiences. They carry both a personal and archetypal meaning, for while the cards bear pictures of deepest meaning, what we do with those images comes out of our own needs and experiences.

Various people, such as P. D. Ouspensky and Joseph D'Agostino, have attempted to write down their own Tarot meditations as an example or guide. For me these descriptions do not really convey the experience of the card coming alive, of becoming a part of the picture. Each person will experience different things in these moments. For instance, with Strength you might find yourself running with the lion, or else the woman's flowering wreath might wrap around you, or you might become the woman herself or the lion; or even, as happened to me once, the woman might release the lion to leap at you and claw and bite you.

Here are some more hints. If you do not have a particular image you wish to work with, you can do a reading or simply go through the deck until a card grips you and pulls you into it. Then place it before you and begin with your normal meditation. Become aware of the picture, putting aside any ideas you might have about it. Keep your eyes closed or opened, depending on what works for you; most people find that at least when the fantasy starts they prefer their eyes closed. Try to see and feel yourself in that place with those people and animals.

As mentioned earlier, if you are giving a meditation to someone else you should give them suggestions to get them involved with the image. You may find, after some experiments, that you want to use such suggestions on yourself. For the Hanged Man I often use the image of climbing a great tree, stopping at different levels to look at the land and the sea beneath me, the sky and the stars above. Or you might simply want a description of the card that you can listen to with your eyes closed. If you wish to use such guides you might find it valuable to make a tape ahead of time so that your conscious mind does not have to occupy itself with remembering what comes next. Try to time the tape so that you leave enough silent spaces for yourself to react. You might include the opening of the meditation on the tape, instructing yourself to relax, breathe deeply, etc. or you might simply leave a long silence. Either way, most people prefer to turn the tape on at the beginning and let the instructions come on without their having to make a conscious decision. You can, of course, use the same cassette over and over again, preparing cues for different cards. Or you might make a general tape, with instructions about relaxing, merging with the card, and so on.

Above all, do not try to direct or control what will emerge. This holds for meditations you give to others as well as for yourself. There is a fine line here. Too little direction and the person's attention will drift away; too much and you will not allow the subject's imagination to create its own world. As with other situations, experience is the best guide. For both yourself and others, try not to anticipate, and not to fear, what you experience. Most people do not respect their imaginations enough. They think they can understand whatever their imaginations show them. If they see sudden images of monsters, or devils, or death, they think it means something terrible coming from inside themselves, something they do not wish to face. But the imagination is far more subtle than that. It works in its own way, by its own rules. Often what seems disturbing at first will transform into something inspiring. Jung called the imagination 'the organ of the unconscious'. If you give it its head it will take you where your conscious mind would not have thought – or dared – to go.

All this holds true especially for the Gate cards, as well as the Major ones. Their wordless quality of Strangeness leads us far beyond the literal meanings associated with them. At the same time, because they do represent certain qualities they can also help us achieve those qualities. If it helps to carry a card around it helps even more to carry a Major or Gate card. They are powerful images, with an effect all their own. The act of looking at the Nine of Pentacles, letting it sink into you, helps to *create* discipline, just as carrying and looking at the Six of Pentacles or the High Priestess will help you focus your awareness in a receptive way.

CREATING A 'MANDALA'

So far, we have considered ways to bring the influence of single cards into our lives. But a reading contains many cards which work together. To make a reading come alive, I have found it valuable to create what I call a 'mandala' – a pattern formed from several cards. These cards can include not only those from the reading but others whose qualities will support the direction the reading advises. This act of deliberately adding cards not in the reading extends again the balance between the conscious and the unconscious. The reading has reached into the unconscious areas of knowledge to present a picture of the situation as it exists now. Through the mandala, and through the introduction of new cards deliberately taken from the deck, we can extend or transform the situation.

Here is an example of a mandala in which no extra cards were necessary. The reading itself provided all the images we needed. The following Work Cycle (Fig. 92) concerned a woman who felt isolated from the people around her despite several apparently good friendships.

The Cross illustrated the situation perfectly: Two of Pentacles reversed crossed by Six of Swords. It showed her central situation of pretending to enjoy life and relations with others (Two of Pentacles) producing a sense of functioning ('the swords do not weigh down the boat') while she remained unable to connect with the people around her. She remained like the woman in the boat, wrapped in her shroud, silent.

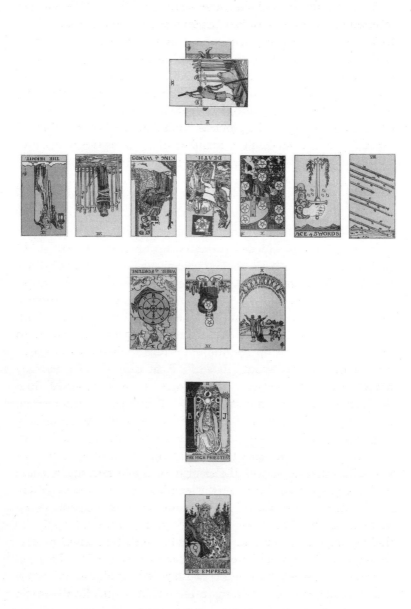

Figure 92 An example of a work cycle reading

Briefly, I interpreted the other cards as follows. The Hermit reversed in the position of Past Experience showed the reality of the friendships. At the same time, comparing it with the High Priestess at the end, it suggested she had not learned to use her sense of aloneness creatively, to develop her individuality. The Eight of Swords reversed as the Expectations showed a desire to understand herself and the situation, thereby becoming free of it. It also reflected the political side of the problem, for a good deal of the woman's isolation came from being a member of a minority group, with experiences not shared by any of her friends. At a certain level she was alone. But instead of appreciating her uniqueness among the people around her she allowed herself to hide her own experiences in an attempt to blend in.

The three Work cards were King of Wands reversed, Death reversed, and Ten of Pentacles reversed. The fact that every card so far had come up reversed; and yet several – such as Eight of Swords reversed – invited a positive reading, showed the need for change. The King described an attitude to take towards herself and others; strong minded, yet tolerant of confusion and weakness. Death reversed, as inertia, indicated a danger in doing nothing. The need to turn it right side up became emphasized when we compared it with the Six of Swords above it. That card shows a journey modelled on the journey of dead souls. To release herself from the boat of isolation, the sense of a half-life, she would have to complete her journey by 'dying'; that is, let go of the personality that had accustomed itself to superficial relationships and inner isolation. The Ten of Pentacles reversed indicated that to do this she would have to gamble with the security of her current situation and push her comfortable but limited friendships to more intense levels.

The Ace of Swords, as the Outcome card showed the strong attitude as well as the sharp perceptive mind she would need, and find, to open up the current situation. The Result of this Outcome, the Eight of Wands, indicated the success of the gamble. The card carries suggestions of love and friendship. It symbolizes a journey – the spiritual boat-trip – coming to an end. Most directly, it signifies the Eight of Swords repression transformed into positive energy.

We then turned over five more cards in a pattern of three below the Work cards, then one and one below the Centre. (There was no special reason for doing this instead of laying out another line. It was simply an intuitive choice – one that proved worthwhile.) The three cards gave more attitudes and approaches to the situation. First, the Wheel of Fortune reversed indicated the changes she wished to make. The reversed position suggested difficulties and reinforced the risk element of the Ten of Pentacles (remember that the Wheel is also 10). The Four of Pentacles came below Death reversed. It implied both the idea of releasing energy and of keeping a structure in her life while she challenged the pattern of her friendships. The third card continued this meaning. Coming below the Ten of Pentacles reversed, the Ten of Cups insisted that while the woman took these risks she must keep an awareness of the genuine love her friends felt for her. It referred also to the idea that she must not doubt the person she lived with, for there she received total support and should answer this gift with trust.

The High Priestess indicated that in a certain sense she would remain alone, for the people around her would still not share her background and experiences. The silence of the High Priestess, however, is not the silence of the Six of Swords. Although silent to others, the High Priestess hints at a strong inner communication, an acceptance and knowledge of the self that a person cannot express in concrete rational terms to other people. The card spoke especially to the woman, who was a poet and had recently written a poem using the metaphor of a private language to express just this idea of deep knowledge available only to oneself.

Below the High Priestess came the Empress, the other side of the feminine archetype. As in the Major Arcana, the two cards complemented each other, for the Empress signified a passionate involvement with life and friendship, not as an opposition to the High Priestess's inner awareness but as a result of it. From a position of self-acceptance the woman could give herself openly to the people around her.

With such a powerful reading the woman wanted to work further with the images. We therefore constructed a mandala for use in meditation and study (see Fig.93). We began with Death as the centre, for the transformation remained the key. Below Death came the High Priestess on the left, signifying the fact that inner communication must accompany the process for Death to produce real results. The Ace of Swords on the right, stood for sharpness of mind. The Empress went above, to bring about the desired new way of relating to the outside world.

We next placed cards in the four corners around the structure, beginning with the Six of Swords and the Eight of Wands in the bottom left and right. The cards showed the journey and its hoped for end. For the top corners we used the Eight of Swords reversed and the King of Wands reversed – the desired action and the attitude needed to produce it Finally, as 'legs' for the mandala, we placed the Ten of Cup below the Eight of Wands, and the Ten of Pentacles reversed below the Six of Swords. The images then looked like this:

Figure 93 An example of a mandala

If you have a set of Rider Tarot cards arrange them as in the diagram and look at it for a while. Notice that for meditation you can concentrate on one card, such as Death in the centre, or let the entire pattern sink into the mind, perhaps moving the images about. Since the mandala contains all the elements, with the trumps in the middle, the woman could maintain balance by taking the image into herself.

If you study such an arrangement new relationships emerge between the cards. The Eight of Swords and Eight of Wands are obvious partners; so are the Ten of Cups and Ten of Pentacles reversed. But the Eight of Wands and the King of Wands reversed will also provide new meanings when we consider them together, as do the Eight of Swords reversed and the Six of Swords. Because we have reshaped the reading into a geometric pattern we can draw lines, triangles, etc., constantly discovering new ideas and new patterns. In a way the mandala creates new readings from the same images.

To construct such a pattern, choose the most important cards from the reading and work from the centre out, trying to build the image organically. Place the cards needed for support at the bottom and the cards symbolizing goals at the top. Do not hesitate to introduce cards not found in the original reading if you find a strong need for qualities these cards represent. If you see a need for Temperance, for instance, place it below the centre; or if the reading shows a need for more developed will-power and discipline you might place the Chariot and the Nine of Pentacles side by side above the mandala, as the goal. In this way, you take charge of the reading, opening it to include what your intuition tells you the person needs.

CHAPTER THIRTEEN

WHAT WE LEARN FROM TAROT READINGS

Most people consult a Tarot reading for specific information. Those who understand the cards a little more may look on the reading as a means of finding a direction. And those who follow a series of readings will see them as a method of keeping in harmony with the changing patterns of life. But to spend a long time reading cards for yourself and others is to discover many things beyond personal information.

We have already seen some of these things. One is people's pessimistic reactions to readings. Another, more important, is the way Tarot readings require – *and therefore create* – a balance between subjective and objective, intuitive and rational, immediate impression and established knowledge, right and left side of the brain. We cannot create such a balance simply by wanting it. We have to let it grow. Tarot readings can help this happen.

But the Tarot teaches us other things as well. It teaches us to pay attention. As we begin to learn the ways in which people act, and the ways in which the world acts on them, we become more and more in the habit of noticing what others do and what we do ourselves. Suppose a person becomes ill whenever a holiday approaches. This could go on for years without the person making the connection and seeing all those illnesses as a subconscious trick to avoid some problem or fear associated with holidays. A Tarot reading can make the person aware of this problem – and makes the reader aware of yet another example of subconscious manoeuvring.

Just the practice of reading the Tarot will help us observe these tricks of behaviour, in ourselves as well as in others.

Once we start paying attention to what we do and what happens as a result we notice all sorts of things, not just through readings, but in daily life; patterns of anger and trust, hope and fear, how our response to situations may come from inside us rather than from the situation itself. We become more conscious of the way we deal with work and friends, of tendencies to shift responsibility either *away* from ourselves ('It's not fair' or 'You did this to me') or *onto* ourselves ('It's all my fault'). We will notice, for instance, that saying 'It's all my fault' is often a trick to avoid seeing what we have actually done. By making it all or nothing, we make it easy to avoid a true assessment of the situation.

Paying attention makes it just a little bit harder to get depressed or to manipulate other people. As we begin to observe the subtle reasons why people cry or become angry or accuse others, we will at least know a little about ourselves when *we* do these things.

Tarot readings make us aware of the wonderful variety of human nature. As the same cards come up in endless different combinations it becomes clear that people can always produce something new. At the same time, the newness will always come on top of underlying patterns. Through readings we learn in general the ways in which the past affects people, the ways in which their hopes and fears help create the future. But specific past situations and future expectations – these will always surprise us.

Here again we learn the habit of paying attention. For if we start interpreting the cards automatically on the basis of authoritative books or past readings then we lose the truth, and the readings become shallow and confused. Keep a book of past readings, yes, but not simply to use it as examples for future work. Instead, the book can help remind us of the variety and the constant newness of human behaviour.

Notice that, as in creating balance, the Tarot does not simply help us to pay attention. It forces us to do so if we want our readings to produce good results. Tarot readings act as a kind of psychic exercise programme which strengthens the perceptive muscles.

What people do with the information they get from Tarot readings teaches us some important lessons about free will. Many people look on the question of free will as an absolute. Either we make constant choices or we act according to destiny. To give it a more modern context, do we do what we do as a deliberate choice at that moment, or as a result of a lifetime (or many lifetimes) of conditioning?

In terms of Tarot this becomes a practical question. If I act freely at any moment, then how can the cards predict what I will do? What meaning can the reading have if my choice remains totally open until the moment I do something? Or does some power force me to act the way the cards predict?

These problems become easier if we give up the absolute all-or-nothing approach to the question. Then we can say yes, we always retain free will, but we rarely use it. Our conditioning, our past experience, above all our ignorance of all these things, tend to manipulate us in certain directions. The reading reflects these influences and shows their likely result. The cards do not compel the situation to turn out in a certain way. They simply reflect the way in which the influences combine in real life. We can make a different decision when the time comes to act. And yet we do not. Over and over again in life, with little conscious knowledge, we surrender our freedom of choice. We allow our history and conditioning to move us. We do this partly from ignorance, and partly from laziness. It is much easier to follow conditioning than to act on truly conscious decisions.

When I 'failed to follow good advice', when I said to myself, 'Now that I've done the reading I can make sure those bad things won't happen', when I went ahead with my original plan so that the predicted problems arose, I demonstrated how I did not use my free will. I avoided it at the same time that I pretended to be acting on it. This sort of thing happens again and again, and the act of doing Tarot readings shows us very vividly the ways in which people deny their freedom. It is this relationship between freedom and conditioning which forms one of the most valuable pieces of knowledge the Tarot can give us.

The Tarot teaches us as well the valuable lesson of context. No matter how absolute a quality may seem to us in the abstract, in reality it affects us only in the context of other influences. Readings demonstrate this fact in a practical way, as with the woman trying to deal with her lover's jealousy. A card usually thought of as positive, the Sun, actually tended towards a bad result, for by hoping for the Sun she did not face the needs of the situation, and in fact allowed other people's ideas to dictate what she wanted.

Along with context we learn the ways in which the elements of life balance each other. We see first of all how the suits and specific cards combine to form a unified situation with no suit better or worse than any of the others. Astrologers often find that clients hope for certain signs and elements to dominate their charts, and will show disappointment or even shame if others appear.

Similarly, for some people who know a little about Tarot, if a reading shows a lot of Wands, or Cups, they will feel comforted; if it shows Swords they will become frightened; and if it shows Pentacles they will think of it as trivial, even insulting. Some will only accept a reading which contains many Major cards, because only the trumps, with their implications of power and spiritual awareness, appear important to them.

But even the Major Arcana forms only one element, meaningless without the others. We study it in isolation for its wisdom and powerful description of existence. But in practice we need to mix the spiritual with the mundane, the happy with the sad, love and anger together to understand the world.

The cards teach yet another balance, one hinted at in the scales of Justice. How does the past relate to the future possibilities? How do we combine the effects of our own decision with the influences of the outside world? What do we mean when we say we take responsibility for our lives? Does it mean we create or control everything that happens to us? As in the case of free will many people like to think of responsibility in an absolute way. Either the world shapes us entirely, or we retain total control over our lives. Tarot readings drive home the point that a person's situation at any moment derives from a combination of these things. Just as a very short person cannot expect to become a professional basketball player, so that same person must not consider his whole life dominated by height.

People who accept this idea in theory may still ask: Which counts most — situation or personal responsibility? Which one really controls a person? But Tarot readings demonstrate the meaninglessness of this and similar questions. In some readings the position of Self or Hopes and Fears will clearly dominate. In others Basis or Environment will prove the determining factors. It depends on the person and the particular situation.

Tarot readings help us develop confidence in our own perceptions. Partly this comes from the knowledge gained, and partly from the need to make choices and stick by them. Which of a card's meanings applies in a particular case? Does a court card apply to the subject, some other person, or an abstract principle, such as the King of Swords signifying law and authority, or the Queen of Cups creativity? As we read more we find ourselves starting to sense the answers to these and similar questions. As a result we gain more trust in our understanding and intuition.

What period does a reading cover? With the Celtic Cross or the Work Cycles, the answer can range from a few days to years, not just forwards, but backwards as well. Sometimes, for an adult, the reading can reach back to childhood. The Tree of Life, too, though it usually shows an overview of the whole life, can sometimes show a shorter period if the person is going through a time of intense change.

The different periods of time covered especially in the shorter readings, depend on two things. First, the person's situation and the question asked. Some things, practical or legal matters and certain emotional situations, can bring forth an answer that makes itself apparent within a few days. With others – the working out of emotional conflicts, deep relationships, spiritual or artistic development – it can take a long time before the reading fulfils itself. This does not mean that the readings will not 'come true' for years. We are not speaking of predictions, but of continuing patterns that slowly unfold as time passes.

Second, the different levels a person may touch when mixing the cards. Sometimes he or she may evoke surface situations which last only a short time. At other times the person may mix the cards and somehow go to the very centre of experience. And even here, the reading may show the deep past, or it may reflect the person's potential for future development.

The level reached may not depend at all on the attitude of the person mixing the cards. Usually this approach does make a difference. Someone who sees a reading as a joke or a game will most likely produce a shallow reading; the person who thinks deeply of a question, mixes the cards carefully, and tries to sense the exact moment to stop and cut the deck, will usually produce a reading of some significance. Yet sometimes even such a careful approach will not go below the surface events of the immediate future, while at other times the most casual shuffler will suddenly find her or himself confronted with a powerful image of an entire life. For the reader such moments carry an intense excitement.

Even the question itself may not matter. People can ask about how their work is going, and receive an answer about their new love affair, especially if that question occupies their mind more than the one they asked. Or, as in the case of the woman who found her sexuality blocked by conflicts with her father, the reading may answer the question by bringing up unexpected material from some other area.

How do we know, then, what the reading tells us? Some things become obvious from the images of the cards. If we ask about work and the Lovers and the Two of Cups appear, then the reading will probably concern not work but love. As a beginning reader, however, you cannot expect to uncover all subtleties. Experience alone will help you find your way to the heart of the labyrinth. As you continue with readings you will find yourself able to sense these things. And the heightened perception will carry over to other areas of your life as well.

Sometimes, no matter what our experience or the sharpness of our intuition, we will make mistakes. We might look at the Lovers symbolically when it predicts a love affair with a person the subject still has not met. From this inability to know exactly what the cards mean we can actually learn a very valuable lesson. We become aware of Ignorance. I have capitalized this term because of its essential quality. While most of the knowledge we build up in life is really quite superficial and external, Ignorance lies at the very base of our existence. First of all, we are ignorant of the true nature of things. What we know of the world is bounded by our sense organs. For us to see the words on this page, light must bounce off them to be collected by our eyes. Then the optic nerve carries impulses to the brain, which converts the impulses into others,

arranging them into meaningful patterns our consciousness under-
stands as language. But we cannot directly know, in the sense of
merging with something out there. We can only convert the
universe into impulses, patterns, symbols.

Similarly, because we exist in physical form, we must work out
our lives in the boundaries of time. This means, among other
things, that we cannot realize all our potential, because we must
always choose to do one thing and not another with the few years
available to us. A person with the ability to become both a dancer
and a businessman will have to choose one over the other. And
which ever he chooses he will have to work for years before he can
actually achieve his goal. Time means also that we often cannot
know the consequences of actions we take, simply because the consequences might not appear until years in the future. Sometimes the
consequences of our actions appear not to us but to other people.
Something we do in a certain place may affect people there long
after we have moved, or even died. Quite simply, time means things
must happen before we can know about them.

Meditation with the Eight of Swords as a Gate can increase our
awareness of Ignorance. Tarot readings – and the mistakes we make
as we try to interpret them – can demonstrate Ignorance more
directly. A Tarot reading actually reaches beyond time, bringing out
the true pattern that includes past and future. The random pattern
of the cards leads us to bypass the limitations of consciousness. And
yet that limited consciousness must interpret the reading. Therefore, at one and the same time, we experience the true state of the
universe, in which all things exist together, and our own extremely
limited time-bound knowledge of it. We experience both truth and
ignorance.

The other side of Ignorance is Certitude, the state of knowing
reality, rather than the impressions and symbols our limited consciousness forms from it. Many people consider ecstasy, or oneness
with the light of God, as the supreme goal of the mystic or occultist.
But as the Major Arcana of the Tarot demonstrates, the lightning
bolt of ecstasy forms only a step along the way. The true goal is Certitude, the state of knowing where before we could only guess.

What is the real cause of any single action? What will its consequences be, not just to the person who has acted, but to others,

both known and unknown? Those few people who have achieved Certitude can see the causes and consequences within the action itself. The rest of us can only guess about these and a thousand other things. We remain Ignorant.

But even if we cannot guess at the true interpretation of a Tarot reading, the reading itself reaches beyond that timebound Ignorant state. The reading carries Certitude, if not the reader. And if we work enough with cards, comparing our interpretations with subsequent events, becoming more and more involved with the pictures, developing our intuition, then sometimes we can get experiences of Certitude, of knowing the true meaning of something. While such experiences carry their own value, they serve us most by giving us a sense of direction. They help us perceive what we want to achieve.

Finally, the practice of Tarot reading teaches us something else. Because the cards are not neutral in their attitude to life, because they embody certain approaches and beliefs, and renounce others, they change us. We begin over time – always over time – to see the balance of things, the steady harmony within the constant shift and flow of life. We become aware of the Strangeness always waiting beyond our ordinary experience, we learn to recognize the gifts we receive from existence, and our own responsibility to understand and use them. Most of all, we begin to grasp the truth the Tarot always urges upon us – that the universe the whole universe, lives. And what we can know of ourselves we can know of everything.

BIBLIOGRAPHY

Butler, Bill, *The Definitive Tarot* (London: Rider and Company, 1975)

Case, Paul Foster, *The Tarot, A Key to the Wisdom of the Ages* (Richmond, VA: Macoy Publishing Company, 1947)

Crowley, Aleister, *The Book of Thoth* (New York: Samuel Weiser, 1944)

D'Agostino, Joseph, *The Royal Path to Wisdom* (New York: Samuel Weiser, 1976)

Douglas, Alfred, *The Tarot* (London: Penguin, 1972)

Eliade, Mircea, *Shamanism* (Princeton, NJ: Princeton University Press, 1964)

Gray, Eden, *The Tarot Revealed* (New York: Bantam, 1969)

Haich, Elizabeth, *Wisdom of the Tarot* (New York: 1975)

Kaplan, Stuart, *The Encyclopedia of Tarot* (US Games Systems, Inc., 1978)

Malory, Thomas, *Work* (ed. Eugene Vinaver; London: Oxford University Press, 1989)

Scholem, Gershon, *Major Trends in Jewish Mysticism* (New York: Shocken, 1941)

— , *On the Kabbalah and its Symbolism* (New York: Shocken, 1965)

Waite, Arthur Edward, *The Pictorial Key to the Tarot* (New York: University Books, [1910], 1959). All quotations from Waite are taken from this book.

Wang, Robert, *An Introduction to the Golden Dawn Tarot* (Wellingborough: Aquarian Press, 1978)

Williams, Charles, *The Greater Trumps* (London: Victor Gollancz, 1932)

INDEX